Basic income is one of the most innovative, powerful, straightforward, and controversial proposals for addressing poverty and growing inequalities. A Basic Income Guarantee (BIG) is designed to be an unconditional, government-ensured guarantee that all citizens will have enough income to meet their basic needs. The concept of basic, or guaranteed, income is a form of social provision and this series examines the arguments for and against it from an interdisciplinary perspective with a special focus on the economic and social factors. By systematically connecting abstract philosophical debates over competing principles of BIG to the empirical analysis of concrete policy proposals, this series contributes to the fields of economics, politics, social policy, and philosophy and establishes a theoretical framework for interdisciplinary research. It will bring together international and national scholars and activists to provide a comparative look at the main efforts to date to pass unconditional BIG legislation across regions of the globe and will identify commonalities and differences across countries drawing lessons for advancing social policies in general and BIG policies in particular.

Series Editors:

Karl Widerquist is a visiting associate professor of Philosophy at Georgetown University-Qatar.

James Bryan is an associate professor of Economics at Manhattanville College.

Michael A. Lewis is an associate professor at Hunter College School of Social Work.

Basic Income Reconsidered
by Simon Birnbaum

Basic Income Reconsidered

Social Justice, Liberalism, and the Demands of Equality

Simon Birnbaum

palgrave
macmillan

First published in 2012 by
PALGRAVE MACMILLAN®
in the United States—a division of St. Martin's Press LLC,
175 Fifth Avenue, New York, NY 10010.

Where this book is distributed in the UK, Europe and the rest of the world,
this is by Palgrave Macmillan, a division of Macmillan Publishers Limited,
registered in England, company number 785998, of Houndmills,
Basingstoke, Hampshire RG21 6XS.

Palgrave Macmillan is the global academic imprint of the above companies
and has companies and representatives throughout the world.

Palgrave® and Macmillan® are registered trademarks in the United States,
the United Kingdom, Europe and other countries.

ISBN: 978–0–230–11406–7

Library of Congress Cataloging-in-Publication Data

Birnbaum, Simon.
    Basic income reconsidered : social justice, liberalism, and
    the demands of equality / by Simon Birnbaum.
        p. cm.—(Exploring the basic income guarantee)
        ISBN 978–0–230–11406–7 (hardcover)
        1. Income distribution. 2. Income maintenance programs.
    3. Social justice. 4. Liberalism. 5. Equality. I. Title.
    HC79.I5B563 2012
    339.2′2—dc23   2011033414

A catalogue record of the book is available from the British Library.

Design by Newgen Imaging Systems (P) Ltd., Chennai, India.

First edition: February 2012

10 9 8 7 6 5 4 3 2 1

Printed in the United States of America.

For Anna

Contents

ACKNOWLEDGMENTS

My work on this book stretches over a long time period. Throughout the project, I have been fortunate to benefit from the comments and encouragement of many colleagues and research groups. I defended a doctoral thesis on the ethics of basic income in March 2008 at the Department of Political Science, Stockholm University. Even though most of the material has been substantially revised, reorganized, and updated since then, this book builds on the arguments and the overall structure of that thesis. Hence, my first thanks go to the supervisors of my work during those years in the doctoral program, Bo Lindensjö and Jouni Reinikainen, and to all of my colleagues in the department for their support.

Bo Lindensjö, who died in 2011, was the person who first drew my attention to the world of contemporary political theory and guided my first steps as a researcher. Bo's encouragement to follow my own path and his firm confidence in my abilities were important conditions for moving the project forward. His mild personality, the wide scope of his own work, and his open mind helped establish an intellectual climate in which it was easy to think freely and creatively. He is greatly missed.

Through my years in the doctoral program I was also privileged to receive the guidance of Jouni Reinikainen. I am very thankful to him for consistently providing me with challenging objections and arguments on all of my drafts, for his enthusiasm about my project, and for always being generous with his time. I also thank Ulf Mörkenstam who kept an eye on my project from start to finish and offered valuable advice on problems and questions that arose through the various stages of this work.

I am grateful to Magnus Reitberger and Per-Anders Svärd for their helpful comments on an early version of the manuscript, presented in September 2007. Gustaf Arrhenius, Ludvig Beckman, and Mikael Eriksson also deserve special thanks for reading the whole manuscript at that stage and for providing me with detailed comments and critical remarks. Mikael Eriksson has provided constructive feedback on just about every piece I wrote during my years as a doctoral student. His friendship and our ongoing conversations on the core themes of my thesis were very important for the development of the project.

Three persons played an especially important role in the explanation for why I repeatedly returned to this material after the defense of my dissertation and developed it into its present form. First, I was very fortunate to have Stuart White as the critical examiner of my work and to benefit from his excellent comments and challenging questions on all parts of the manuscript. Second, it is unlikely that this work would have existed in its current form if I had not met Philippe Van Parijs and other members of the BIEN community in Barcelona in 2004. Nobody who reads this book will fail to notice my admiration for the work of Van Parijs and his influence on my way of thinking. His warm and generous way of responding to my research, and of welcoming me to the international basic income debate at this very early stage, was incredibly inspiring. And third, I am deeply grateful to Karl Widerquist, who read my doctoral thesis carefully and encouraged me to develop this material into a book.

I thank STINT (The Swedish Foundation for International Cooperation in Research and Higher Education) for supporting a six-month stay in Oxford and the Department of Politics and International Relations at the University of Oxford for welcoming me as a visiting graduate between September 2006 and March 2007. In particular, I want to express my gratitude to the members of the Nuffield Political Theory Workshop and the Political Theory Graduate Workshop for all their helpful comments and questions on the material I presented there.

I am indebted to Gustaf Arrhenius, Daniel Butt, G. A. Cohen, David Miller, Jens Johansson, Jonas Olson, Emre Ozcan, Ben Saunders, Adam Swift, and, above all, Stuart White who all contributed, in different ways, to make those months in Oxford supportive and fruitful. The friendship and comments of David Casassas, who was a visiting fellow at the Centre for the Study of Social Justice during part of my stay in Oxford, and our work on joint projects during this time also meant very much and helped shape the future direction of my work.

After the defense of my thesis, I was given the opportunity to return to some of the key arguments of that work and to related projects, thanks to two postdoctoral fellowships in stimulating and friendly research environments. The first was a Hoover fellowship at the Hoover Chair of Social and Economic Ethics at the Catholic

University of Louvain, October–December of 2008, and the second was a postdoctoral fellowship in Bergen at the Stein Rokkan Centre for Social Studies, September 2009–January 2010, with funding from the Nordic Centre of Excellence (NordWel).

I thank the representatives and participants of these research groups and institutions for those valuable months. In Louvain-la-Neuve, special thanks are owed to Philippe Van Parijs, Yannick Vanderborght, Axel Gosseries, and Nenad Stojanovic (Nenad was also a Hoover fellow—and my flat mate!—during this period). In Bergen, I benefited from the feedback, warmth, and hospitality of many people, including Nanna Kildal, Tord Skogedal Lindén, Even Nilssen, and Johan Strang.

In 2011, I joined an interdisciplinary research project on intergenerational justice (led by Tommy Ferrarini), with colleagues at the Institute for Social Research (SOFI), at Stockholm University and Uppsala University (Tommy Ferrarini, Kenneth Nelson, and Joakim Palme). This project, to which the present book is a contribution, enabled me to reconnect to some of the core themes of my previous work, such as the question of justice in relation to inherited assets and the role of reciprocity. I thank my colleagues in this research group for stimulating discussions, and I especially thank Tommy Ferrarini for his comments on the manuscript. Financial support from FAS (Swedish Council for Working Life and Social Research) is gratefully acknowledged.

Additional thanks to SCAS, the Swedish Collegium for Advanced Study in Uppsala, for giving me the opportunity to spend the fall of 2011 as a SCAS fellow. Those great months made it possible for me to attend to the remaining details of the manuscript in a focused way, as well as to initiate related projects in a very inspiring environment. I also wish to thank the Department of Political Science and Stockholm Resilience Centre (and its Baltic Nest Institute) at Stockholm University, especially Ulrika Mörth, Carl Folke, Christoph Humborg, and Henrik Österblom for enabling a smooth transition from my work on this book to my current duties at these institutes, and for their patience with my parallel commitments.

Several drafts of arguments in this work, and related articles, were presented at conferences and workshops in Barcelona, Bergen, Copenhagen, Klekken, Louvain-la-Neuve, Manchester, Oxford, Stockholm, Uppsala, Växjö, Århus, and Örebro. In addition to those mentioned above, I have benefited from useful comments and/or discussions with Hans Agné, Jan Otto Andersson, Daniel Attas, Björn

Badersten, John Baker, Andreas Bergh, Niclas Berggren, Karl Birnbaum (my grandfather), Kristina Boréus, Erik Christensen, Jurgen De Wispelaere, Eva Erman, Max Fonseca, Andreas Gottardis, Pierre Guillet de Monthoux, Michael Howard, François Hudon, Mats Höglund, Per Janson, Magnus Jedenheim-Edling, Robert Jubb, Sune Laegaard, Claes Linde, Kasper Lippert-Rasmussen, Karolin Lundström, Aaron Maltais, Søren Midtgaard, Taro Miyamoto, Peter Mølgaard Nielsen, José Noguera, Sofia Näsström, Kieran Oberman, Marcus Ohlström, Carole Pateman, Diane Sainsbury, Guy Standing, Attila Tanyi, Robert van der Veen, Martin Westergren, and Jörgen Ödalen.

I am also grateful to Susanna Lindberg and Merrick Tabor for both helping out to improve my English at different stages of my work on this book. I also thank Karl Widerquist (the series editor), an anonymous referee, and the editorial staff at Palgrave Macmillan for their feedback and assistance.

On a more personal note, I extend my thanks to Sven Olsson, my grandfather. Sven died in 2006 when I was in Oxford. Few have participated with such an enthusiasm in my work as Sven, who was an amazing supporter and a very dear friend. Through his unconditional love, his devotion to science, and the excessive importance he ascribed to my research, he has been a great source of inspiration.

Finally, I thank my whole family for their support. Specifically, I would like to mention my father, Anders Olsson, who has helped me with many aspects of this work and provided plenty of useful advice in discussions on a day-to-day basis. Also, warm thanks to Agnes Monus—my father's wife—for generously offering me to use her art for the cover of this book, and for the efforts she devoted to adapt her work for this context. Most importantly, I thank my partner, Anna Saarikoski. I am deeply grateful for her love, encouragement, and friendship throughout this project and the 15 years I have known her.

Two chapters of this book are revised and adapted versions of articles that were previously published elsewhere. I thank Taylor and Francis for their permission to republish material from "Radical Liberalism, Rawls and the Welfare State: Justifying the Politics of Basic Income" (in chapter 2), originally published in 2010 in *Critical Review of International Social and Political Philosophy* (CRISPP) 13 (4): 495–516 (http://www.informaworld.com). I am also grateful to the editors of *Politics, Philosophy and Economics* and SAGE for their permission to use material from the article "Should Surfers Be Ostracized? Basic Income, Liberal Neutrality and the Work Ethos" (in chapter 6), originally published in 2011 in *Politics, Philosophy and Economics*, 10 (4): 396–419.

Introduction and Overview

CHAPTER 1

Basic Income, Liberal Egalitarianism, and the Study of Social Justice

1.1. Introduction. Welfare Reform, Basic Income, and the Universal Welfare State

A universal welfare state is often described as a type of welfare state in which rights to income security are primarily based on citizenship or permanent residence. Comprehensive forms of welfare universalism rest on the idea that a substantial set of welfare rights should cover all members of society and that the welfare state will thus remain a concern for everyone. Such a welfare state does not mark out a separate group of needy people from the rest of the population.

Universal provision manifests that we are all—rich or poor—equal in relation to state-provided services and support. Each member of society is entitled to resources in times of need. Access to essential services or income support is a universal right and, hence, it does not depend on the (unpredictable) charity of the rich, and it does not involve stigmatizing forms of provision (Kildal and Kuhnle 2005; Korpi and Palme 1998; Rothstein 1998; Sainsbury 1996).

In the domain of income support, the most universal strategy possible would be to implement a basic income. A basic income is an income unconditionally granted to all permanent members of society on an individual basis, without any means test or work requirement. In the typical basic income proposal, every citizen or permanent resident, rich or poor, is given a tax-free basic income, on which income from other sources can be added (Van Parijs 1992a). Basic income and similar proposals can take many different forms and have been defended from normative positions all across the political spectrum.[1]

In this book I will examine whether a commitment to *liberal-egalitarian justice* (by which I primarily refer to objectives identified and defended in John Rawls's theory of justice, to be introduced in sections 1.2 and 1.6) should lead us to embrace such a radicalized form of the universal welfare state. The academically most influential work on basic income in recent years is Philippe Van Parijs's sophisticated and comprehensive justification of such a reform as the cornerstone in his liberal-egalitarian conception of distributive justice (Van Parijs 1995). In Van Parijs's view, implementing the highest sustainable basic income would be the best way of turning a mere formal, libertarian freedom—in the form of a well-enforced structure of rights— into "real freedom for all." Whatever may happen through our lives, and whatever we might want to do, the basic income would guarantee a firm material foundation on which we can always rely.

Examining Van Parijs's claim will force us to respond to normative questions about the nature of the ideals of justice on which our welfare arrangements are (or should be) based. What is the relationship between social rights, individual freedom, and work obligations? And what is the relationship between universal welfare rights and individual responsibility? Before turning to competing views on such fundamental moral questions, we need to say something more to explain the contemporary context and political relevance of such theoretical debates.

Basic income and similar proposals have a long history that dates back at least to Thomas Paine's plea for a universal basic endowment in *Agrarian Justice*, 1796 (for a collection of historical writings, see Cunliffe and Erreygers (2004); for helpful overviews of the history of basic income, see Vanderborght and Van Parijs (2005) and Widerquist, Lewis, and Pressman (2005)). In this book, however, I will mainly be focusing on contemporary contributions to this debate. I will consider the many ways through which the normative justification and criticism of this idea have matured and gained precision since it was reintroduced in the European context in the early 1980s and gradually turned into a debate with global reach. Some of the social conditions that have made the demands for such an unconditional basic income, and similar policies of strong universalism, appear increasingly relevant in the past few decades result from the economic and social tendencies toward greater material inequality and labor market flexibility.

First, since the 1980s, the situation of growing material inequalities and the return of mass unemployment in many advanced welfare state economies, committed to the norm of full employment, have generated discourses on the "two-thirds society" and the "new social question." In increasingly service-based and skill-demanding economies, welfare states of the world face steadily rising domestic inequalities in income and wealth and—in many cases—high levels of persistent unemployment (White 2007, 151–152).

The failure to make labor markets absorb everyone who is looking for a meaningful and adequately paid job led to widespread exclusion from nonstigmatizing forms of social insurance in which eligibility is based on prior labor market attachment. The political and social climate in which the basic income idea was rediscovered, and took root in many European countries in the 1980s and 1990s, was a situation in which the need to attend to new divisions between insiders and outsiders of the labor market became increasingly urgent (Van der Veen and Groot 2000; Kildal 2001; Standing 2004).[2]

Hence, political pleas for basic income have often started off from the observation that a person's labor market position cannot (consistently) be the basis of income security, and useful social participation, if significant parts of the population are permanently excluded from the labor market or only weakly attached to it. More generally, if we hold on to the core values that have guided egalitarian welfare states for many decades, any strategy that offers better prospects for employment only at the price of exacerbating existing trends toward growing economic inequalities, power asymmetries, and greater social insecurity (say, by combining the removal of minimum income schemes with wage flexibility) will seem highly unsatisfactory.

The second major social trend that has helped spark an interest in such policies of strong universalism is the way in which patterns of employment and conditions for family and civil society relations have gone through major changes in recent decades. In most OECD economies, an increasing share of workers depends on precarious employment, that is, temporary, fragmentary, and discontinuous forms of work. While such forms of employment offer opportunities for work and participation, "flexible" workers (sometimes referred to as the "precariat") who depend on such jobs, but lack any workplace-independent income security to rely on, remain in conditions of exploitable dependency (Standing 1999; 2001; 2011).

The fact that people are more often expected to change jobs, careers, and the local community (or even nation) they call home many times during a lifetime, and the fact that a given family unit is less often expected to last for life, have reshaped the conditions for policies to meet objectives of maintaining income security and economic equality. In light of such tendencies, Robert Goodin has argued that the nonstate pillars of social security—the market, the family, and the community—are all "crumbling" (Goodin 2000).

Without supportive universal distributive arrangements, processes of flexibilization and the associated destandardization of social risks leave many people increasingly vulnerable during the frequent gaps between jobs, family transition, periods of unemployment, care work, retraining, and so on.[3]

A third important basis for the argument that there is a great social need for forms of social security that are not based on one's labor market attachment and previous earnings is that society inevitably depends on considerable amounts of socially necessary, informal, and nonremunerated work. The need for attending to the economic conditions for people to devote time and effort to productive activities that are not primarily organized by either the market or the state has always provided an important reason for taking an interest in the basic income proposal. This link between basic income and activities conducted in parts of the economy referred to as the "autonomous sphere," the "social economy," or "third sector" has often been articulated by groups that emphasize the need to facilitate and recognize informal care work, democratic participation, local exchange systems, environmental care, and various forms of cultural work (Gorz 1999).

More recently, the many ways in which the Internet has transformed our economies and forms of interaction have generated new lines of argument for linking basic income to the aims of recognizing and supporting unpaid contributions to economic progress and innovation. The latter has been powerfully illustrated by the great social and economic importance of unpaid mass collaboration phenomena such as the development of open source software and Wikipedia (Wright 2010).

By connecting the right to basic social protection to membership of the relevant community rather than one's attachment to the labor market, the case for a basic income suggests a policy path in which social rights do not reflect and strengthen divisions between the insiders and the outsiders of the labor market. It offers an innovative strategy for the aims of expanding the opportunities of the least favorably positioned (in the labor market and elsewhere) while simultaneously reducing material inequalities and promoting personal independence.

1.2. Competing Ideals and the Future of Welfare Universalism

While proposals for universal and unconditional distribution of this kind play an important role in academic debates, they occupy—with some exceptions—a relatively marginal role in political debates and actual policymaking.[4] Indeed, many of the developments just out-lined have been responded to, or partly generated by, accounts of justice that demand more stringent requirements that all citizens who are able to work must do so in order to be eligible for social rights. Demands for every welfare recipient to apply for jobs more actively and/or to undertake work or work-like activities under supervision, and often with compensation below minimum wages, is the essence of liberal-conservative justifications of "workfare" (work for your wel-fare) or "welfare-to-work" policies (Mead 1987; 1992; 2005).[5]

In the influential ideals of welfare contractualism, which have also played a very central role in Third Way-style social democracy, there are "no rights without responsibilities" (Giddens 1998, 65). Income security is not an unconditional right of citizenship but something that one must earn. The central practical implication of this view is that work obligations in return for social assistance, or income rights more broadly, are seen as a necessary part of any fair and nonexploit-ative social contract (cf. White 2000).

The idea of placing the obligation to make a productive con-tribution at the center stage of social justice also comes in more egalitarian versions, often linked to radical interpretations of social democracy. *Egalitarian reciprocity* objects to one-sidedly impos-ing duties of contribution on the needy. It is concerned with the requirement that the "idle rich" should not be allowed to escape obligations of contribution, and that duties are imposed against the background of genuine equality of opportunity and conditions for meaningful work to all (Schweickart 2002; Van Donselaar 1997; 2003; 2009; White 2003a).

In order to secure the requirements for relations of mutual advan-tage between the members of a cooperative scheme, egalitarian reci-procity demands that we attach highest priority to policies such as employment-generating investment and activating educational pro-grams for meaningful work. Hence, if a strong notion of welfare universalism is to be embraced within such a conception of justice—whether under capitalist or socialist arrangements—it must be tied to distributive schemes under which everyone will (normally) con-tribute substantially in the form of employment or other productive activities.

The need for a political theory of basic income springs primarily from the fact that many people, in all parts of the political spectrum, have strong moral objections to unconditional forms of distribution to adult persons who are capable of working (Van der Veen 1998, 141–142). Agendas based on various forms of welfare contractualism may be held morally superior to any ideal that accepts substantial amounts of unconditional and universal distribution in cash, since redistribution to the voluntarily unemployed provides "something for nothing." The latter type of arrangement may, thus, be held to exploit those who work.

In order to assess arguments for or against attaching work requirements to income security, and to provide normative standards to guide policymaking with respect to basic income, it is necessary to explore the moral intuitions and principles underlying such objections head on. As should be clear from my introductory remarks above, arguments for and against different agendas on these issues are not merely (or even primarily) based on defensive factual claims about how best to meet given normative objectives under (partly) new social and economic conditions. While policy debates on these matters often place reactive economic arguments on feasibility, political necessity, or conditions for short-term economic competitiveness in focus, they must eventually rely heavily on arguments about values and the long-term commitments and priorities we ought to make. It is this normative dimension of the debate on the future of universalism and work conditionality that this study attends to.

In this book I want to challenge accounts of social justice that defend a strict connection between welfare rights and work obligations. The general purpose of the research project is, more precisely, to explore and defend a politics of unconditional universalism based on a Rawlsian ideal of *radical liberalism* (a term I borrow from Ackerman (2003)). Counter to liberal-conservative ideals of welfare contractualism and the politics of workfare, and counter to ideals of egalitarian reciprocity with its politics of work-based equality, radical liberalism (as I shall characterize it) holds a substantial universal and unconditional tier of social rights to be one of the ideal requirements of liberal-egalitarian justice. Such an ideal is radical in the sense that it demands far-reaching equalization of opportunities. But it is also distinctively liberal by insisting that people must be left free to use their resource shares for a much wider range of purposes and life plans than those typically accessible through existing social rights.

Building on the tradition of a universal welfare state, such an ideal demands that a substantial component of (re)distributive mechanisms should be attached to citizenship (or residence) rather than any more particular role or need. In the context of existing welfare states, this view—with its objective of providing each citizen with a substantial stake of the economy on which they can securely rely—also connects naturally to the general policy orientation that flows from John Rawls's case for an egalitarian form of *property-owning democracy*.

Following James Meade, Rawls argued that justice must ideally achieve resource equalization ex ante rather than (merely) corrective adjustments ex post (he associated the latter approach with "welfare state capitalism"). By opting for this radical agenda, attacking arbitrary inequalities at the root, and providing all with an independent share of wealth, the institutions of such a regime would seek to make sure that the least advantaged will not be the objects of charity, compassion, or pity. Instead, the aim of the property-owning democracy is to "put all citizens in a position to manage their own affairs on a footing of a suitable degree of social and economic equality" (Rawls 2001a, 139; cf. Meade 1964; O'Neill 2009).[6]

For those that share broadly "Rawlsian" commitments to an interpretation of justice that (a) seeks to respect a wide range of different conceptions of the good life (nonperfectionism), that supports (b) the firm protection of basic individual liberties associated with the liberal tradition, and (c) the objective of countering morally arbitrary inequalities, I shall suggest that such a radical-liberal view has considerable force relative to its reciprocity-based alternatives (part I). Along the way, this view will be confronted with, specified, and qualified in response to objections about responsibility (part II) and feasibility (part III).

In particular, I will emphasize the need to link these arguments to a broader framework in which close attention is paid to the duties of promoting and maintaining the conditions for realizing justice, the requirements of stability and instrumental virtues, and, finally, a number of desiderata linked to the prior protection of people's basic autonomy. Once placed in this broader picture, I want to argue, then, that such a radical-liberal interpretation of Rawlsian ideas offers a powerful, normative foundation for justifying and renewing welfare universalism.

The arguments of this project evolve from an examination of Rawlsian ideas of justice and an effort to respond to the question of what they imply for the issue of work conditionality in the set of social rights that serve to guarantee everyone an adequate share of income and wealth. What are the implications of basic Rawlsian commitments for the moral status of basic income and similar policies of strong universalism? And how should the central Rawlsian ideas and concepts best be specified and interpreted when confronted with such issues?

There are several reasons for this choice of theoretical framework. Rawls's theory of "justice as fairness," as presented in *A Theory of*

Justice (1971) and specified in a number of books and articles, especially *Political Liberalism* (1993) and *Justice as Fairness: A Restatement* (2001), is the most influential theory in the academic literature on social justice. It offers a very forceful justification of many of the fundamental ideals and objectives that are widely shared in existing welfare states (Kangas 1998). However, while Rawls's own theory is the starting point of the project, the idea is not simply to derive ad hominem arguments based on exegetical studies on Rawls. It is to work out normative arguments on how best to justify and specify general Rawlsian commitments in dialogue with a broader literature on liberal-egalitarian justice and welfare reform.

While this project may not be very interesting to someone who rejects such Rawlsian ideals altogether, I think the ideas are general enough to have wide appeal in democratic welfare states. The moral convictions that serve as crucial normative footholds in debates on distributive justice and welfare conditionality can be fruitfully interpreted, specified, and assessed using concepts and ideas from Rawls's theory of justice. Those ideas can also helpfully capture and clarify many of the actual policy disputes in existing welfare states that set out to be both egalitarian and liberal in the ways indicated above.

Hence, Rawls's theory provides us with a rich normative framework that can establish substantial common ground between competing theoretical ideals from which many of the relevant disagreements can be approached.[7] I will seek to substantiate that claim in section 1.6. The more specific objective of my book, then, is to explore and defend a set of arguments for why the ideal of radical liberalism and the politics of basic income seem both desirable and feasible if one accepts certain general normative commitments of the Rawlsian framework.[8]

The remainder of this first chapter is organized as follows. In section 1.3 I shall provide a closer introduction to the basic income guarantee and the set of ideas covered by that term. In sections 1.4–1.5 I discuss the need for theories of justice, methodological considerations, and assessment criteria in the study of liberal-egalitarian justice and welfare reform. The relationship between the kind of justice-based approach adopted here and other forms of policy assessment is examined. I characterize a policy-oriented—"institutional"—form of ideal theory and argue that it offers a suitable analytical framework for assessing arguments on the moral status of such an idea. Having established relevant criteria for normative assessment, I move on (in sections 1.6–1.7) to introduce some of the central Rawlsian concepts and debates around which my study is structured and to briefly examine the notion of reflective equilibrium as the procedure for testing rival principles. The final section of the chapter (1.8) gives a general over-view and summary of the argument that lies ahead of us.

1.3. THE BASIC INCOME PROPOSAL

Considering the centrality of the basic income proposal in this proj-ect, I should start by defining that concept and explain some of the general attractions of this idea. "Basic income guarantee" (BIG), as I will explain here, is a general term used to describe any scheme of income support that offers resources unconditionally to all members (permanent residents or citizens) of the relevant political community, that is, including adult persons who are capable of working. To be more precise, they are offered to every full member of society (a) on an individual basis, (b) without any selective economic means test, and (c) without any requirement to work or demonstrate a willing-ness to do so.

Hence, such schemes represent a distinctive form of citizenship-based security where full membership of the relevant political com-munity is a sufficient condition for eligibility (De Wispelaere and Stirton 2004). Since none of these programs are based on special needs or employment status, they differ in crucial ways from social assistance, social insurance payments, and programs targeted at indi-viduals who are unable to work.

Criterion "b" is flexible enough also to include various forms of "negative income tax" proposals under the general label of a basic income guarantee, even though it should be noticed that such pro-posals have often been household-based rather than individualized. The negative income tax (NIT), to which I will return below, offers (more or less) automatic payments to low-income groups without any work conditions, but these payments are gradually reduced when the individual's earnings from other sources increase, that is, it is based on a form of "universal means-testing" (Fitzpatrick 1999, 75; see e.g., Friedman 1962).

The term "basic income" (BI) will be reserved for *a specific form of basic income guarantee* that I will be mainly concerned with in this book. Basic income differs from the negative income tax in the sense that it provides explicit payments of the same nominal amount to everyone (i.e., rich and poor), *irrespective of earnings from other sources* (Van Parijs 1992a; 1995, 57). Focusing on this version of the basic income guarantee then, what is it, more precisely, that makes it dif-ferent to most existing forms of income protection? This individual, universal, and unconditional payment contrasts with the typical, residual household-based, and means-tested form of social assistance that is normally paid only to people without access to savings, assets, or means from other members of the household.

Unlike most forms of social assistance, the basic income is fully individualized, and normally it is not reduced when income from other sources is added. Hence, in the typical basic income proposal there is no "poverty trap" imposed on basic income recipients that may result in very limited (if any) economic incentives to work for those who depend on the guaranteed social minimum. In contrast to most social assistance schemes—where income support is reduced with the full amount of an increase in one's labor income—even a small supplementary source of income or a part-time job would always give people a higher net income.

Finally, a basic income also differs markedly from job-based social-insurance-type programs. Unemployment insurance will typically be accessible only on a conditional basis to those that have a prior labor-market attachment, are available (and actively applying) for paid work, and demonstrate a willingness to take a job if offered. The logic of the basic income is also different from schemes that offer social insurance payments or pensions to people who are sick or in early retirement on condition that they are (demonstrably) unable to work (and therefore incapable of undertaking job-like activities). In contrast to any such *behavior-conditional* and *activity restricting* forms of social insurance or pension schemes, a basic income would give no reason to worry that one's activities or improving health would jeopardize one's eligibility for basic income security. There are no behavioral conditions or activity restrictions attached to the basic income. It is paid to all, with no strings attached.

For the above reasons, a basic income can be defended as an instrument of redistribution that secures a firm, opportunity-expanding and activating income floor for everyone. Thereby, it has the potential to help build the commitment to solidarity and freedom on wider and more inclusive foundations than arrangements based on various forms of work conditionality. It should be emphasized that the universalism of these transfers does not, of course, imply that everyone would actually be a net beneficiary of the basic income. After all, some capital endowment or income must be taxed (directly or indirectly) in order to finance the basic income. This normally involves significant redistribution from those who are (relatively) rich to those who are (relatively) poor, that is, wealthy individuals will pay much more in tax than they receive as basic income.

The level of a basic income could be high or low and need not be sufficient on its own to cover basic needs (Van Parijs 1992a, 4). However, most people drawn to the basic income proposal accept the introduction of a full basic income as a long-term objective, where full (as distinct to a partial basic income) is meant to signify that its level is sufficient to cover basic needs. For the normative purposes of the present research project, the basic income I will have in mind is high enough to provide each citizen with the basic means for a "modest but decent standard of life" (Pateman 2006) and would, thus, leave a very marginal (if any) role for social-assistance-like schemes. In addition to such a basic income there would, of course, still be a need for various targeted benefits to people with special needs and, possibly, some form of income-related social insurance appropriately adjusted, simplified, and coordinated with the basic income (see ch. 7).

There are, however, a number of possible deviations from the basic income proposal, and so we should also identify the most important pathways for constructing similar proposals without diverting from the general definition of a basic income guarantee above. In particular, I wish to stress the possibility for variation within the following three dimensions: duration of the program, interval between payments, and the time of final payments. Most defenders of a regular basic income advocate a permanent "from the cradle to the grave" scheme. However, in the literature there are also proposals for a "time limited basic income." This would typically offer every member of society (the opportunity to activate) an unconditional and adequate income, but only for a limited period of her life (White 2003a, 173–174). A regular basic income may thus be "full" but time-limited in the sense that the program is designed with the purpose of covering basic needs (in the absence of income from any other sources) during a fixed and limited period of time: say 1, 3, or 5 years.[9]

The "interval between payments" dimension captures the frequency and concentration of payments within the relevant period of time. It specifies whether the basic income guarantee is provided in the form of a regular stream of income (for example, weekly or monthly installments) (Van Parijs 1995) or, instead, fewer large payments. When the proposal consists in providing only one or a few lump-sum payments (Ackerman and Alstott 1999), basic *capital* is a more accurate term to use.

What about the time of (final) payment(s)? As we have seen, not all advocates of a basic income guarantee suggest that it should be distributed in the form of direct ("explicit") payments of the same nominal amounts to all, with no strings attached. When they are, they are normally redistributive since those who are better off will tend to pay much more in taxes than they receive as a basic income (the distributive outcome would, of course, depend on the details of tax arrangements and the sources of taxation). Nevertheless, some find it unnecessary or even provoking to make payments not only to net beneficiaries of the scheme but also to all those who would end up financing it. "Why pay Bill Gates?" (Block 2001).

Those who argue for ex post versions of a basic income guarantee suggest that it should take the form of an income tax reduction or tax credit (reducing the income tax one is obliged to pay) in normal cases, while those with low or no incomes may instead choose to regularly receive the benefit as an explicit payment in advance. This means that "tax-liabilities and the universal benefit are set off against each other annually" (Van der Veen 1998, 141). In cases where the value of the universal benefit turns out to exceed one's tax liabilities, the tax system is reversed. Instead of being required to pay a positive amount of money in income tax, people in the lower income bracket(s) receive money in the form of "negative taxes."

The crucial difference between ex ante and ex post versions of the basic income guarantee is that the former is paid to every member of society with no strings attached while the latter is based on some form of universal means testing or tax/benefit integration. In the latter category of proposals, the final sum of taxes or benefits will thus need to be adjusted in the light of knowledge about people's incomes from other sources. As long as "refundable tax credits," "credit income taxes," or "negative income taxes" are relevantly universal and unconditional, they will—according to my definition—all be included under the general label of a basic income guarantee.

1.4. Why Do We Need a Theory? Policy Assessment and Distributive Justice

Debates on the future of universalism, work-conditionality, and basic income must be informed by arguments that operate on different levels of abstraction, of which some are highly practical whereas others address more fundamental normative issues. Even though this project is concerned with policies and institutions, most of the arguments under study belong to the latter category. It is clear that a theory-driven and relatively abstract project, focusing on the moral aspects of the debate, cannot claim to offer an exhaustive basis for assessing the desirability of such proposals.

A relatively general account of how particular proposals or policy agendas relate to competing criteria of social justice will be insufficient as a basis for decisions on what to do under real-world conditions. Clearly, matters of economic feasibility, power, strategy, institutional and normative continuity, and a wide range of contingent and context-specific conditions will matter in crucial ways to the immediate relevance, political attractiveness, and short-term feasibility of such policies.

However, the exploration of the deeper moral issues at stake is clearly a necessary part of any full and satisfactory assessment of such ideas. There is also a sense in which such a project seems more fundamentally important than more contextually targeted and empirically richer forms of policy assessment that take further real-world feasibility constraints into account. Even if the policy orientations under consideration may be politically unfeasible, or likely to be counterproductive due to normative resistance against them, this does not by itself give a relevant reason to reject such views at the level of ideal theory. If a policy path of strong universalism seems desirable from the point of view of justice, but turns out to be politically unachievable, this gives us a reason for seeking to make the policies feasible by promoting the necessary institutional requirements or to shift focus in long-term budget priorities. At the same time, we would need to engage in discussion on how best to meet the underlying ideals and objectives under present circumstances.

Of course, normative conflicts and problem-solving in particular situations may often be resolved without reference to fundamental principles of justice. People may often agree about the choice of a political path in particular situations without being in full agreement about the normative sources from which this rightness flows (Lindensjö 2004). This insight is central to Amartya Sen's recent argument for the claim that so-called transcendental theorizing, beginning its normative analysis with an attempt to work out a conception of a perfectly just society, is neither necessary nor sufficient for advancing justice in the real, imperfect world (Sen 2009). And yet, the importance of spelling out the structure of our principles and convictions with precision will become apparent as soon as convincing arguments about the effectiveness of a particular reform for meeting some particular social aim are dismissed by someone with the disarming reaction: "so what?" (Van Parijs 1992a, 25).

The (supposedly) beneficial consequences of a redistributive reform for countering income inequalities will not matter to someone who considers the inequalities under study to result from individual choices for which people must be held economically responsible. The possible impact of unconditional schemes for expanding opportunities to perform nonmarket activities, or to reach greater independence in personal or labor market relations, will not impress anyone who believes that the good life, or the right norms of fairness, requires every person to be self-supporting through her own labor market activities. This is essentially why and how the study of particular policy issues leads us in the direction of a more fundamental and abstract normative analysis that serves to justify, clarify, and set out the relation and priorities between competing values and objectives.

The practical need to accept this task becomes particularly clear once we reject various versions of the claim that history is inevitably on the side of universal needs satisfaction, suggesting that history is destined to move in the direction of a general expansion of social rights, and/or that affluence will make the circumstances under which it is relevant or urgent to speak of justice fade away by providing all individuals with what they need (White 2003a, 6–7). Justice theorists tend to follow David Hume in taking the conditions of moderate scarcity and competing claims on resources as the fundamental circumstances under which principles of justice are needed.[10]

Counter to the expectations of historical materialism, or the optimism attached to social rights expansion during the 1950s and 1960s, such conditions are likely to remain inevitable features of the human condition. Hence, disputes on the requirements of justice are bound to be more than abstract theoretical quibbles of limited practical relevance. This observation is underscored by the growing awareness of ecological limits for global material expansion and the urgent need to address global climate change. As observed by G. A. Cohen: "Marxism thought that equality would be delivered to us, by abundance, but we have to seek equality for a context of scarcity, and we consequently have to be far more clear than we were about what we are seeking, why we are justified in seeking it, and how it can be implemented institutionally" (Cohen 2000, 115).

1.5. FEASIBILITY REQUIREMENTS AND IDEAL THEORY

A meaningful assessment of the desirability of basic income will require an analytical framework that systematically links philosophical standards of justice to the empirical evaluation of competing institutional arrangements and policy orientations. In this study I will adopt a framework of *institutional ideal theory* to serve this end. By institutional ideal theory I refer to a level of analysis placed on a level of abstraction in between John Rawls's very general account of ideal institutions and the more empirical approach that Bo Rothstein, following Lundquist, refers to as "constructive theory" (Rothstein 1998, 16–17).

The former, associated with Rawls's *A Theory of Justice* (the main target of Sen's criticism above), sets out to specify ideal institutions and policies in the context of a hypothetical, perfectly just society, under the assumption of favorable circumstances. The latter seeks to leave the philosophical ivory tower in order to offer useful policy prescriptions on the basis of an empirical account of what can be feasibly achieved by the state under real-world conditions. While these two approaches are both useful to different and complementary purposes, it seems that none of them are fully suitable to the objectives of this work. I will characterize the approach of institutional ideal theory by explaining why.

The concept of ideal theory builds on the Rawlsian notion of a well-ordered society, which is a society in which all, or nearly all, agree to live in accordance with the same public conception of justice (Rawls 2001a, 13). In contrast, nonideal theory is concerned with how best to deal with injustice under conditions where compliance to justice is absent or only partial. In Rawls's form of ideal theory we seek to identify the most plausible principles of justice, under the assumption that everyone else would also accept and act upon the principles under consideration (Rawls 1971, 245, 453ff.). The aim that defines this form of ideal theory, then, is to work out an ideal of a perfectly just society and thereby establish a normative standard, or point of reference, for identifying injustices under actual institutions in the (presumably) unjust world or society that we actually inhabit (Simmons 2010).

However, Rawls's own ideal-theoretical way of approaching the issue of ideal institutions has a number of limitations when it comes to the assessment of concrete policy proposals such as basic income. Methodologically, he draws a strict demarcation line between principles and objectives of particular institutional regimes, on the one hand, and the effectiveness of the institutions to actually meet such objectives, on the other: "A regime's ideal description abstracts from its political sociology, that is from an account of the political, economic, and social elements that determine its effectiveness in achieving its public aims" (Rawls 2001a, 137).

On his own general account of ideal institutions, they are assumed to successfully realize intended objectives, and hence his analysis does not address competing approaches to unemployment or particular social policy arrangements in any detail. The institutional guidelines advanced by Rawls are typically meant only as "rough and intuitive" and developed under simplifying assumptions of "favorable conditions." Hence, they leave more specific policy issues to the legislative stage where the relevant empirical facts and contextual information needed for a meaningful and accurate assessment of our options are available (Rawls 2001a, 135–136; 1996, 184).

Such an abstract and empirically thin approach to the study of principles of justice and competing institutions or policies is useful if we wish to set out a very general and utopian ideal that is normatively compatible with a wide range of specific arrangements and contextual circumstances and remains theoretically compatible with widely different empirical theories on political sociology and institutional design. However, an ideal-theoretical framework that does not address reasons for and against the effectiveness of competing institutional arrangements for meeting certain moral principles and objectives is not very helpful to our purposes. An analysis pitched at a level of abstraction where real-world problems, such as the challenge of unemployment, unavoidable feasibility constraints, institutional imperfection, or the unintended side effects of social policies, play only a marginal role will be unable to capture and provide guidance in many of the central disputes on justice considered here.

Such a form of normative analysis—in which we abstract from the circumstances under which many of our debates on justice become particularly pressing—is not well suited to provide a basis for useful policy guidelines when assessing rival views on how to deal with real-world conditions. Establishing a close dialogue between criteria of justice and the relevant policy arguments for competing institutional options requires an approach that is more closely adapted to the social and economic conditions of the societies we address. Observations about the limitations of Rawlsian ideal theory for producing politically relevant and applicable policy guidelines have led a number of practically oriented authors to attack such abstract forms of political theory. Ideal theories have been criticized as unfruitful forms of armchair theorizing, far too distanced from actual political realities and the "nonideal circumstances" we confront (e.g., Farrelly 2007; Mills 2005; see also the contributions to Robeyns and Swift 2008).

In one version of that criticism, "constructive theory" has been advanced by a number of authors who seek to identify an approach to policy assessment that combines normative theory with insights from empirical research on concrete policy implementation, and the impact of competing political institutions (e.g., Rothstein 1998; see also Lundquist 1993; Premfors 2000). This form of theory places the question of feasibility in the foreground. It aims to offer conclusions about what can successfully be done by state institutions and thereby attempts to establish a solid empirical foundation for providing useful and relevant guidelines for what to do here and now.

Clearly, the extent to which institutional arrangements and particular policies meet such political feasibility conditions and seem both possible and desirable will often depend on their propensity to gain broad acceptance and, thus, function well in each particular context with all its particular normative expectations and traditions (Swift 2003). For example, Bo Rothstein has suggested—in this constructive vein—that the basic income proposal seems problematic because a majority of people might regard nonworking basic income recipients as free riders. He suggests, on such grounds, that the introduction of a basic income scheme may violate a very important condition for the "contingent consent" upon which any widely supported welfare state institution is based (Rothstein 2000, 138).

Surely, in the context of real-world policymaking, it would be foolish not to take such considerations on normative continuity in relation to people's views and expectations into account. Nevertheless, while various forms of constructive theory have a crucial role to play, it is important not to conflate the search for ideal options with short-term political relevance and explorations into the perceived legitimacy of competing reforms within existing communities. What "can" successfully be done is often determined by more or less contingent circumstances. If the feasibility constraints imposed by popular opinion are viewed as conditions that are necessary for an acceptable theory to accommodate, we will tend to naturalize normative and institutional conditions that are both undesirable and (in the long run) avoidable.

Political feasibility conditions fixed by, say, presently fashionable discourse and widespread opinions would, thus, be dealt with as natural facts of human life, rather than conditions that could, and perhaps should, be done away with. From the point of view of ideal theory, then, we should not allow people's actual operative attitudes or convictions to enter into the characterization of just institutions solely on the grounds that they are likely to constitute important real-world feasibility constraints. The crucial matter is whether the attitudes and convictions in question (such as the perceived link between basic income and free riding discussed by Rothstein) are *morally justified*.

While sharing with constructive theory the concern for bringing less favorable circumstances and practical considerations to our attention, the policy recommendations that flow from institutional ideal theory need not be feasible in the more narrow political sense of tracking popular opinion, or of being likely to gain political support and legitimacy in our existing political communities. The guiding objective is not primarily to develop conceptions that are well suited to existing opinions or institutional traditions and, thus, desirable to implement here and now (all things considered). Instead, it tries to provide a more general and forward-looking yardstick for how institutions and practices should ideally address certain challenges and conditions that are bound to stay with us. Political philosophy is a source of inspiration and guidance in efforts to reach beyond the present human condition. In my view, then, constructive analysis—as interpreted above—must not be regarded as an alternative, but as complementary to more ideal-theoretical accounts of justice.

Institutional ideal theory seeks to provide an analytical framework in which our principles of justice are systematically related to institutional arrangements and practical considerations, such as administrative, technical, or economic issues of feasibility, the effectiveness of proposals to achieve our objectives, and the stability of the ideal in question (a desideratum to which I return below). It does so for the purpose of fleshing out an ideal social arrangement, under assumptions of broad compliance to the standards considered.

Our analytical focus is, thus, placed on the implications of considerations of justice for our public rules and practices.[11] The exploration of institutional ideals remains an exercise in ideal theorizing in something close to the Rawlsian definition, in the sense that it seeks an interpretation and specification of principles of social justice under assumptions of broad compliance to the general ideals and arrangements under consideration. In this case, however, the analysis refers more loosely to the compliance with ideals and arrangements rather than compliance with a fixed set of principles.[12]

The way we approach feasibility conditions will vary greatly depending on whether the analysis takes place in ideal or nonideal theory. Sometimes—as in constructive theory—feasibility conditions are primarily used to explore whether certain arrangements might be possible and desirable to advance under actual normative and institutional conditions (i.e., under fully realistic assumptions, taking people and societies as they are). Sometimes—as in Rawlsian ideal theory—the central feasibility test is, instead, whether a given ideal would be workable *under conditions of compliance to justice*, that is, once the ideal under consideration has been realized. In other words, a feasibility condition may primarily draw our attention either to the (nonideal theory) question of whether it is possible to get from here to there (and, if so, how?), or to the (ideal theory) question of whether the ideal would be viable, once in place.

One of the most important aspects of feasibility in institutional ideal theory belongs to the latter category and is closely related to Rawls's considerations on the stability of justice. Rawls repeatedly returns to the importance of paying close attention to the social and psychological consequences of the public acceptance of the principles of justice. What are the consequences for the public political and social culture and the trust and cooperative virtues necessary to sustain the preconditions for, and systemic needs of, a just society? (Rawls 2001a, 86, 116–119, 124–126). Would a particular ideal of justice, if fully implemented, tend to support or erode the conditions on which its justification relies? Would it be likely to win spontaneous allegiance over time?

In our present context, it is important to ask whether the attitudes, dispositions, and behavior encouraged by a particular radical-liberal scheme—such as a full basic income—and the moral commitments on which it is based are likely to support or weaken the social, economic, and cultural conditions on which its stable realization depends. On this broad, policy-oriented account of stability, this requirement largely coincides with the criterion of "viability," as recently defined by Erik Olin Wright. Wright's criterion asks whether "proposals for transforming existing social structures and institutions" would, if implemented, "actually generate—in a sustainable, robust manner—the emancipatory consequences that motivated the proposal" (Wright 2010, 21). In exploring the normative issues of work conditionality and basic income in the context of institutional ideal theory, the outcome depends on a systematic and integrated analysis of the following questions:

1. Which set of principles of justice should be chosen in a procedure of (wide) reflective equilibrium? (I will discuss the idea of reflective equilibrium in section 1.7).
2. What is the ideal set of institutions and policies for meeting these principles of justice under the general, objective circumstances in which history has placed us, taking feasibility into account?

The next step after having completed such an exploration in institutional ideal theory would be to address the following question of "constructive" theory:

3. How should the relevant principles of justice and social ideals be supported in nonideal theory, that is, under conditions of noncompliance to justice? What would be the fair and sensible way of meeting requirements of justice under nonideal conditions while, at the same time, moving closer to the ideal we should be aiming for? I will only briefly attend to these questions in chapter 7 of this book.

1.6. Introducing the Theoretical Landscape: Five Dimensions of Rawlsian Justice

Let us now turn to some of the normative debates on social justice that lie before us and to the theoretical perspectives I will rely on to shed light on the policy issues at hand. Since the publication of John Rawls's *A Theory of Justice* (1971), there has been a hugely influential strand in political theory that takes justice to be the most important virtue of social arrangements (Rawls 1971, 3). In the Rawlsian tradition, justice typically refers to (something like) "the way in which the major social institutions distribute fundamental rights and duties and determine the division of advantages from social cooperation" (Rawls 1971, 7).

This is not to say that such a view holds justice to exhaust the requirements of morality or that it outweighs every other moral concern. In my view, however, the value of justice does not compete with or need to be weighed against fundamental values such as liberty, equality, or efficiency. Instead, justice is understood as an "organizing concept," which incorporates, interprets, and justifies the role and meaning of such basic values when we address the distribution of burdens and benefits of our major institutions and social arrangements (Kymlicka 1992, xiii).

This is the theoretical tradition from which my project takes off. Rawls's theory of social justice promised to find an interpretation, justification, and unity to the requirements of an impartial normative commitment to each person's right to freedom and equality within a fair system of social cooperation. Rawlsian accounts of social justice rest on the idea that citizens who are advancing their political arguments about fair terms of cooperation to each other should find it reasonable for others to accept them when addressed as free and equal persons, and consequently not as "dominated or manipulated, or under the pressure of an inferior political or social position" (Rawls 1997/1999, 578). On this view we are required to attach equal concern to each person's interest, and to do so in a way that is not bound up with any particular "thick" conceptions of the good life.

This means that justice must be given an interpretation that does not attach an unjust privilege to any particular controversial conception of what a good life consists in. In order to respect people's diverse convictions and their freedom to live by widely differing ideals of the good life, we ought to be "nonperfectionists" in relation to competing ways of life.[13] Other terms used for the same idea is that we should be "neutral," "impartial," or "ecumenical" with respect to different accounts of the good.

It would not be plausible to require that we abstain from appealing to particular ideals of the good life in every minor political decision, or to abstain from promoting one's firm ethical beliefs in all the voluntary associations of society. Instead, the idea is that we should—as a matter of respect for diverse ideals and the fundamental values of liberty—avoid to settle matters of *basic justice or constitutional essentials* by imposing on others any particular conception of the good life or human perfection with which many people may reasonably disagree (Ackerman 1980; Barry 1995; Dworkin 2000, 153ff.; Kymlicka 2002; Larmore 1996, chs 6, 7; Rawls 1988/1999, 457ff.). Nonperfectionism suggests that in fundamental matters of distributive justice we should be primarily concerned with the distribution of so-called all purpose means that we all need (whatever ideals of the good life we may identify with), rather than justifying distributive arrangements in ways that are biased in favor of some particular way of life.

Broadly speaking, Rawls's theory takes equality in people's expected shares of all-purpose means to be the intuitively compelling point of departure. Inequalities in access to such resources are, to a large extent, viewed as the result of conditions for which individuals cannot reasonably be held responsible and are, in this sense, arbitrary from a moral point of view. However, it also holds that if inequalities generate incentives that will tend to improve the economic prospects of the least advantaged members of society (relative to what they would have enjoyed under more strictly egalitarian arrangements), such inequalities should be accepted. Hence, this *efficiency-sensitive egalitarianism* still leaves considerable leeway to justify deviations from full equality.

I will not offer a close examination of Rawls's theory in relation to the questions under study until chapters 2 and 3. In the following, however, I shall briefly introduce five central (broadly) Rawlsian debates on liberal-egalitarian justice in which our policy debates will be situated and briefly indicate how they all bring important normative resources for the study of justice, work conditionality, and basic income. One important project is to identify the particular all-purpose means or opportunities that egalitarian liberals should be concerned with, or, in other words, what the central "currency of egalitarian justice" should be (Cohen 1989; Sen 1980). In what way and to what extent should we stay out of conceptions of the good life when seeking to specify the relevant means? Depending on whether we emphasize income, leisure, wealth, the social bases of self-respect, or some other set of advantage(s)—such as welfare, resources, or capability to achieve certain valuable functionings—and depending on how we weigh the relevant advantages against one another, we will arrive at different conclusions about the desirability of basic income (*the currency of egalitarian justice*).

More specifically, considering the basic income proposal brings our attention to the implications of liberal neutrality in relation to different views about work and the good life. Does the liberal concern for state neutrality in relation to different conceptions of the good mean that it would be objectionably sectarian to take a stand on the ethical value of employment?

If that is the case, this could indicate that there is something ethically biased and illiberal about popular justifications for primarily targeting resources to promote opportunities for paid work and consumption, rather than also allowing people to use resources for non-market activities or leisure. That is indeed the view of many liberal proponents of basic income. Others have voiced arguments for why work might belong to the bases of self-respect, without which nothing seems worth doing (*work and liberal neutrality*).

A forceful strategy for critics of basic income is to argue that justice implies preferences for work and that it would be unfair to ascribe leisure preferences the same weight or relevance as work preferences when specifying the requirements of liberal-egalitarian justice. This introduces a third important debate on liberal-egalitarian justice, namely, to what extent obligations to contribute in return for social resources are built into the cooperative framework that provides the context for Rawls's theory of social justice. As we have seen, Rawls held that the task for a theory of social justice is to respond to the question of how to distribute the fruits of social cooperation within a fair cooperative scheme.

Explaining the meaning of such a "cooperative" account of the context and content of social justice and linking it to principles of reciprocity might suggest the following: The only persons who can ever make firm, *justice-based* claims on the relevant resources are normally those who cooperate in the sense that they make (or, at the very least, express a willingness to make) a productive contribution to their communities.

Different ways of specifying such a claim have been offered to reject principled, justice-based arguments for a substantial basic income. On the other hand, it is not obvious that all justice-relevant resources result from social cooperation, or what the concepts of cooperation and contribution (more exactly) entail, or that it is equally plausible under all social circumstances only to include "productive" cooperators among those to whom social justice applies. Hence the question: Is there any "reciprocity-free" category of wealth to which all can claim a share, regardless of their willingness to work or contribute? Philippe Van Parijs's case for basic income depends strongly on the assumption that there is indeed such a category of resources. I will refer to this aspect of justice as that of wealth sharing. On the other hand, critics of that view have questioned that there is such a category of resources or, to the extent that there is such a pool of assets, that all members of society have a justified claim to their value (*reciprocity vs. wealth sharing*).

These disagreements on the currency of justice, liberal neutrality, and reciprocity versus wealth sharing are intertwined with a fourth debate revolving on the relation between luck, exploitation, and responsibility. On one influential interpretation, Rawls's conception of justice is best justified if grounded in a general concern with counteracting morally arbitrary inequalities of "brute luck." On this interpretation and justification of liberal equality—dubbed "luck egalitarianism" by Elizabeth Anderson (1999)—relative disadvantages that result from conditions of brute luck are unchosen, undeserved, and therefore arbitrary from a moral point of view (e.g., Arneson 2000; Cohen 1989; Roemer 1994). Given the observation that many (perhaps most) conditions of the real world that determine people's access to social resources and opportunities (such as one's early socialization, talents, emotional and intellectual support) seem to be fully beyond our control, this luck-egalitarian position helps justify the strongly egalitarian tendency in Rawls's project.

This luck-egalitarian reading of Rawlsian intuitions on responsibility is helpful to the articulation of competing intuitions with respect to basic income. While luck-egalitarians hold that social justice requires equalization for circumstances beyond our control, it also holds that inequalities of outcomes for which people might reasonably be held responsible must be respected. Basic income can seem objectionable from this point of view because it entitles every person resources even if she freely decides not to work.

Moreover, people differ in their abilities to contribute depending on the productive capacity with which they have been endowed through talent, upbringing, educational support, and so on. Once we take into account that one's ability to contribute seems to matter to the justified resource claims one could have, there might be other grounds for holding this type of policy as objectionable. Not only does it extend the right to income security to those who can work but simply choose not to, it also fails to differentiate people's rightful resource claims depending on whether or not the talents and social background they have been endowed with would make it easy or difficult for them to support themselves in a meaningful way.

In specifying and addressing such objections, there is an important interaction between luck-based criteria of responsibility and (1) debates on how liberties may restrict objectives of economic equalization, and (2) the possible limits of luck-egalitarianism in dealing with (supposedly) self-inflicted disadvantages. With respect to 1, there is a strong liberal presumption for counteracting inequalities in ways that do not interfere with people's control over their own self, body, and talents. In other words, liberal equality must not justify the "slavery of the talented" in order to consistently neutralize the impact on people's options that are (largely) due to bad brute luck. "Natural" inequalities in health, talent, beauty, or whatever benefits our personal endowments may offer are often morally arbitrary in the luck-egalitarian sense. However, a liberal account of social justice must find a way to interpret egalitarian objectives in a way that is also sensitive to the universal freedom of occupational choice and other fundamental liberties.[14]

With respect to 2, theorists who are critical of (the full application of) luck-egalitarian principles have stressed that it seems unfair and/or disrespectful to deny resources to people whose choices (rather than circumstances) have led them into destitution. More broadly, to make the enforcement of needy people's rights and responsibilities depend on the seemingly harsh, intrusive, and moralizing judgments necessary to apply such responsibility-tracking distinctions may be inconsistent with the aspirations of liberal-egalitarian conception of social justice (Anderson 1999; Scheffler 2003; Wolff 1998; see also Knight and Stemplowska 2011) (*luck, liberty and responsibility*).

The final—fifth—debate on Rawlsian justice that I want to mention at this stage has been increasingly attended to in the wake of G. A. Cohen's writings on the site of distributive justice (Cohen 2000; 2008).

What agents or institutions would be responsible to bring about and maintain a (relevantly) just distribution? How should we specify the division of labor between public institutions and the informal norms of society? Placing issues of work conditionality and basic income in relation to this theoretical debate helps bring attention to the interaction between formal work obligations (and the norm of liberal neutrality in state policies) and the informal expectations or social "ethos" with respect to work and contribution in society at large.

In order to stimulate work and contribution—which is crucial to any feasible conception of justice—we can rely on different kinds of rules and incentives. Some authors that support basic income have argued that we must build (some version of) a strong societal work ethos—guiding people's individual behavior—in order to help neutralize arbitrary inequalities and boost the prospects of the least advantaged (*justice and the egalitarian ethos*).

On closer scrutiny, then, the feasibility of the basic income option may depend on (or benefit from) strengthening the importance of informal mechanisms for stimulating work effort. As I hope to show, confronting radical-liberal standards with the justice-based case for a work ethos helps clarify the social ideals under study and to expose forceful objections to the neutrality-based argument for unconditional transfers.

To sum up, this study in institutional ideal theory places the radical-liberal case for a basic income, and the question of whether social rights must be linked to work conditions, in relation to five "Rawlsian" debates on distributive justice: (1) The currency of egalitarian justice, (2) work and liberal neutrality, (3) reciprocity versus wealth sharing, (4) liberty, luck, and responsibility, and, finally, (5) justice and the egalitarian ethos. These dimensions of contemporary debates on social justice all help shed light on the moral status of universal and unconditional distribution.[15]

Of course, there are many other theoretical debates on social justice that are relevant to the study and assessment of basic income that I cannot attend to here. One particularly important issue that I must bracket is the geographical scope of liberal-egalitarian justice. How are we to think of the relationship between global or international justice and the internal justice of national (or similarly demarcated) communities? And—given a plausible account of justice and boundaries in ideal theory—how are we to deal with issues of migration and movement across borders with respect to social rights? Should we not be primarily concerned with the least advantaged in the world rather than the (less urgent case of) inequalities within relatively wealthy nation-states?

For the most part, my discussion will assume the context of an economically advanced, democratic nation-state, and the arguments are primarily addressed to other citizens of such communities. Many of the arguments should also be relevant to debates about basic income in communities that face different circumstances. However, the questions and emphasis of the exploration are shaped by the fact that this book is written from within the context of the European Union, and more precisely, a Nordic welfare state. The project is primarily motivated by the objective to identify a just way of tackling the challenges of inequality, unemployment, and labor market flexibility within such a wealthy, national (or similarly bounded) democratic community. Like most people, I assume that this will remain a relevant and important task for the foreseeable future.

In view of global inequalities and the presence of dire world poverty, however, such an emphasis might seem parochial and morally misguided (Caney 2005; Moellendorf 2002; 2009). In response, my present focus on domestic inequality is certainly not to deny the moral importance or urgency of distributive justice beyond existing national boundaries. Indeed, I leave open the question of which political units (if not humankind as a whole) the principles of liberal-egalitarian justice should ideally apply to.

One way of justifying a domestically bounded starting point would be to rely on moral arguments in favor of strong national units and identities as desirable components of a relevantly just world. On such views, the demands of justice within our particular national or regional communities are bound to have a special moral status. There are a number of familiar justifications of such a position. Perhaps we should attach a moral priority to people's democratic right to collective self-determination (or, more generally, the freedom of different communities to live by radically diverse views on social justice and much else). Perhaps there are special duties that arise through particular forms of interaction with one's compatriots that we do not have with others (cf. Miller 1995; 2007; Rawls 2001b).

I will discuss some of these criteria in chapter 3. I wish to stress, however, that our present focus on the case of domestic justice need not depend on (and is not meant to imply the endorsement of) such a bounded account of the scope of egalitarian commitments. Accepting a strong, justice-based call to reduce global inequalities, and perhaps even an ideal theory in which the same, fundamental principles of social justice apply to humankind as a whole, would be likely to cause tensions and trade-offs in relation to the project of domestic egalitarianism. However, there are also a number of complementarities between these projects. Indeed, the best way of softening the tension between domestic equality and the case for more open borders would be to improve the conditions to lead a good life regardless of where in the world one happens to be born. And it is likely that intra-national redistribution (along with building new international institutions to enforce cosmopolitan objectives) is often necessary for advancing opportunity-equalizing objectives worldwide.

As pointed out by Van der Veen and Van Parijs, there is a good empirical case to be made for why domestic welfare universalism tends to prevent or soften existing protectionist resistance to the economic restructuring needed to help equalize conditions across the world (for relevant measures, see, e.g., Brock 2009; Tan 2004). Here I will only mention two relevant mechanisms. First, it is not likely that people in the richer parts of the world will readily accept a development route that would tend to move a wide range of jobs to developing countries if that will threaten their income security and, thus, if it is not linked to a socially smooth transition path (se also ch. 7). Second, empirical studies suggest that people in universalistic and generous welfare states tend to be more favorably inclined toward development aid and global solidarity (Van der Veen and Van Parijs 2006, 11ff.).[16] I must, however, leave further discussion of these important matters to another occasion.

1.7. REFLECTIVE EQUILIBRIUM

This section offers a brief account of reflective equilibrium. It serves the purpose of describing, in a general way, how I will go about when approaching the task of moral assessment and my view of the relevant criteria for deciding when certain principles seem morally justified. On Norman Daniels's account of the "method of reflective equilibrium," this approach to moral justification suggests that we should try to find a stable and coherent state of equilibrium between three classes of propositions: (a) a set of well-considered moral judgments, that is, "convictions" or "intuitions" about what is right or wrong in particular cases; (b) a set of general moral principles or rules that may organize and govern those judgments; and (c) a set of relevant philosophical and empirical background theories we believe to support "a" and "b" (Daniels 1996, 22; Rawls 1971, 19–21, 48–51; Tersman 1993, 49–51, 56, 68).

The first step in this search for an optimal fit between principles and convictions is to formulate a set of consistent judgments and principles that mutually support each other. The concept of "considered" moral judgments implies that the relevant members of "a" must be resistant to various conditions that may normally be thought to distort the ideal use of a person's moral sensibility. In other words, the convictions need to be filtered so that we dismiss convictions guided by wishful thinking, prejudice, and other circumstances or mental conditions that are likely to make us arbitrarily disregard important evidence against some beliefs.

Such well-considered convictions constitute a provisional foundation for the rest of our beliefs. However, according to the equilibrium approach to moral justification, no moral convictions or principles are, in principle, immune to revision. We are thus asked to explain our strong convictions of justice in concrete cases by considering alternative sets of moral principles that may support them and to introduce new concepts and examples in order to clarify the structure and content of our arguments. In doing so we may be persuaded that some of our initial judgments are in fact untenable or incoherent in relation to the rest of our beliefs.

The "procedure" or "method" of reflective equilibrium is essentially that of going back and forth between these sets of propositions and trying to resolve tensions and contradictions between them until a coherent equilibrium is reached. Sometimes this will convince us to revise our set of moral principles to accommodate our considered convictions. Sometimes we will, instead, be moved to revise some moral judgment that seems inconsistent with plausible moral principles.[17] As the starting point of this procedure is a set of initial moral judgments, reflective equilibrium may seem bound to lead to conclusions that are conservative in the sense that the justified principles are those that support intuitions that seem natural and convenient for us to accept from within the particular cultural context we are embedded.

In order to explain why this is not the necessary outcome of this procedure, it is useful to introduce Daniels's widely accepted distinction between narrow and wide reflective equilibria. A narrow equilibrium is a state of a person reached by finding an optimal fit between a set of consistent principles and her considered moral judgments. However, moral thinking is not merely a matter of mutually relating judgments to principles at hand that may support or explain them and to minimize inconsistencies between them. A wide equilibrium may be the result of major theory-driven revisions of a belief system in a process where (ideally) all alternative sets of principles and their supporting arguments, as well as relevant philosophical and general empirical background theories, have been thoroughly examined:

> In this case, we suppose this person's general convictions, first principles, and particular judgments are in line; but now the reflective equilibrium is wide, given the wide-ranging reflection and possibly many changes of view that have preceded it. Wide and not narrow reflective equilibrium is plainly the important concept. (Rawls 2001a, 30–31)

One difficulty in this process is that equilibrium can sometimes be reached by either deciding to reject an intuition that is inconsistent with the rest of our beliefs or by revising our moral principles to accommodate that intuition. When torn between such options, how do we know which of them to choose? How do we know that the (wide) equilibrium within reach is *the right* equilibrium or, more broadly, that there is such a thing to be found?

Will Kymlicka is probably correct when holding that "the only way to show that it is possible to advance compelling arguments for the rightness or wrongness of principles of justice is actually to advance some compelling arguments" (Kymlicka 2002, 7). Considering the meaning of "rightness," in this context it should, however, be observed that the acceptance of the above criteria for justified beliefs is not necessarily to accept the further claim that a conception that successfully meets them is objectively true (thereby linking reflective equilibrium to the acceptance of moral realism, in some form). Needless to say, there are many rival accounts of the nature of morality and the possibilities for moral knowledge.

As emphasized by Brian Barry, however, such competing meta-ethical views need not affect which substantive moral views we take to be justified, or the actual practice of assessing them (Barry 1989, 258; cf. Rawls 1975a/1999, 290). In the present context, I identify our central, immediate aim of normative political theory as that of resolving moral tensions and contradictions by tracking down, structuring, and critically scrutinizing the basis of our political beliefs. It is to help provide guidance when facing fundamental normative trade-offs and when torn between conflicting judgments in matters of basic justice.

1.8. Overview of the Argument

I begin the argument by formulating a tentative justification of basic income based on a radical-liberal interpretation of central commitments expressed in Rawls's theory of justice (part I). The exploration then moves on to introduce a series of challenges to that view based on responsibility (part II) and feasibility (part III). Responding to those challenges will serve to clarify and reshape the structure of this conception and its implications in dialogue with a broader literature on liberal-egalitarian justice. It will also introduce various qualifications to the case for an unconditional distributive scheme in order to accommodate important objections. The final chapter briefly situates the argument for radical liberalism and the politics of basic income in the context of nonideal theory and real-world politics.

Part I

The first part of the book develops a general argument in defense of basic income, guided by the aims of maximizing the economic life prospects of the least advantaged while simultaneously promoting and protecting their status as equals at every stage of their lives. Chapter 2 provides a normative assessment of the basic income strategy relative to options based on an obligation to work, given the overall purpose of "maximinning" economic opportunity.

Different ways of defining and weighing competing primary goods, and of specifying the time frame for the analysis of economic prospects, will generate different policy implications with regard to the role and design of minimum income schemes. In the procedure of balancing competing primary goods, while also realizing other prioritized requirements of justice as fairness, I argue that we have reasons for attaching special importance to people's access to effective freedom and the social bases of self-respect or, for short, their basic autonomy.

Building on recent works on relational equality and the bases of self-respect, the argument identifies circumstances of exploitable dependency and the lack of a context for social recognition as key obstacles to a society in which people can identify and interact as equals. The importance of universally protecting (a) a solid foundation in support of a nonsubservient self-conception and (b) access to meaningful activity triggers both reasons for and against attaching work requirements to the social minimum. On balance, however, it is argued that these prioritized concerns provide an important reason for *continuously* counteracting economic inequalities in an *independence-preserving* way, and that basic income has crucial advantages in this respect.

Chapter 3 continues the Rawlsian exploration of the case for basic income in a more defensive vein. The chapter identifies a set of conceptual and normative bases for questioning the acceptability of unconditional schemes within Rawls's organizing idea of society as a fair "system of cooperation." The chapter reconstructs and analyses a number of ways in which this fundamental idea, and the notions of reciprocity and productive contribution with which it is closely linked, may potentially block the argument for basic income.

It is argued, however, that the best way of specifying the meaning and normative weight of cooperation-based and reciprocity-guided justice is unlikely to stand in the way of the possibility and attractiveness of a justice-based plea for basic income. The chapter distinguishes between thick and thin accounts of the cooperative requirement. My argument suggests that a thick interpretation of cooperation, which connects full cooperation very tightly to labor market participation, introduces problematic tensions in relation to other important Rawlsian commitments and fails to accommodate powerful intuitions of justice.

However, the most fundamental justice-based objection to unconditional distribution remains to be explored head on. Would not the taxation required to fund the opportunity-equalizing and equal-status-protecting scheme sketched in chapter 2 depend on the systematic exploitation of hardworking people? Even if the conclusions of part I would prove solid, the "exploitation objection" suggests that the protection of people's status as equals may come at a very considerable and, perhaps, unacceptable moral cost. Addressing the relationship between unconditional transfers and individual responsibility is the central task for part II of the book.

Part II

The exploitation objection leads us to an exploration of the account of equal opportunity set out by Philippe Van Parijs in *Real Freedom for All* and the rich debate sparked by this work. Van Parijs presents a detailed and sophisticated attempt of providing a solid, principled, first-best justification of basic income based on the idea of "gift equalization." This argument might give us a powerful, broadly luck-egalitarian argument for why the charge of exploitation is mistaken (or, at least, its weight exaggerated).

Following Van Parijs, we may link our tentative justification of basic income, and the arguments for maximizing the economic prospects of the least advantaged, to the existence of a large category of resources to which nobody has a prior responsibility-based claim (such as natural resources and inherited assets). For this argument to work, however, it must be able to explain both why the pool of such resources is sizeable enough to fund a substantial basic income and why access to them should not be restricted to people who are willing to use them productively.

In chapter 4, I develop a critical examination of Van Parijs's argument and some of the most important objections in the debate on *Real Freedom*. A reconstruction of his justification of basic income is followed by an exploration of the so-called restriction objection, of which I identify a strong and a weak version. The case for restriction holds that redistribution of the relevant "gifts" is required only to those that are willing to work and, thus, the involuntarily unemployed. I argue that Van Parijs's view survives the strong version of the objection (according to which the arguments for restriction applies to all assets of this kind) and harbors a number of qualifications to accommodate some of the concerns to which this objection points. At the same time, however, this exploration also argues that even Van Parijs's own account of gift equalization needs to incorporate important qualifications to the defense of unconditional payments, based on the long-term stability of justice (see section 1.5). Fleshing out the requirements of such demands leads to the conclusion that the normative status of basic income in this "gift distribution" framework is weaker and depends more heavily on the consequences of such a reform than *Real Freedom* indicates.

Van Parijs's way of arriving at his radical view that justice requires "the highest sustainable" basic income rests heavily on one interesting and controversial argument, namely, that so-called employment rents, incorporated in the wages of privileged jobs, belong to the category of resources to which all are equally entitled. It is possible to go along with the arguments of chapter 4 without endorsing the inclusion of scarce job assets in the category of resources to be dealt with as gifts to which all have an equal claim. This observation provides the starting point for the examination of a weak version of the restriction objection, according to which basic income–type transfers may be a suitable way of "maximinning" access to the value of some external assets, but that only those who are willing to work are entitled to the value of jobs.

Chapter 5 identifies and examines a number of moral criteria that may potentially break down the analogy between jobs and (other) gifts. In response to these objections, it is argued that Van Parijs's view remains a very powerful candidate for specifying luck-egalitarian, opportunity-equalizing objectives for our political purposes of formulating an institutional ideal. I also argue, however, that it is not able to fully accommodate our considered convictions of social justice, or to explain the advantages of the basic income, unless combined with our considerations of equality of status in part I. The real-libertarian account of equality of opportunity and individual responsibility needs to be constrained and reshaped by our prior concern to consistently support the social and economic foundations of basic autonomy. It seems, then, that *Real Freedom*, once placed within a broader framework of stability (ch. 4) and basic autonomy (ch. 5), provides powerful normative resources to save the tentative conclusions of part I from the charge of exploitation.

Part III

In light of the exploration of the radical-liberal argument for basic income in parts I and II, part III of the book places the issue of feasibility of such ideals in focus. The argument for unconditional wealth sharing is now confronted with questions about the social and economic conditions relied upon to make such a scheme "stable" or "viable," once in place. The starting point of chapter 6 is the observation that some adherents of an unconditional and universal tier of distribution make an informally enforced obligation to work—along the lines of G. A. Cohen's egalitarian ethos—a crucial component of their social ideal.

As shown in parts I and II, supporters of liberal neutrality (nonperfectionism) have powerful arguments for why there is something illiberal about linking access to "gifts" to work conditions. The central liberal motivation for basic income is to provide greater freedom to choose between different ways of life, including options attaching great importance to nonmarket activities and disposable time. As argued by Philippe Van Parijs, even those spending their days surfing should be fed.

This chapter examines Van Parijs's dual commitment to a real-libertarian justification of basic income and the public enforcement of a strong work ethos, which serves to boost the volume of work at a given rate of taxation. It is argued—contra Van Parijs—that this alliance faces the neutrality objection: the work ethos will largely offset the liberal gains of unconditionality by radically restricting the set of permissible options available. It would remove many of the options that made the acceptance of "real freedom" attractive and will be more consistent with a nonperfectionist standpoint than its rivals, thereby neutralizing such liberal gains.

A relaxed, nonobligatory ethos might avoid this implication. This view, however, is vulnerable to the structural exploitation objection.

Using feminist reservations against basic income as illustration, I argue that feasibility may here be achieved only because some choose to do necessary tasks to which most people have the same aversion. In light of these objections, the chapter examines whether there is a morally untainted feasibility path consistent with liberal objectives. In order for gift equalization to avoid the threat against neutrality while at the same time remaining economically feasible and nonexploitative, I defend the need for an ethos of contribution (which is much broader than a narrowly job-centered "productivist" ethos, and would cover many informal, nonremunerated efforts).

Reconnecting to the arguments about equality of status and basic autonomy, I also defend, on feminist grounds, the relevance of objections to universal cash transfers under conditions where other, prioritized, elements of justice (such as the provision of various social services) are not in place. In contrast to "libertarian" accounts of gift equalization, our emphasis on *social* equality leads us to attach particular importance to the requirement that people's preferences and projects can always be formed within a context of choice in which the bases of their status as equals is sustainably maintained. Hence, the book's pluralistic account of the egalitarian ideal leads to a policy agenda in which the principle of unconditionality is not sacrosanct, and in which policy implications will depend on contextual considerations on the outcome of the interaction between public policy and social structure.

Finally, chapter 7 discusses some of the political recommendations that may follow from the radical-liberal views explored and defended in this book. An important part of the process of clarifying and assessing arguments for and against the feasibility of a basic income regime is to spell out with precision the empirical mechanisms through which a basic income is expected (by its adherents and critics) to help bring about a certain outcome. The chapter develops a contribution to this theoretical project. The first part reconnects and seeks to specify some of the stability-based requirements from chapters 4 and 6 and offers a fuller characterization of the set of public-spirited virtues that a desirable and stable radical-liberal ideal must reproduce. This analysis also identifies a number of possible mechanisms through which the politics of basic income may indeed be supportive to such needs and, thus, stand this feasibility test.

The second part of the chapter places the arguments for basic income in the context of nonideal ("constructive") theory and a set of practical policy issues. In particular, the challenges of political legitimacy, sustainability, and gender equity are examined. The chapter is concluded by contrasting proposals in which basic income–type schemes are gradually introduced to reform and complement the welfare state, to those that wish to take very significant steps to replace it with a basic income model. In the face of budgetary constraints, it is argued that programs in which there is a modest basic income, combined with social insurance arrangements and various benefits in kind (associated with existing, universal welfare states), are much more promising than radical replacement strategies.

PART I

A Society of Equals: Radical Liberalism, Self-Respect, and Basic Income

CHAPTER 2

Equality of Status and Its Priority: A Rawlsian Case for Basic Income

2.1. RAWLSIAN JUSTICE AND THE WELFARE STATE: TWO CHALLENGES

Preventing unemployment, substantial inequality of resources, and unequal opportunities in the labor market are widely shared concerns in economically advanced welfare states. In recent years there has been an influential trend in both egalitarian and conservative thought emphasizing, in a much more pronounced way, the importance of linking income security to work requirements in tackling those challenges. In such ideals of welfare contractualism a minimum income is not an unconditional right of citizenship but something that one must earn (e.g., Giddens 1998; Layard 2005; Mead 2005; White 2003a). In order to remain eligible for a guaranteed minimum income, people must demonstrate that they are available for work, actively applying for work, and prepared to undertake other activities.

This chapter begins the exploration of an alternative, radical-liberal option by presenting a Rawlsian case for an unconditional basic income. It is probably uncontroversial to say that Rawls's justice as fairness is the most theoretically influential conception of social justice. With its concern for countering inequalities that seem arbitrary from a moral point of view, and to do so in ways that respect basic liberties and remain consistent with a wide range of conceptions of the good, Rawls's view offers a very forceful justification of many of the fundamental ideals and objectives that are broadly supported in existing welfare states.

I am, of course, not the first to seek a justification of basic income on liberal-egalitarian grounds. In recent years, however, many proponents of basic income have suggested that a solid nonperfection-ist case for basic income must rely in crucial ways on non-Rawlsian views, such as left-libertarianism (Widerquist 2006a), Dworkinian ideas about equality of external resources (Van Parijs 1995), or a republican account of freedom (Raventós 2007; Pettit 2007).

Against this background, the project of mounting a case for basic income on Rawlsian foundations responds to two challenges. The first is to argue that the politically influential ideal of welfare contractualism is actually, on balance, more difficult to reconcile with widely shared Rawlsian starting points than a basic income alternative. The second challenge, more narrowly concerned with other justifications of basic income in the literature, is to demonstrate that the Rawlsian framework holds sufficient resources to make a powerful case for an unconditional basic income.

Radical liberalism—as I shall characterize it—holds a substantial universal and unconditional tier of distribution to be one of the ideal requirements of liberal-egalitarian justice. To repeat, such an ideal is radical in the sense that it demands far-reaching equalization of opportunities. It is also distinctively liberal by insisting that people must be left free to use their resource shares for a much wider range of purposes and life plans than those typically accessible through traditional distributive schemes (involving a work-test or other forms of behavioral conditionality).

This chapter is organized as follows. First, briefly introducing the Rawlsian framework, I articulate and examine the most important reasons for and against work-conditionality and basic income available from Rawls's difference principle (section 2.2). Having identified some difficulties of grounding basic income in the difference principle, I then turn to develop a set of arguments for why a basic income strategy seems preferable to approaches that consistently tie the social minimum to work obligations.

Sections 2.3–2.4 spell out my Rawlsian grounds for why (a) the promotion of opportunities for meaningful activities and the conditions for nonsubservience of the least advantaged matter in crucial ways to a plausible account of Rawlsian justice and (b) why a basic income regime would do better than its main alternatives within these dimensions. In sections 2.5–2.6 I respond to objections that accept the normative premises of my argument but insist that an obligation to work is required to meet the very same moral objectives. Finally, the chapter is concluded with some clarifications and caveats (section 2.7).

2.2. The Difficulty of Grounding Basic Income in the Difference Principle

According to John Rawls, the right principles of justice for a fair scheme of cooperation are identified behind a veil of ignorance. Behind the Rawlsian veil, we lack information about our specific ethical aims, talents, family attachments, and so on, but we do have general knowledge of all relevant empirical facts needed to make a decision on what principles and institutional arrangements to accept. We know that we must be prepared to live a complete life in a society guided by the principles of justice chosen, but we do not know if we will turn out to be rich or poor in marketable talents, or whether we will be religious or atheists, leisure loving surfers or hardworking Protestants, and so on.

This thought experiment of the "original position" is employed to bring out the meaning and implications of an impartial and equal concern for the interests of all, regardless of their circumstances or conceptions of the good life. Given the high stakes involved in this very special choice and given the assumption that the decision is final (we must be prepared to live a full life under the chosen set of principles, whatever the outcome), Rawls famously argued that the most rational rule for decision-making behind the veil of ignorance is maximin, that is, "to adopt the alternative the worst outcome of which is superior to the worst outcomes of the others" (Rawls 1971, 152–153). In other words, we should select the institutional arrangement that provides an outcome that is as beneficial as possible for the least advantaged. Rawls proposes the following two principles of justice:

1. Each person has the same and indefeasible claim to a fully adequate scheme of equal basic rights and liberties, which scheme is compatible with the same scheme of liberties for all.
2. Social and economic inequalities are to satisfy two conditions: (a) they are to be attached to positions and offices open to all under conditions of fair equality of opportunity; and (b) they are to be to the greatest benefit of the least advantaged members of society (Rawls 1996, 5–6; 2001a, 42–43).[1]

In this chapter I shall be primarily concerned with the second part of the second principle, usually called the difference principle, and leave aside details and priority problems with which this set of principles presents us (I introduce some aspects of principle 1 in section 2.3). In assessing competing arrangements from the point of view of the difference principle, the worst off are, roughly, identified by looking at the least advantaged person's share of so-called primary social goods (more precise formulations will follow).

If, behind the veil of ignorance, we are left with no knowledge of our own ethical convictions, Rawls's idea is that our account of advantages or resources should be more or less untied from any particular ideals of the good life. Hence, social primary goods are things that a rational person is normally presumed to want "whatever else he wants," or, as he later specified, that people need in their status as "free and equal citizens" and "fully cooperating members of society" (Rawls 1971, 62, 92; Rawls 2001a, 58). For Rawls, this includes, among other things, income, wealth, powers and prerogatives, and the social bases of self-respect.

What are the implications of Rawls's view for the issue of work requirements and the social minimum? Let us start by reviewing some possibilities in dialogue with the earlier literature on this issue. In *A Theory of Justice*, Rawls actually mentions the negative income tax (which automatically provides a nonwork-tested guaranteed income for anyone below a certain income threshold) as part of the institutional structure that justice as fairness may recommend. He also links the difference principle to the objectives of providing all with an adequate social minimum (1971, 275, 277, 285).

It is not difficult to identify powerful arguments in support of such an orientation toward unconditional transfers. After all, under any scheme of income support based on stringent forms of means testing and/or a work-test, there will always be some individuals falling through the safety nets. By contrast, a fully universal basic income, paid directly to each member of society, should be more or less watertight by avoiding most causes of low or partial take-up of the relevant benefits (cf. Van Parijs 1995, 94–96; 2003a, 216–222).

A basic income scheme does not involve any intrusive procedure that may easily generate feelings of shame among the needy. There is no informational or administrative complexity that may give rise to difficulties to decide whether or not someone is actually eligible for support. Nobody would be prevented from knowing their rights or fail to activate support because of stigmatization, lack of relevant information or skills. Hence, by opting for this radically universalistic strategy we would have done what we can to make sure that nobody in the relevant community falls below the level of the guaranteed income.

For reasons to be explained, this is not, however, the interpretation that Rawls himself favored once faced with various objections to the difference principle. In 1974 Richard Musgrave stated the critique that Rawls's initial formulation of that principle involved an objectionable bias in favor of those with a strong preference for leisure or nonmarket activities. He argued that it would unfairly support healthy adults who *choose* to indulge in a life of leisure at the expense of their hardworking fellow citizens (Musgrave 1974).

Using Rawls's way of identifying the least well-off, we would find not only low-paid workers or involuntarily unemployed in that category but also leisure-oriented persons who can work but simply *prefer* not to. The objection about the difference principle's alleged insensitivity to people's responsibility for work-leisure choices has later been repeated by many other critics, including in Will Kymlicka's influential discussion (Kymlicka 2002, 73–74).

Can it be right (to take an example later discussed by Rawls) that a person who prefers surfing along the beaches of Malibu all day to the unglamorous reality of full-time work should be entitled to access public funds in the form of generous income rights on an unconditional basis? A full reply to this question is not possible until we have examined how best to specify the demands of individual responsibility in liberal-egalitarian justice, questions I will not address in detail until chapter 4. There are, however, a number of other central interpretive decisions that help determine the difference principle's response to the claims of our surfers.

In fact, no decisive suggestion on the normative status of basic income seems to flow from Rawls's own interpretation of his principles of justice. One reason is that Rawls's egalitarianism is distinctively pluralistic. The substance to be equalized or maximinned is not *one* clearly identifiable and measurable currency, but a flexible index of primary goods. Rawls offers little guidance on how to ideally weigh the various types of goods against one another and seems to suggest that the implications of justice as fairness for our present concerns must be worked out at the legislative stage where information about the particular situation, context, and relevant traditions is available.

It must be observed, however, that Rawls offered arguments to tighten the link between the principles of justice as fairness and the case for attaching work requirements to the social minimum. In response to the kind of criticism voiced by Musgrave and Kymlicka, Rawls repeatedly held that a promising way to deal with the Malibu surfers would be to include leisure in the index of primary goods: "twenty-four hours less a standard working day might be included in the index as leisure. Those who were unwilling to work...would have extra leisure stipulated as equal to the index of the least advantaged. So those who surf all day off Malibu must find a way to support themselves and would not be entitled to public funds" (Rawls 1996, 181–182, n9; 2001a, 179).

Accepting Rawls's idea of adding leisure to the list of primary goods and to weigh income, work, and leisure in the way suggested would thus enable us to say that once we operate with a more complete notion of relevant goods, poor people who are *voluntarily* unemployed do not actually belong to the least well-off. In the absence of redistribution, they have lower income than those working full time, but they have much more leisure. This suggests that in comparing the income prospects of the least advantaged under different arrangements, we should mainly be concerned with the least well-paid full-time *workers*; that is, typically "unskilled laborers" (Rawls 1971, 78).

Before examining this option further I want to identify another and perhaps more forceful response available for Rawlsian critics of BI who wish to avoid the Musgrave-Kymlicka type of charge. Rawls offered many different ways of specifying the difference principle (for an excellent overview, see Van Parijs 2003a). But the formulation of the principle he tends to accept in most passages is actually concerned with average *life prospects* of the worst off. Rawls wants to maximize the expected lifetime share of primary goods of a representative member of the group holding the least favorable *social position* (Rawls 1971, 64, 98, 285; 1982/1999, 362–363; cf. Schaller 1998, 371).

If accepted, this interpretation may give arguments to strengthen the view that our Rawlsian arguments for a generous, watertight basic income scheme rest on objectionable moral priorities. The difference principle would actually seem less vulnerable to the Musgrave-Kymlicka objection than such critics (and Rawls himself) tended to believe because the implications they are concerned to avoid may not follow.

If the difference principle is applied to lifetime expectations linked to the least advantaged positions, this would be compatible in principle with distributive arrangements under which people's actual monthly incomes would, in some periods, be very low and even fall temporarily below a certain poverty threshold *if* we could safely expect that the incentives of such a scheme would help maximize the long-term prospects of (representative members of) the relevant group. Indeed, focusing on *representative* members of a group allows the conclusion that some, less representative, individuals may actually be allowed to slip through the safety net altogether. Also, attaching some productivity-enhancing behavioral conditionality to the social minimum would arguably be required if (again) the expected (say) total earned incomes of the least favorable worker were to expand as a result in the long run.

Hence, a "life prospect" perspective of this kind, with an emphasis on income and wealth expectations, harbors powerful reasons for rejecting any basic income policy that would significantly reduce work incentives. By opting for a basic income policy that allows people to choose more freely what kind of work to accept, and how much to work, a lower volume of labor output could be expected compared to policies more closely tied to stimulate employment, human capital investment, or other productive activities. If the lifetime expectations of income and wealth for the least advantaged are thereby worsened, the basic income option would seem far from optimal from our Rawlsian standards.

All this may have left us with some uncertainty about the relevance of a solid, regular guaranteed minimum of some kind (work-tested or not) and, thus, the relevance of our initial remarks about conditionality and low take-up. However, if we are serious about introducing leisure as a primary good—as suggested by Rawls in response to the Musgrave-Kymlicka type of argument—adherents of the basic income approach actually have good reasons to question that the outcome of the life prospects comparison is something that should be held against their view. It is true that Rawls's argument on leisure as a primary good helpfully provides us with a reason for why we must not regard a full-time worker and a full-time surfer (having the same income level) as equally situated from the point of view of justice.

However, as pointed out by Philippe Van Parijs, this would also offer the bases of an argument *in favor* of basic income-oriented policies when assessing the life prospects linked to the least advantaged social positions. True, the economic incentives and cultural dynamics of a feasible basic income regime may not be optimal for maximizing the expected lifetime shares of income and wealth of the relevant group. But access to a subsistence level basic income *is* (all other things being equal) likely to offer better opportunities for all to bargain for working conditions that provide more leisure (e.g. through part-time work and career breaks) compared to institutions that consistently tie income rights to work obligations (Van Parijs 2003a, 219–220; Van Parijs 2009b, 5–6).

So, perhaps a basic income regime would provide less income and wealth but more leisure to holders of the least advantaged social position, compared to an egalitarian "obligation to work" regime facing similar conditions. Hence, taking leisure into account is likely (depending, of course, on empirical assumptions) to lead the application of the difference principle in a direction more favorable to the basic income option. However, it also leaves its implications with respect to welfare conditionality highly indeterminate. For someone who turns to the difference principle for guidance on how to address these controversial policy decisions, this is a disappointing result. Policy recommendations now seem to depend on the weights we decide to attach to income and wealth, on the one hand, and leisure, on the other. Justice as fairness remains silent in this matter.

2.3. A Broader Agenda: Equality of Status and Its Significance

So, are there considerations on any other, more fundamental normative commitments that may help unbreak this tie between unconditional and conditional options? Yes, I think so. First, any plausible conception of justice needs to make sure that people can effectively make use of the basic rights and liberties covered by Rawls's *first* principle, having lexical priority to equality of opportunity and the difference principle. Rawls plausibly holds that effective freedom, in this sense, requires some form of minimum income, ensuring that everyone's basic needs are met (Rawls 1996, 7; Casal 2007, 323–324; Schaller 1998, 376). This argument about effective freedom provides independent grounds for why any balancing of different primary goods in maximinning life prospects must operate on the foundation of some kind of sufficiency floor, ensuring that people can always satisfy their basic needs.

In addition, it is well-known that Rawls gave powerful arguments for why the social bases of *self-respect* may constitute the most important primary good, because if we lack self-respect "nothing may seem worth doing, or if some things have value for us, we lack the will to strive for them." Rawls's account of self-respect includes, first, "a person's sense of his own value, his secure conviction that his conception of his good, his plan of life, is worth carrying out. And second, it implies a confidence in one's ability, so far as it is within one's power, to fulfil one's intentions."[2] Hence, the parties of the original position "would wish to avoid *at almost any cost* the social conditions that undermine self-respect" (Rawls 1971, 440, emphasis added).

For focus and simplicity I shall, for our present purposes, merge these two prioritized elements of Rawlsian justice, the effective freedom to exercise one's basic liberties and to access the bases of self-respect, into the broader requirement of *basic* or (in the words of Cécile Laborde) *minimal autonomy*.[3] To be autonomous in this basic or minimalist sense is, then, to access the key conditions needed to meaningfully make use of one's basic liberties and to approach *competently* and *confidently*—that is, well-informed and with a lively sense of self-worth—the tasks and ways of life at one's disposal. As argued by Laborde, "we do not have a (basic and universal) interest in pursuing a life of autonomous assertion, but we do have a (basic and universal) interest in avoiding ethical servility" (Laborde 2006, 371; see also Laborde 2008).[4]

Basic autonomy, in turn, can plausibly be regarded as one of the key requirements of a wider and more fundamental idea of equality of status, addressing all the conditions necessary to place people in a position from which they can interact as social and political equals. While noticing that equality of status may potentially have far wider implications, some of which I will attend to in chapter 6, the remainder of this chapter is mainly concerned with the *economic* demands of *basic autonomy*.[5] The important observation for now is that our reconstruction of the Rawlsian commitment to basic autonomy helps bring attention to normative demands that we have reasons to ascribe priority in relation to many other aspects of social justice.

Rawls's own (rather abstract and general) account of the difference principle does not offer much guidance on how to address situations of unemployment and job inequalities or, more generally, to deal with the side effects of our best instruments for promoting participation in paid work. It should be clear, however, that once we introduce the challenge of preventing unemployment *and* take basic autonomy into account, our conclusions are likely to diverge substantially from those stated in section 2.2. If we go along with the moral priority of basic autonomy, this suggests the differences between regimes in expected access to income, wealth, or leisure over the course of a life to be less important than differences in the satisfaction of basic needs and the bases of self-respect. How, then, could considerations on these concerns, and self-respect in particular, affect the choice between basic income and work-test schemes?

I shall argue that *social recognition* and *nonsubservience* are two key elements in a plausible account of the social bases of self-respect. Providing people with access to (and not preventing them from taking part in) meaningful forms of participation, with opportunities for social recognition, is, no doubt, very important if we want to promote social conditions for the development of a person's confidence in her abilities to pursue tasks within her powers and a lively sense of her own worth (J. Cohen 1989).[6]

Section 2.2 mentioned how problems of stigmatization may prevent distributive programs from reaching intended, low-income recipients. But surely, the problem that transfers based on certain forms of classification may be interpreted as visible markers of inferior status (and thus bound up with feelings of failure, guilt, or shame) is something that looks morally troubling, quite apart from its potentially negative effects on the take-up of income support. Catriona McKinnon argues, in this vein, that the social bases of (Rawlsian) self-respect demand that people can pursue their projects with a "non-subservient self-conception" (McKinnon 2003, 146).[7] Prima facie, distributive arrangements under which some people have no option but to live under conditions of exploitable dependency and, thus, (to use a republican phrase) at the mercy of others seem objectionable from this point of view (cf. White 2006b, 71–72).

With this general reconstruction in place, it is easy to understand Rawls's repeated emphasis on meaningful work and personal independence in his characterization of the ideal of a well-ordered society:

> no one need be servilely dependent on others and made to choose between monotonous and routine occupations which are deadening to human thought and sensibility. Each can be offered a variety of tasks so that the different elements of his nature find a suitable expression... The division of labour is overcome not by each becoming complete in himself, but by willing and meaningful work within a just social union of social unions in which all can freely participate as they so incline. (Rawls 1971, 529)

To get a clearer idea of the broader picture in which these demands of social recognition and nonsubservience should be placed, it is also worth noticing that the demands of basic autonomy help us attend to an important ambiguity in the justification of the difference principle. I find it natural and attractive to interpret the Rawlsian presumption for maximin as based, at least in part, on an attempt to balance brute-luck equalization against considerations of efficiency (cf. Van Parijs 2009a; White 2007). There is an important sense in which inequalities of economic life prospects due to circumstances of brute luck are "morally arbitrary" and should be counteracted in a just society (see 1.6). Nevertheless, pursuing the path of brute-luck equalization will only seem sensible, all things considered, insofar as this helps improve the prospects of the least fortunate (Birnbaum 2010a).

At the point where steps toward greater equality would tend to make the least advantaged groups economically worse off than before ("leveling down"), redistribution of primary goods should come to a halt. Now, as long as we are focusing narrowly on economic prospects, it seems that such an agenda for *efficiency-sensitive egalitarianism* should lead us (all things considered) to focus *primarily* on the absolute living standard of the disadvantaged, not so much on how well members of this group fare relative to others in their community.

However, it should be clear that an important argument for ascribing instrumental value to the reduction of economic inequality arises once we take into account that relative economic positions—with the power asymmetries, dependencies, and social roles with which they are associated—matter greatly to the social bases of self-respect. Rawls himself points to the possibility that "a person's lesser position as measured by his index of objective primary goods may be so great as to wound his self-respect" (Rawls 1971, 534). At this stage, let me just mention one relevant mechanism (I will discuss other aspects of this point in the following section; see also section 5.6 in ch.5). Whether or not people can access the resources to live up to *basic social norms and conventions* in their society and thereby (as stressed by Amartya Sen) "appear in public without shame" clearly depends not only on how much resources they have in absolute terms, but also on how much they have (and of what) relative to others in their community (Sen 1991, 71). When we attend to the bases of self-respect, then, continuously moderating economic inequality—the size of the economic gaps in a given society—may sometimes seem even more important than maximizing the absolute economic prospects of the least well-off (Pogge 1989, 162–163; White 2007, 6–7, 104).

2.4. A Rawlsian Case for Basic Income

In this section I will argue that a basic income approach has crucial advantages relative to its conditional rivals when trying to meet the Rawlsian agenda set out in section 2.3. My central argument is that a basic income scheme can help satisfy basic needs and improve the economic prospects of the least advantaged in ways that *also* (1) promote their opportunities for social recognition and (2) secure important conditions for each person's nonsubservience at each stage of her life.

In contrast to distributive schemes that rely on stringent forms of means testing and/or work conditionality, a firm layer of unconditional and universal payments offers a path to realize our Rawlsian objectives without causing fundamental trade-offs between them. The potential of a basic income scheme to help support access to meaningful employment for the least advantaged stems primarily from the fact that its unconditional nature makes it possible for those receiving it to reject or leave unsatisfactory jobs. People can thus place much more emphasis on the content of the activities offered (cf. Williams 2006).

Social assistance and social insurance schemes typically allow payments only on condition that recipients are prepared to take a job if offered, whether or not they find it rewarding. The fact that people are given this kind of bargaining power by the basic income payment would thus reduce the availability of people competing for highly unattractive jobs at low wages. It would thereby strengthen economic incentives for employers to improve working conditions and/or offer higher wages for such tasks.

Those who are sympathetic to workfare policies may now object that this bargaining power would not, on balance, support the recognitional bases of Rawlsian self-respect if it would greatly reduce work incentives for the less advantaged. If people are not only free to reject unsatisfactory jobs but also economically discouraged to take *any* job, this economic equalization may tend to lock healthy people into unemployment, isolation, and idleness. The general thought is that the reservation wages under such a scheme would be very high because of the high effective marginal tax that people in the lowest income brackets would face under such a scheme.

Such an argument, suggesting a trade-off between redistribution and social recognition, may have considerable force when targeted against the forms of welfare dependency experienced under a means-tested social assistance scheme with lax or no work requirements. But it is crucial to see that a sensibly designed basic income scheme is something very different. Since a basic income without a so-called poverty trap is not (like social assistance payments) reduced as income from work or capital is added to it, people are free to *combine* paid work, savings, and basic income in a flexible way. It could thereby introduce extensive opportunities to subsidize self-employment, to accept a part-time job, or to take jobs that are low-paid (and perhaps not viable in the absence of basic income) but intrinsically rewarding.

It could also make "job sharing" between the involuntarily unemployed (who want to work more) and the involuntarily employed (who want to work less) more feasible. Having the basic income to rely on would provide greater freedom to take a career break in order to improve one's skills, or to engage in a wide range of nonremunerated activities beyond the wage-based economy that one finds attractive.

Through these mechanisms a basic income policy (perhaps linked to the removal of some labor market regulations that may become redundant with a basic income in place) can help equalize resources while at the same time promote access to meaningful activities for the least advantaged.

A possible trade-off between economic equalization and social recognition is also present in various inactivity traps facing those who have become categorized in conditional distributive schemes as (more or less) permanently *unable to work*. Individuals who find themselves in these situations—early retirement, sickness, limited employability—are often unavoidably encouraged by the rules of inactivity-conditional schemes to regard themselves as unable to work or contribute in order to remain qualified to receive the necessities of life.

To the extent that people would risk losing their access to a steady, reliable stream of income if they try to take a job, or accept other work-like activities in civil society or the domestic sphere (thus indicating that they may actually be able to work after all), such programs clearly introduce incentives to become or stay unable to work and, thus, inactive in order not to jeopardize their income security. Through these inactivity traps, dependency on such schemes may often be harmful to the opportunities for social recognition and, thus, the *confidence and self-esteem* of the least advantaged, especially when the categorization involved is found stigmatizing.

Having a basic income to rely on, and having the freedom to combine the basic income with paid work, should not only make meaningful (part-time) employment more accessible for those having difficulties to cope with a full-time job, it would also become economically smoother and less risky to move out of conditional programs based on inability to work. By avoiding stigmatization and by not basing eligibility to receive an income on the kinds of classification and inactivity mentioned, the basic income scheme offers economic security without fostering a personal identity as (more or less permanently) incapable of work or other contributive activities.

Having established some key advantages of the basic income option for counteracting inequality of economic resources *while at the same time* supporting the recognitional bases of self-respect, let us now turn to the conditions for nonsubservience. Consider the obligation to work and conditional income rights from the point of view of individuals without steady jobs who are frequently in need of income support or help from partners, friends, or relatives. Even when individuals in such conditions do manage to get the *income* they need to cover their basic needs, they still live in circumstances of exploitable dependency.

The nonsubservience condition of self-respect is not very clearly articulated in Rawls's own writings. It is, however, as indicated by his remarks on independence and meaningful work quoted above, implied at several stages of his argument. This interpretation can, for instance, help justify and explain Rawls's view that an egalitarian form of property-owning democracy would be superior to welfare state capitalism. Rawls emphasized the need for widespread ownership of wealth and human capital ex ante and thereby minimizing the need for the means-tested benefits ex post that he associated with welfare state capitalism.

A property-owning democracy, endowing people equally from the start, would move beyond the reactive focus of many welfare state arrangements and minimize chronic dependency on welfare by putting "all citizens in a position to manage their own affairs on a footing of a suitable degree of social and economic equality." Under Rawls's alternative, then, we must ensure that the least advantaged are endowed as free and equal citizens and not be placed in a position in which they are objects of "charity and compassion, much less our pity" (Rawls 2001a, 139; cf. Krouse and Macpherson 1988). James Meade's writings, on which Rawls's brief characterization of property-owning democracy relied, were even more explicit about the crucial link between personal independence, bargaining power, and nonsubservience:

> The essential feature of this society [the property-owning democracy] would be that work had become rather more a matter of personal choice. The unpleasant work that had to be done would have to be very highly paid to attract to it those whose tastes led them to wish to supplement considerably their incomes from property. At the other extreme those who wished to devote themselves to quite uncommercial activities would be able to do so with a reduced standard of living, but without starving in a garret. (Meade 1964, 40–41)

In fact, Meade defended the basic income proposal in many writings over the course of several decades (including his final book—*Full Employment Regained?*—published in 1995), usually conceived as an individual share of the return from socially owned capital (a "social dividend"). As he observes in another passage:

> A man with much property has great bargaining strength and a sense of security, independence, and freedom...He can snap his fingers at

those on whom he must rely for income, for he can always rely for a time on his capital. The propertyless man must continuously and without interruption acquire his income by working for an employer or by qualifying to receive it from a public authority. *An unequal distribution of property means an unequal distribution of power and status even if it is prevented from causing too unequal distribution of income.* (Meade 1964, 39, my emphasis)[8]

Following this Meade-Rawls agenda for independence-preserving equalization "ex ante," let me point out two more specific reasons based on nonsubservience why a basic income should be a part of such a radical-liberal path beyond welfare state capitalism. First, as argued by Jonathan Wolff, there are numerous "harmful effects on respect-standing and self-respect caused by shameful revelation" under work-based conditionality. One of them is that people are subjected to situations of demeaning exposure where one must not only admit to oneself *but also make a convincing case to public authorities* that one has not been able to find any job "despite one's best efforts" while others could easily do so (Wolff 1998, 114, 121–122; 2010). In this way, heavy reliance on conditionality may easily breed, or reinforce, a deep sense personal failure and inferiority.[9]

Second, the impossibility to withdraw from a relationship on which one depends for one's livelihood is likely to help silence the propensity to articulate to oneself and voice ideals and complaints to others, whether in the home, the workplace, or the forum (cf. Okin 1989, 136).[10] On Rawls's view, "we expect and indeed want people to care about their liberties and opportunities so that they can achieve their good. We think they would show a lack of self-respect and weakness of character in not doing so" (Rawls 2001a, 85). However, it is not surprising if people display this "lack of self-respect" when they systematically depend on another for the satisfaction of their basic material needs. Placed in such a situation, people will often need to strategically anticipate the reactions of the latter and suppress their own wishes and concerns (see also Lovett 2010, 131–134).

Having a firm, reliable, and relation-independent basic income to access gives a person (in the words of Karl Widerquist) the "the power to say no" to partners, bosses, and welfare bureaucrats, or anybody else she may depend on for a living (Widerquist 2006a). I conclude that this basis of immunity against the more urgent forms of demeaning exposure and exploitable dependency seems of great importance if we attach priority to people's opportunity to express and act upon their wishes with strength and confidence. Hence, if we follow Rawls in his concern for "maximinning" life prospects in ways consistent with the attachment of special weight to the social bases of self-respect and, more broadly, the protection of basic autonomy, there is a strong case for continuously securing a robust economic basis for each individual's personal independence.[11]

2.5. Are Work Requirements Needed to *Support* Self-Respect?

I shall now move on to consider a counterargument against this radical-liberal interpretation of Rawls. In the Rawlsian context, the arguments on basic income in section 2.4 are open to the objection that self-respect would actually require the right *and* obligation to do paid work, and to enforce the latter through work requirements (Farrelly 1999, 291). According to a position defended by Donald Moon, and explored by Raymond Plant, self-respect is "something that people have to achieve according to the norms of respect in a particular society" (Moon 1988; Plant 1993, 42). For Moon, only independence and self-sufficiency through paid work could truly offer the bases of self-respect in most existing economies (largely organized through wage-contracts).

There are two main routes for specifying this objection about self-respect. The *ethical objection* is based on arguments about recognition and essential conditions for a good life. The *exploitation objection*, which captures an important element of the responsibility-based intuition expressed in the Musgrave-Kymlicka objection above, is based on the idea that self-respect is damaged by basic income because such a policy does not require us to fulfil our duty to make a productive contribution in return for economic benefits (Schweickart 2002, 76, 101). This latter type of objection is important and powerful but complex and must be dealt with separately (I will return to it in chs 3–5, see also McKinnon 2003, 152–156).

In the remainder of this chapter I can only examine the ethical version of the objection. To spell out this objection from self-respect, it can be forcefully argued (and Rawls is one of those who have done so) that access to a paid job is normally a social and psychological condition for people to develop a lively sense of their own moral worth and a deep confidence in their abilities to pursue their objectives. One could add that it may also, especially at an early formative stage of one's adult life, play a very important role to facilitate the development and exercise of morally crucial (in Rawls's words) "social capacities of the self" such as the communicative skills, the sense of responsibility, and the moral sensibility needed to lead a satisfying and just life in fair cooperation with others (Phelps 1997, 12–15; Rawls 1971, 442; 1982/1999, 366; Rawls 1996, lix; cf. White 2003a, 60).

These arguments help express an important and widely shared view in political debates on work and welfare, namely, that people need *work* to find recognition and develop basic abilities, not only passive income support. Moon has asked the following rhetorical question: "If people hold the norm that they should be independent (in the sense of self-supporting), then how can the state provide them with the means of subsistence without violating their self-respect?" (Moon 1988, 35).

Also, many of those who criticize unconditional income support from the point of view of self-respect worry about the lack of self-confidence of people who are unemployed in existing welfare regimes and argue that they are unlikely to make the choices necessary to move out of such a state in the absence of external guidance and activation (Mead 1987, 2005). For instance, Richard Layard argues that unconditional welfare transfers tend to make people end up in a state of "grey resignation." Hence, we need a politics of welfare-to-work under which "you can only get benefits if you look really hard for work" and where you "have to take advantage of what you are offered" (Layard 2005, 67, 173–174). For their own good—for the protection of their self-respect—people must be required to remain activated: it is better to have some job than not having a job at all.

Do these arguments shake our conclusions in the previous section? First, we should observe that the "Hegelian" outlook advanced by Moon, deriving justice from actual moral norms and expectations, is bound to generate a justification of something very close to the status quo. If failure or unwillingness to be self-reliant through paid work is generally associated with a certain social stigma and if people in need tend to internalize such work expectations, it is clear that having a job will be extremely important to access the relevant primary goods. To be sure, those who do not work will not access the sources of self-respect to the same extent that those who have proper jobs if people in general view those who claim resources but who do not work as free riders or even parasites. As Jon Elster points out, the feeling that one is a free rider or a parasite is likely to be devastating to self-respect (Elster 1988, 67; see also Anderson 2004).

However, the fundamental normative issue to consider must be whether the political community and reasonable citizens *should* express such universal expectations to be independent and self-reliant through paid work in the first place. In seeking to work out an institutional ideal, we need to explore what principles and moral expectations people should be committed to rather than taking their operative moral convictions as given.

If we are concerned about the prospects for the least well-off, attaching particular importance to the bases of self-respect, and if *one* very important cause of people's lack of self-respect is the attitudes and expectations others express with respect to their labor market status, the following obvious question arises: Is it not radically counterproductive to accept an ideal in which income security and opportunities for useful participation are so strongly tied to paid employment; where the social conditions of people's sense of self-worth is essentially based on their role on their labor market position, and where people who are not fully "self-supporting" through their own earned income are stigmatized as free riders and parasites?

Still, the argument for why activation policies are required responds to an important social concern that would not simply disappear if our political community would take a milder stance to people who don't have jobs and offer them better living conditions. For many (perhaps most) people, paid work imposes a welcome structure on the flow of time, a daily routine, a sense of belonging, possibilities to find meaningful activities outside the family, friends, challenges, and, thus, social recognition (Arneson 1990; Elster 1988, 62; Phelps 1997). The claim that access to meaningful paid work or some other form of social contribution whose value is personally rewarding and widely recognized within at least some (as Rawls calls it) "community of shared interests" is a crucial component of the social bases of self-respect can be given plausible backing from general ethical and psychological arguments (Rawls 1971, 442; 1982/1999, 366).

There is quite an argumentative leap, however, from accepting this claim to also accepting Layard's case for a welfare-to-work approach. The importance of meaningful work was one of the fundamental reasons advanced *in defense* of an unconditional basic income (in section 2.4) as an instrument to improve the possibility to bargain for good working conditions while at the same time lowering the barriers to labor market participation. When considered from the point of view of social recognition and nonsubservience, employment-based strategies seem plagued with difficulties and negative side effects of the kinds I have already discussed, unless combined with, and restricted by, the independence-enhancing and opportunity equalizing instrument of (something like) a basic income.[12]

Such limitations can hardly be categorized as minor, contingent flaws that will be smoothly swept away once the most well-designed employment program has been put into place. It should also be observed that insofar as paid work *is* a crucial component of the recognitional bases of self-respect, this is essentially because self-respect is a by-product of *doing something that others find valuable* rather than the activity of paid work (or workfare-activity) itself, that is, regardless of whether or not the activities undertaken are in genuine demand and widely perceived as a valuable contribution (cf. Elster 1988, 74–75).

2.6. Why the Ethical Argument for Work Obligations Is Ideological and Illiberal

More fundamentally, if we attach priority to people's access to paths for social recognition (as a basis of self-respect), it remains unclear why the best option is to spend scarce social resources to create and administer work-like activities to all, and for pushing everyone into the structure of paid employment, whatever his or her preference with respect to that activity. I will leave to one side qualms about whether using money to create activities for the unmotivated and making people apply for jobs they don't want are well spent from the point of view of economic efficiency. For the present argument, the important point is that self-respect-based ethical justifications of such arrangements conflate paid work and meaningful activity, thereby concealing how work obligations can stand in the way of, rather than supporting, people's access to useful tasks.

One important advantage of a basic income strategy relative to an obligation to work regime is that it would build the bases of self-respect on wider and more inclusive social foundations. Consider the case of John. John lives under a basic income regime that enables him to lead a life he finds rich and fulfilling. He spends his typical week by working a few hours a day at a local café (supplementing his basic income), fishing with his friends, playing guitar in a band, and coaching a children's football team. Now, his liberal-conservative government tells him that the structure of paid work is in fact a condition for self-respect and *therefore* it intends to remove the basic income.

This means that John will be required to spend his days in a factory (accepting the only full-time job he can get) that he would do anything to escape. This will leave little time or energy left for the things he finds enjoyable and rewarding in life. However, the politicians in John's political community assure him that it is better for his self-respect to have a full-time job (or workfare activity) that is not very stimulating than not having one at all.

Now, there may be other reasons for why John should be required to work more in order to receive an income, but our *ethical* argument for workfare or "welfare-to-work" fails because it suggests that John should be thankful rather than insulted by this way of justifying such a political move. For those who share Rawls's concern to move away from jobs that are (to repeat the quote used earlier) "deadening to human thought and sensibility," the influential discourse according to which a job (or workfare-activity) is always better than an income (or that any job is better than no job) is counterproductive.

It does not allow us to say that a condition where many people are enabled to lead lives like John's—thanks to the basic income—is preferable to conditions under which these individuals have no option but to be employed full-time in exhausting and soul-destroying forms of labor, just to remain occupied. Many actual jobs do not offer social contacts or challenges, or they lack in other ways the properties commonly used to explain the essential role of paid work to recognition, confidence, and the development of crucial social capacities. And many forms of activity (actual and conceivable) outside the labor market most certainly do possess these attributes.

There are, of course, work-based options attaching great priority to promote better working conditions for all than typical workfare policies. Under such options the relevance of the example offered might fade. For example, we could link the social minimum to an obligation to accept adequately paid, meaningful work (or activities to qualify for one) by putting massive resources into education, public sector employment, wage subsidies, and even supporting the development of worker-owned and worker-managed firms (Arneson 1990; White 2003a).

Nevertheless, even if that would be the position from which we launch the ethical argument for linking work obligations to the minimum income—and abstracting from our various arguments against work conditionality in sections 2.3 and 2.4—it would still be the case that (a) people's preferences will differ with respect to the options available and (b) other forms of socially valuable activities beyond the wage-based economy offer conditions for personal development, of being useful to one's community, access to social networks outside the family, developing skills and capabilities, and so on, especially when the value of such activities and contributions are widely recognized (Gorz 1999; Pateman 2005). As Erik Olin Wright argues in defending the basic income alternative:

> This would include things like childcare, eldercare and home healthcare services, recreational services, and a wide array of cultural and art activities. The production of these services in the social economy, it must be emphasized, is social, not private: the issue here is not moving

childcare or eldercare services from market or state provision back to the family. Rather, the social economy is built around the public provision of such services by collective association rather than by the state or market. (Wright 2005, 200–201)

The point, here, is not necessarily to endorse Wright's particular account of the "social economy" and its value. It is simply to illuminate why paid work should not be dealt with as a condition of self-respect in our Rawlsian ideal, and to stake out a general path toward a more inclusive, accessible, and liberal basis for meaningful, self-respect-conferring participation. The ethical self-respect-based argument against basic income in section 2.5 is stated in a language consistent with nonperfectionism (by appealing to the *primary good* of self-respect). However, this hides the way in which an obligation to do paid work, based on the objective to promote universal access to recognition and useful activities, runs counter to people's ethical interests on many reasonable conceptions of the good. Once unpacked and subject to closer scrutiny, then, this type of argument looks bound to clash with the liberal ideal of nonperfectionism.

The structure that paid work imposes on time is welcomed as a crucial condition of personal development and human flourishing by some, whereas others find that particular property of paid work detrimental to the realization of their conception of the good, a prison from which they cannot escape. Through the history of ideas, particular forms (or the very institution) of waged work have been hailed as primary sources of self-fulfilment by some and deemed as tantamount to slavery by others.

In making a decision behind a Rawlsian veil of ignorance on the choice of ideal political institutions, we are left unaware of what ethical value we may attach to the forms of paid work available to us and, thus, which of those categories we might find ourselves closest to. It is, to put the point mildly, hard to make a plausible *liberal* case for paternalistically pushing people into activities they strongly dislike, find humiliating, or do not identify with in order to promote their access to the bases of self-respect. This is particularly clear when bringing our concerns of nonsubservience into attention.

Surely, the ethical justification of the obligation to work, thus construed, has an objectionably moralistic flavor. Nonemployment can be disastrous or liberating depending on the circumstances. In conclusion, the ethical argument from self-respect against basic income is objectionably illiberal and may, as illustrated through the case of John, easily turn ideological in the pejorative (Marxian) sense (see also

Attas and de-Shalit 2004). Anyone who is embarrassed about claiming to be in possession of superior ethical knowledge (and ascribe false consciousness to those who disagree) will need to find some other way of supporting his or her anti-basic income intuitions.

2.7. CONCLUDING REMARKS: BEYOND THE OBLIGATION TO WORK?

Rejecting the ethical objection from self-respect does not mean rejecting norms and arrangements to promote the thinner and more flexible Rawlsian objectives (that we have identified along the way) to offer each person "a variety of tasks so that the different elements of his nature find a suitable expression" and the possibility to participate in an association of "shared ends." Even so, this does not completely disarm the objection we have just considered. After all, there is nothing in the basic income proposal itself to guarantee that everyone will actually be able to find and undertake meaningful tasks—in the labor market or elsewhere—rather than "sink into apathy and cynicism" (Rawls 1971, 440; cf. Farrelly 1999, 293–294).

In particular, there may be remaining worries about basic income related to the argument about responsibility- and solidarity-fostering abilities at an early stage of a person's adult life. One of the reasons advanced by Edmund Phelps for rejecting basic income is that "all too many young people would lack the vision and the will to resist yet another year of avoiding life's challenges and risks" (Phelps 1997, 111). It is far from obvious, from a nonperfectionist point of view, that we should be troubled by this freedom to "reject challenges and risks" (why should we privilege a risk- and market-oriented way of life?). But it would also be too hasty to categorize this objection as flowing from an objectionably perfectionist bias in favor of employment-centered activities.

Linking Phelps's concern to the Rawlsian assessment of life prospects, one could build a case for why a short period of relatively constrained life situations at a formative stage of our adult lives should be accepted, all things considered (after all, few take compulsory schooling as objectionably illiberal). For example, certain "in-kind" benefits and conditional transfers in the form of educational opportunities, or other meaningful, participation-based schemes, could be better than an unconditional basic income in cash for our long-term prospects, not only within the dimensions of income and wealth (as discussed in section 2.2) but also from the point of view of self-respect and the cooperative capacities (mentioned in section 2.5) on which any feasible welfare regime relies.

In assessing the relevance and force of this case for introducing elements of conditionality, it is, of course, important to stress the opportunity-expanding potential of basic income with respect to a wide range of activities. However, the work-independent security of a basic income would make it possible to reject such opportunities and responsibilities. This could sometimes be a source of legitimate concern when we attend to the bases of self-respect in a long-term perspective. Stimulating young people's development of their capacities, and widening their horizon, clearly looks crucial if people are to be endowed with the opportunities to make well-informed choices and pursue meaningful paths for social recognition.

Let me close with three remarks on this. First, this objection would remain idle for a long time since an economically feasible basic income without a poverty trap would need to remain relatively modest for the foreseeable future. Hence, in addition to people's own motive to find and accept opportunities that provide them with a socially rich and stimulating life (which should normally be very strong!), there would remain significant economic incentives in place to work in order to achieve a more comfortable standard of living.

Second, we must concede that unless educational institutions, wage-setting mechanisms, the norms of social participation, and legal conditions for undertaking work-like civil society activities are suitably modified and coordinated to stimulate and channel the possibilities of basic income in constructive directions, some of the stated Rawlsian advantages (from the point of view of recognition) of basic income would clearly weaken. If a basic income is largely justified through considerations on self-respect, and is to remain supportive to the set of capacities and virtues on which a just society depends, it should walk hand in hand with a social infrastructure of participation and an ethos of contribution (for helpful remarks on this theme, see Van der Veen 1998).

Third, the ethical objections about self-respect against basic income help remind us of the importance of attending to the ways in which public expectations help shape the conditions for social recognition. The participation-enabling and opportunity-equalizing potential of the basic income will be a much less powerful mechanism for expanding the range of meaningful choices beyond the wage-based economy unless combined with a corresponding change in the attitudes expressed through public institutions to projects and forms of contribution outside the formal labor market. Taking these qualifications into account, I conclude that our Rawlsian explorations on equality of status and basic autonomy leave us with a powerful case for basic income.

CHAPTER 3

Are Only Contributors Entitled to Social Rights? Cooperation, Reciprocity, and the Boundaries of Social Justice

3.1. BASIC INCOME AND THE IDEA OF SOCIETY AS A FAIR SYSTEM OF COOPERATION

One idea that plays an important role in several attempts to reject a strong unconditional component in welfare state arrangements, and to back the present trend toward workfare and activation, is the view that social justice must be grounded in the idea of society as a productive system of cooperation for mutual benefit. In his critique of the basic income proposal, William Galston appeals to the Rawlsian point of departure that a theory of social justice is about "the fair organization of...a cooperative venture and a fair allocation of its joint products" (Galston 2001, 33). On this view, it seems, nonparticipants have no relevant claims on the fruits of this venture (at least not on grounds of social justice).

Similarly, Edmund Phelps maintains that the resource-claims of people who can work, but simply choose not to do so, must be rejected for the reason that they are incompatible with the Rawlsian picture of society as a "cooperative enterprise...for the purpose of mutual private gain." In his application of this cooperation-based account of justice, Phelps quotes Calvin Coolidge's words that "the business of America is business" (Phelps 2001, 54–55).

These cooperation-based objections against basic income are brief. However, the general idea they express harbors a number of powerful arguments with strong popular resonance. The idea of a fair system of cooperation plays a foundational role in the Rawlsian project. His remark that "citizens are seen as cooperating to produce the social resources on which their claims are made" may seem difficult to combine with a defense of basic income (Rawls, 2001a, 50; cf. Rawls 1971, 112). It is clear, then, that anyone who wishes to explore the relationship between basic income and a liberal-egalitarian ideal needs to consider the meaning and role of this notion about the cooperative context of social justice or, for short, *cooperative justice.*

The general view I shall explore holds that (willingness) to contribute productively—primarily in the form of paid work—is a necessary feature of social cooperation for "mutual gain." Hence the conclusion that a distributive program that provides social resources to *all* of society's members on an *unconditional* basis (i.e., irrespective of their productive contribution) is incompatible with social justice. Yet, as indicated by the above quotes, this line of argument is often ambiguous and can be specified in numerous ways. My objective in this chapter is to identify, disentangle, and assess three distinct ways of spelling out—independently or combined—our Galston-Phelps type of objection that unconditional distribution is incompatible with cooperative justice.

The outcome of my reconstruction and assessment of the arguments for this view will shed doubt on the potential of these strategies to offer a compelling rejection of basic income. The three elements of this challenge that I will discuss are: (a) a cooperation-based account of the circumstances under which the duties of social justice arise, (b) a productivist ideal about the shared ends and interests ("the common good") of citizens in a just society, and (c) a reciprocity-based criterion for identifying who is entitled to share in the fruits of the cooperative venture.

The chapter is organized around the development of a set of defensive arguments that reconstruct and respond to these three dimensions of the challenge from cooperation-based justice. My first argument defends the claim that a plausible understanding of "thick" cooperation, stressing the importance of *economic* participation, has deep pragmatic difficulties to justify views according to which distribution must be directed only to those that express a willingness to perform various remunerated services (sections 3.2 and 3.3). These problems of a narrowly employment-centered understanding of productive cooperation leads us in the direction of a less demanding account in which a "willingness to work" test is not necessary to ensure the satisfaction of contributive requirements.

One reply to this conclusion reformulates the cooperation-based objection by drawing on "b." My second claim, however, suggests that a closer study of the implications of arguments "a" and "b" provides us with reasons for why those who advance this objection should turn to a thinner account of cooperation, in which political requirements of cooperation are emphasized whereas work participation is not necessary for inclusion in the community of social justice (section 3.4). The implication of this argument is that the option of unconditional transfers from productive to (allegedly) nonproductive members is not banned from the notion of "fair cooperation" even *if* meaningful and enforceable distinctions were possible to make between workers and nonworkers.

Finally, a possible reply to *this* conclusion offers yet another way of reformulating the objection by drawing our attention to "c," thereby shifting focus from the relational circumstances that may (help) define the scope of social justice to a reciprocity-based account of its *content*. In reply to this version of the objection, I argue that economic reciprocity—if given the meaning and weight necessary to provide a firm liberal-egalitarian rejection of BI—has difficulties to accommodate powerful intuitions based on the notion of *wealth sharing*. This idea must, or so I will argue, play a central role in a plausible conception of social justice (section 3.5). Moreover, attempts to ground the most fundamental rights of social justice in principles of economic reciprocity create a deep tension with the principled protection of individual liberties of central importance to the liberal-egalitarian project (section 3.6).

3.2. What Kind of Participation Matters? Thick versus Thin

> It would be incoherent to say that the contributors to society's enterprise, in generating a social surplus, have—as defenders of a UBI [universal basic income] suggest—the obligation to share it with those who have not contributed. What do the latter have to do with it? If we earth people should discover Martians unwilling to trade or collaborate with us, do they nonetheless have a claim too? (Phelps 2001, 55)

Many people will, no doubt, share the intuition that there would be something very odd about the claim that even Phelps's Martians would be entitled to a basic income. One way of explaining this intuition is to advance the relational view that the duties of social justice (as distinct to humanitarian, or other—typically less demanding—moral duties) do not arise between persons unless they are mutually connected through specific bonds of interaction. On this view, people must cooperate in certain systematic and nontrivial ways within the group of people in question before they can have rights and duties of egalitarian justice in this community.[1]

However, such a general requirement of cooperation could clearly be interpreted in a variety of ways. I will distinguish, broadly, between economic and political accounts of cooperative justice. The economic account, implied by the Galston-Phelps position, holds that participation in economically productive cooperation constitutes a form of human interaction of special moral significance. The key criterion of this view is that people who can work *contribute productively* in the relevant scheme or, at the very least, make a sincere attempt to do so.

This, it may be argued, is the fundamental basis for why inequalities within a context of mutual, dense ties of economic cooperation may appear objectionable in a way that inequalities between different, economically isolated groups (that are aware of each other's existence and social conditions but do not collaborate economically in any systematic way, e.g., Phelps's Martians) do not.

But this view is clearly not the only possible way to fill the idea of cooperation with meaning and normative weight. On a *political* account of cooperation, the fact that residents of a given community take part in peaceful, law-abiding, and coordinated interaction within a given scheme, and are mutually contributing to uphold the supporting state structure (on which—as followers of Hobbes remind us—so many of each person's opportunities, prospects, and talents depend), may provide the key explanation for why they are entitled to the rights and duties of social justice. Hence, cooperators contribute to the maintenance of such a scheme and provide public, mutual recognition of each other's claims and duties. Based on this broad distinction between two different forms of cooperation, we may distinguish, further, between thick and thin versions of the cooperative requirement. A thick view of cooperation would suggest that *both* economic and political conditions are necessary to satisfy for duties of social justice to apply. A thin account holds that fulfilling the demands that flow from one of these forms of cooperation is sufficient. An example of a thin, *economic* account of cooperation in the literature is the view that the existence of dense economic cooperation between different individuals and groups (economic "interconnectedness" or "interdependency" are criteria that are commonly employed in this family of ideas) is the key criterion for determining the scope of social justice (Beitz 1999, 154). An example of a thin *political* account of cooperation is the view that political reciprocity, in the form of mutual acceptance of the role of a full law-abiding citizen (or resident) within the same political unit, would be required *and enough* for social justice to apply (e.g., Sangiovanni 2007, 28).

3.3. WHY THICK COOPERATION IS CONSISTENT WITH BASIC INCOME

In view of these preliminary distinctions, let us now consider a thick account of the circumstances under which our duties of social justice are triggered. For reasons to which I will return in section 3.4, this seems to capture the sort of requirement implied when the criterion of cooperation is used to reject the relevance of unconditional payments in the context of existing nation-states. It might seem obvious that a basic income, justified on grounds of social justice, has no role to play within such a framework since it includes no requirement of productive contribution. This, however, is too hasty a conclusion.

Why? A first attempt to avoid this outcome builds on one of the ambiguities in the notion of economic cooperation. Even nonworkers who receive a share of resources do, of course, participate economically in their roles as *consumers* and *investors*. On such grounds, some may wish to suggest that even nonworking recipients of a basic income would always tend to satisfy the relevant criteria, simply by putting their income to use within their society. Hence, requirements of economic cooperation *would* be satisfied.

The problem with this suggestion, however, is that residents who benefit from *any* distributive scheme, whether conditional or unconditional, selective or universal, regional or national, and so on, would normally satisfy this requirement more or less automatically. Indeed, the more money people receive, the more they would be able to cooperate (by consuming or saving) in this sense. But the question, of course, is to whom such payments are owed in the first place. This proposed, broad interpretation of the cooperative requirement fails to fulfill its intended purpose of providing a contribution-based criterion, independently of any existing transfers, to help distinguish those who are entitled to the egalitarian concerns of social justice from those who are (allegedly) not.

Instead, I wish to identify an internal problem with Galston-Phelps's conclusion, which has to do with the difficulty of distinguishing producers from nonproducers. Starting out from Phelps's interpretation that cooperation to help produce a certain "social surplus" primarily means *paid* work, I will make two points. First, it is true that basic income payments would reach both producers and nonproducers. But an economic criterion of cooperation does not prevent us from accepting unconditional transfers *if* we have firm empirical grounds for assuming that a scheme of the type discussed in chapter 2 has many attractive social consequences while having no major negative impact on people's work commitment.

Empirical research on the effects of a basic income guarantee on people's labor supply (to which I return in ch. 7), based on the negative income tax experiments in USA and Canada in the 1970s, suggests that there are certainly no earthquakes to expect. While working-time reductions and sabbaticals would be made more accessible for some people under a BI scheme, the overall vision of most basic income proponents is also one in which the BI would help lower thresholds to labor market participation considerably and, thus, enable a greater number of people to access gainful employment (thereby helping to spread work more evenly across the population) (e.g., Groot 2004). As long as the basic income is closely linked to aims of labor market inclusion, and BI recipients would generally remain firmly committed to work (albeit in new ways and in new forms), the acceptance of a thick account of cooperation does not stand in the way of embracing a basic income scheme.

Second, it would clearly be incorrect to assume that work in the *formal labor market*, that is, organized through wage-contracts, is the only type of cooperative activity that contributes significantly to the social product on which competing claims of justice are made. For example, the economic return from a given volume of paid work could vary enormously depending on the density and quality of productive networks of informal care and other nonmarket relations upon which well-functioning labor markets depend; the quantity and quality of human capital and the informal educational efforts on which this depends; the availability of capital to invest; as well as the presence and strength of a stable legal-economic framework and citizens' general compliance with and support of the scheme of cooperation in question.

The cooperation-based argument for conditionality is concerned with the risk of reaching unintended recipients, that is, noncontributors. But if we are moved by the broadly egalitarian starting points of the Rawlsian project, and take the importance of the many nonmarket contributions into account, it seems to me that a more prioritized concern should be (at least when basic needs are at stake) the risk of excluding people who do contribute in very important ways to the system of cooperation, but who do so in informal and, thus, less measurable or direct ways (cf. Goodin 1992, 207–208; Pateman 2003; Widerquist 1999; see also White 2003a, ch. 5).

In sum, even *if* we were to accept that only people who (make an effort to) contribute productively can normally have claims of social justice in the relevant community, this does not automatically imply that there is anything problematic about accepting payments to people who choose to spend less time in employment or, in some cases, even choose to abandon the labor market altogether.[2]

To elaborate on this second point, one category of people that should be included among those who contribute productively is the group performing substantial volumes of socially necessary, nonremunerated, informal activities, such as child rearing, caring for sick or elderly people, and many forms of volunteer work. As Raymond Plant points out, "I am only able to act as an independent person in the market because there is in fact a whole infrastructure of relationships on which I am dependent if I am to act" (Plant 1993, 47). There is a complex social interconnectedness of productive activities inside and outside the market, where nonmarket production in the form of educational and cultural work, political activities, and a wide range of "social capital" producing activities in networks and associations are bound to play a very important role.

To exemplify, a productive and well-functioning cooperative system depends on the existence of a rich cultural structure, well-nourished family relationships, as well as secure, confident, and well-educated children with a lively sense of justice. Building and maintaining the social infrastructure and associational ties upon which a productive economy depends clearly requires that a great deal of effort and attention be devoted outside the world of employment (Nussbaum 2003, 511–514).

Without such informal contributions, the taxable market incomes of supposedly "self-supporting" individuals would either become impossible or shrink substantially. Conventional market-based accounts of productive contribution, narrowly focusing on formal, measurable contributions in the form of taxable income, often tend to conceal this fact and to treat resource-claiming individuals whose contributions belong to the categories listed (more often women than men) as "dependent" free riders (Pateman 2006). However, it would be much more accurate to say that those who are "independent" and "dependent" in this market-based discourse are *mutually interdependent*.[3]

To some extent, all existing welfare states do, of course, seek to address the social need for these forms of contribution by organizing some of them through tax-funded services and by providing certain targeted payments to informal contributors. This path for avoiding resource rights to noncontributors may, for example, take the form of transfers to people who provide particularly clear and widely recognized contributions beyond the wage-based economy (say, payments to parents with newly born children or to people who care for an elderly relative or partner).

However, in many cases it would clearly be impossible or undesirable to pursue these strategies. Many of these time-consuming
activities are performed because people find them inherently rewarding and many of them are difficult to distinguish clearly from leisure activities. Paying people to assist their elderly parents, to babysit
their neighbors' children, to build and maintain Internet sites of great
social and educational value, to teach a cousin how to play the guitar,
or to maintain the infrastructure and vitality of various sports associations or religious groups on a voluntary basis would, no doubt,
lead to very many arbitrary distinctions.

Targeted payments based on such fine-tuned distinctions may also
affect the motivation for, and meaning of, some activities in ways that
are negative to their quality of human relationships that we would
like to be based on love, affection, and friendship (Gorz 1999). But
whether or not that is the case, the option of using such instruments
on a very large scale seems blocked by the more practical consideration
that we do not want the intrusive and costly bureaucracy of surveillance needed to verify whether these activities are actually performed
or not. (I will return to some of the challenges that confront the projects of recognizing informal contributions and to work out criteria
for useful activities in chapters 6 and 7.)

The idea of including *all* citizens (irrespective of their labor market
contribution) within the scope of social justice may clearly cause tensions in relation to a thick account of cooperation in which great importance is ascribed to full-time employment. However, if the key idea that
motivates this account of cooperation is that people must normally (seek
to) offer a productive contribution, this should not lead people who are
drawn to this criterion to dismiss the relevance of unconditional transfers. Any society in which many contributions of great importance are
not organized through employment contracts—and I have just suggested that most societies are, inevitably, of this kind—need to consider
if not a broader account of productive cooperation must be preferred.

3.4. Against Thick Cooperation: The Priority of Political Bonds

In order to improve the precision of our analysis of the nature,
strength, and justification of cooperative requirements, let us now
return to the question of *why* certain forms of cooperation may generate special duties of social justice. Why would our moral relationships
to those who (attempt to) make a productive contribution differ so
fundamentally from the duties we may have to others?

Perhaps the most powerful explanation for why *economic* inter-action may be central to the existence of duties of social justice is provided by Rawls when he observes that "social cooperation makes possible a better life for all than any would have if each were to live solely by his own efforts" (Rawls 1971, 4). In specifying the type of cooperation he has in mind, Rawls remarked that "social coopera-tion, we assume, is always productive, and without cooperation there would be nothing produced and so nothing to distribute" (Rawls 2001a, 61; see also 2001b, 19, 24–25; Rawls 1971, 102–103, 343; for an excellent exploration, see Barry 1989, ch. 6).

On this view, then, social justice concerns, primarily, the distribu-tion of the huge social surplus generated through the complementari-ties of people's different talents and the specialization made possible by combining their efforts within a given cooperative scheme. In order to specify these criteria of mutual benefit, however, a few questions need to be addressed. What does benefit mean? Benefit in relation to what counterfactual baseline? Benefit within what dimensions of human life? Rawls is, of course, correct when he says that the possibility for any individual to lead a satisfactory life and even to fully develop some of the most basic human capacities depends, among other things, on the presence of a cooperative scheme of *some* sort. However, it does not necessarily have to be cooperation of a thick kind, if this is interpreted as a form of cooperation in which all participants are interconnected through firm political bonds *and* labor market participation.

Even if people could access some external assets to work on (such as a plot of land) with a family or small group of people, and to develop certain skills, we can sensibly assume that they would have great dif-ficulties to make a comfortable living and to lead a rich and fulfilling life if their efforts and interaction take place under more or less cha-otic forms of social life, *or* if they simply lack access to a broader com-munity of people, with a great variety of abilities and interests, that they can meaningfully cooperate, interact, and live with in a peaceful and coordinated way.

Everyone (even if taxed very heavily) benefits from membership of most actual forms of organized and peaceful systems of social coopera-tion if the baseline of comparison is either a condition of failed coop-eration (i.e., where people interact but do not mutually support the state) or a situation of noncooperation in which people are producing (more or less) individually what they need. This universal and mutual gain from cooperation may not be obvious if conditions in a given political unit are exceptionally poor, and if many people who claim resources do not, in fact, contribute productively in any relevant way.

It should be clear, however, that satisfying such a basic threshold level of cooperation for mutual benefit *in an economically advanced, mature, and well-organized democracy* does not require that all able-bodied persons who claim resources work (full-time) throughout their active ages. As Robert Goodin points out when he identifies a "postproductivist" regime type among existing welfare arrangements, some welfare states have provided substantial social resources to a large number of able-bodied citizens who do not work, or work less than full-time (Goodin 2001).

According to Goodin, it has been possible to do so while still maintaining highly productive, stable and economically competitive welfare states. The *political* feasibility of postproductivist arrangements in highly globalized economies is, no doubt, contested. Nevertheless, Goodin's argument helps illustrate that it would clearly be implausible to say that economically advanced communities that provide basic security also to cooperating (in a thin, "political" sense) individuals without employment are anywhere near to sink below the threshold level where *all* participants benefit relative to noncooperation. Hence, in order for societies collectively to live up to this weak productive requirement of mutual advantage, it need not hold that *each resource-claiming individual who is capable of work* must be a full participant in the employment society.

Now, it seems to me that anyone who wants to reject basic income within the context of existing nation-states, on the basis of an economic account of the circumstances under which duties of social justice arise (such as Phelps 2001), will need to do so by advancing a thick account of cooperation (i.e., in which economic cooperation is not sufficient but will also be complemented with political forms of cooperation). Why? In a globalized economy, in which economic collaboration and mutually beneficial trade across borders is very intense, the criteria of economic interaction that serve to exclude economic noncontributors from the bonds of justice within a given nation-state are also likely to *include* the many economic contributors to this surplus in other parts of the world.

Contrary to international economic cooperation in today's world, people's contribution to establish and uphold a given state, in which they can specify and realize a common conception of justice, *does* provide the basis of a special bond between the members of any particular state that they do not share with others. The state also specifies and coordinates economic cooperation (e.g., through the instruments of taxation, investment, and redistribution) in ways that give rise to a bounded, deeper form of economic collaboration that members of a state do not share with other people in the world.

When placed in such a context of cooperation, our question is whether demands for labor market participation must be universally satisfied *in addition* to our requirements of political cooperation. But once economic cooperation is interpreted in this thick, state-mediated way, the different forms of cooperation become more difficult to distinguish. Well-functioning markets and property rights depend strongly on the legal structure of stable states and the compliance, trust, and security they uphold. In this sense, economic cooperation needs to build on stable political cooperation. This means that people's contribution to the latter will be crucial to the success of the former. Hence, it is not clear that a person who remains without employment but who contributes to the political background conditions for stabilizing their cooperative scheme (e.g., through law abidance and relevant informal contributions) can be excluded from the realm of social justice *even if* the central argument for why duties of social justice arise is based on the economic benefits of social cooperation.

Still, some will, no doubt, find the requirements discussed above too lax. After all, the economic benefits of a given productive scheme are likely to be *greater* with a more demanding account of contribution under which work would normally be required (cf. Galston 2005, 120–122). How could such a view be justified? As mentioned above, another type of argument in defense of a tighter link between cooperation and employment (argument "b" listed in 3.1) is implied by Phelps's repeated appeal to a particular understanding of what "society is for" (Phelps 2001, 51). He endorses the view (which he ascribes to Rawls) that "society is a cooperative enterprise in which individuals come together to participate in the interactive economy *for the purpose of mutual private gain*" (my emphasis) and quotes Coolidge's words that "the business of America is business" (Phelps, 2001, 54–55, 58). The aim of building a common national project around the objective of productive cooperation also connects in a natural way to many popular political arguments used to justify work conditionality *as a means to build and enforce strong mechanisms of social cohesion.*

Perhaps work is universally required because it belongs to the set of common values that constitute the desirable common good of a liberal-egalitarian community that binds us (or should bind us) together. Participation in this shared economic project of our cooperative scheme provides a powerful source of unity, social integration, and a sense of common purpose. In present workfare discourse, it is, for instance, often said that people who are not employed (for whatever reason) are "excluded" and must be integrated into working life in order to be part of society's common project.

I have two remarks on this version of the objection. First, such an account of the common good seems difficult to combine with the liberal requirement of respect for diverse ways of life (nonperfectionism). Endorsing this economistic view of the purpose of (our) society takes us beyond a morally important concern to maintain production and productive capacity to maintain the necessary conditions for the realization and stability of social justice for current and future generations. Instead we are all asked to embrace a controversial ideal of productivism ("business") with which many may reasonably disagree.

Mutual private gain through the joint pursuit of wealth is said to constitute the (main) purpose of human organization and social cooperation. This account of the central purpose and the common good of the cooperative scheme not only excludes people who do not identify with such ethical ends (say, people who regard nonmaterial pursuits, such as climbing mountains or spiritual contemplation, as their main concern in life) from the status as fully cooperating citizens but also leaves a minor social role to individuals who are *unable* to take part in the relevant labor market activities, thereby reducing their status to that of spectators of "the" common project.

Second, such a productivist account of the common good is not sufficiently broad and flexible to accommodate our considered convictions on justice with respect to technological development, social inheritance, and the requirements of intergenerational justice. Building a productivist ideal of society into the common good of fair cooperation in this way rejects in advance the relevance of many reasonable social justice-based resource claims that may arise from people who care little about business, market interaction, or (beyond some level of basic necessities) private material gain.

This would suggest, implausibly, that people who would not receive an income from employment or other (relevantly) productive activities could *never* be allowed to claim any share of resources on grounds of social justice.[4] This may include, for instance, claims to share in the value of natural resources, inherited capital, or, more broadly, the returns from increasing productive capacity. Is the only legitimate way to benefit from social cooperation and increased productivity always to engage in lives structured by production-and-consumption-oriented lifestyles? Are those the only lives, projects, and purposes that could ever be allowed to benefit from resources within the framework of "fair social cooperation"?

A firm "yes" to these questions is difficult to defend unless one wants to reject a rich and powerful tradition of political thought defending the desirability of moving beyond productivist accounts of social progress as inherently incompatible with cooperative justice. From Marx (1845/1998), to Mill (1848/1965), Russell (1932/1996), or Keynes (1963)—to name a few important works—the possibility of channeling the benefits from increased productivity to all, in ways that would embrace the expansion of people's access to discretionary time, and the freedom from toil, are key indicators of social progress.

Indeed, Rawls belongs to those who warn us about the value of accumulating wealth beyond a certain point, arguing that this would be more likely to become "a positive hindrance, a meaningless distraction at best if not a temptation to indulgence and emptiness" (Rawls 1971, 290; 1975b/1999, 275–276). The postproductivist vision is that productivity gains should enable societies to gradually reduce the necessary volume of labor very significantly.

In the context of intergenerational justice, Rawls repeatedly stressed that his view on the obligations toward future generations is perfectly compatible with (which is not, of course, to say that it requires!) a steady state economy in which capital accumulation has ceased, as envisaged by—for example—John Stuart Mill or by contemporary ecologists (for a recent version of the latter, see Tim Jackson's *Prosperity without Growth*, 2009). This is not the place to discuss the relationship between economic growth, sustainability, and intergenerational justice. It should be clear, however, that a plausible liberal-egalitarian account of cooperative justice must be *flexible enough to remain consistent* with the possibility of realizing Rawlsian principles of justice in the context of a post-growth economy.

Now, the requirement that a fixed volume of work must always be offered, under conditions where productivity is steadily increasing, is (all other things being equal) bound to result in a growing economy. Thus, a cap on production output on ecological grounds, when labor productivity is increasing, implies fewer available jobs unless combined with working-time reductions, sabbatical breaks, and so on (Jackson 2009, 180–181). A thick version of cooperative justice, in which strict requirements of universal labor market participation are needed for inclusion in the community of social justice, would radically constrain the type of discretionary time-oriented, postproductivist arrangements that may be legitimately considered within the context of fair cooperation.

I conclude that the need to make the characterization of a "system of cooperation," as the context of social justice, compatible with other firm, liberal convictions, such as respect for a very wide range of reasonable conceptions of the good (nonperfectionism) and the possibility of various postproductivist options, supports the rejection of a narrowly employment-centered account of cooperation. To achieve the required flexibility, a thinner account is needed. As we have seen, this conclusion is fully consistent with the position that the contribution to the maintenance of a stable and productive cooperative system can play a key role to help define both the circumstances under which duties of justice arise and the common ends that we may reasonably ask the participants of such a system to share.

3.5. Reciprocity and the Challenge of Manna from Heaven

There may, however, be another way to support a firm connection between cooperative justice and welfare conditionality. Suppose that we accept a thin, political account of the conditions that give rise to the duties of social justice, and the shared ends of such a system of cooperation. This conclusion still leaves open whether the *justification and content* of egalitarian justice, owed to all the members of this system of cooperation (workers or not), would require that entitlement to most benefits should ideally be conditional upon willingness to work.

Perhaps the most natural route for justifying that only workers can normally have rightful claims on social resources within a system of cooperation is based on a moral principle of reciprocity: "each citizen who willingly shares in the social product has an obligation to make a relevantly proportional productive contribution to the community in return" (White 2003a, 18; Galston 2005). Stuart White explains the fundamental moral intuition of "fair reciprocity" in a powerful way: "If we share in the social product created by our fellow citizens, then, as a matter of respect for them, we have an obligation to make a reasonable effort to see that they benefit from our membership of the community as we benefit from theirs" (White 2003b, 84).

Clearly, many of the arguments about the concepts of "work" and "contribution" advanced in the previous sections imply that any plausible application of "fair reciprocity" may well need to accept some room for unconditional transfers on pragmatic grounds. In the following, however, I will focus on a more fundamental difficulty for this type of rejection of basic income. It will be argued that the role of economic reciprocity is more limited than many supporters of welfare contractualism suggest and, rightly understood, does not block the acceptability of unconditional payments on grounds of social justice. Such a conception of justice has obvious difficulties to capture our intuitions of justice under conditions where something is simply *given* to us by nature, previous generations, inherited technological progress, or any other factor or conditions relevantly unrelated to the labor input by currently active "fellow citizens."

To take a simple case, consider (again) the distribution of assets left to us by previous generations. It is not clear that a principle of reciprocity has much to say about such a case. There can be no obvious reciprocity-based claims or duties related to any such assets since current inhabitants of the society in question did not create them. At the same time, it would be odd to say that an unequal distribution of such assets does not trigger redistributive claims of social justice, or, taking our remarks on productivism and nonperfectionism into account, that the only persons that could ever have a relevant justice-based claim on such assets are people who want to use them for certain productive purposes.

To elaborate on this claim, it is interesting to consider some of the arguments offered by Samuel Bowles and Herbert Gintis for why (what they refer to as) "strong reciprocity" is a common human motivation. Experiments with so-called ultimatum games, carried out at widely differing locations worldwide, demonstrate that when people are asked to divide a given set of assets (i.e., to which there are no prior claims), they tend to act upon the conviction that the fair thing to do is to divide them (more or less) equally (Bowles and Gintis 1998/1999).

These are one-shot games under conditions of mutual anonymity in which one person ("the proposer") is provisionally given a certain amount (in some experiments, up to three months' earnings). She must, however, offer a share of this amount to another unknown person ("the responder"). If the responder accepts the offer she will receive the portion offered and the proposer keeps the rest. However, if the responder rejects the offer, they both end up with nothing. People who find themselves in such situations (regardless of social context) tend to display a strong tendency to forgo personal benefits to act in accordance with convictions of fairness. Most proposers offer 40–50 percent. Responders would, obviously, be better off with some amount than no amount, so rejection of any positive amounts would seem irrational. In spite of this, they tend to reject offers (thereby ending up with nothing) that give them much less than an equal share, as a way of punishing proposers for their unwillingness to share.

What is important to our present concerns is the following: the moral intuition expressed by people in such situations is not to *reciprocate* (again, how could it be?), but to *share equally*. By contrast, Bowles and Gintis include such behavior of sharing in their rich set of empirical evidence to support the sociological claim that reciprocity is a basic human motive, and that egalitarian policies should be consistently tied to principles of reciprocity in order to remain feasible and gain public support. Yet (and here I build on Van Parijs 1998/1999), this broad interpretation of reciprocity amounts to a problematic form of conceptual stretching that helps conceal the complexity of the intuitions of social justice at stake in such situations. In effect, it provides potentially misleading conclusions on how best to respond to those dispositions in the design of egalitarian policies.

If the notion of economic reciprocity is to have a clearly distinguishable and specific core, it is not well suited to articulate this moral intuition of *wealth sharing*. In contrast to principles of economic reciprocity, this notion of wealth sharing—helpfully illustrated by the outcomes of ultimatum games—provides a powerful normative foundation to defend an element of unconditional and universal distribution on grounds of social justice.

In response, some might argue that economic reciprocity can, in fact, contrary to first impression, plausibly capture and guide this requirement of social justice. In the case of inherited resources, one argument appeals to the demands of intergenerational *stewardship* (Becker 1986, 230–231; Page 2007, 232ff., White 2003b). True, we cannot possibly have an obligation to reciprocate to the dead. Nevertheless, it may still be plausible to hold that we should, as a matter of reciprocity, "match their efforts for us by making a similar effort for future generations" (White 2003b, 85). Edward Page argues that people are bound by reciprocity duties to protect resources "for posterity *in return for the benefits inherited from their ancestors*" (Page 2007, 233, my emphasis).

Surely, the fact that what we receive is in some cases produced by past generations cannot reasonably imply that we are, morally speaking, at liberty to do whatever we like with such assets (such as consuming, degrading, or destroying them without taking into account the interests of future citizens). Those who defend a layer of unconditional distribution must show that recognizing such rights for present generations (possibly funded in part through inherited assets) does not jeopardize the obligation of justice to meet the interests of future generations.

However, in contrast to the views expressed by Becker, Page, and White, I do not believe that such an intuition on the demands of justice flows from a principle of reciprocity. As an explanatory view on the psychological sources of moral motivation, it might (or might not) be correct to say that our propensity to pass on to future generations depends on the attitudes or efforts of our parents to us, or of our grandparents to our parents, and so on. The dark side of such a possible psychological chain of intergenerational reciprocity is the implication that if we were (for some reason) treated *badly* by previous generations—if they did not take our interests into account—we might have similar difficulties in caring for the interests of future human beings.

But whether or not there is any truth in such a psychological claim, the point is that it would be highly implausible to suggest that the obligation of present generations to care for future human interests, as a matter of justice, depends in any way on whether past generations took the interests of current generations into account. Hence, current generations should "match" efforts by previous generations only insofar as those efforts conform to a sensible view of what the protection of the interests of future generations requires. This observation suggests that the moral content of our obligations with respect to future generations and the distribution of inherited resources is not explained or plausibly justified by principles of reciprocity.

Still, one may wish to challenge the *practical relevance* of intuitions on wealth sharing by arguing that there can never be any such manna-like assets to distribute. Reciprocity-based supporters of welfare contractualism will be quick to point out that resources are always extracted or processed within an institutional context. Whatever the source and history of the assets in question, a structure of productive cooperation is clearly required to put any rights to resources into place. The fact that even rights to (seemingly) manna-like assets are *institutionally generated and enforced*, rather than falling from the skies, might render any suggestion of unconditional wealth sharing, free from duties of economic reciprocity, problematic.

Stuart White remarks that they may therefore trigger obligations of reciprocity to make a productive contribution to support the legal and political system without which even such assets, or the set of resource rights they protect, would be unavailable to us (White 2003b, 86). This rightly draws our attention to the fact that our mutual contribution to the maintenance of a well-functioning state and, thus, the public assurance of equal subjection to norms of justice are likely to be crucial preconditions for a stable and fair realization of *any* project of social justice. This may sensibly be described as a requirement of reciprocity in a distinctively political sense.

Yet, in our attempt to characterize the *content* of the conception that we ought to realize in this political project, I see no way in which this affects the relevance of taking into account that some assets, such as our example of inheritance, are more like manna than others. The importance of institutional arrangements to generate, protect, and enforce rights to a share of such resources does not affect the need to accommodate the intuitions that their manna-like and reciprocity-free character trigger when we seek to design a fair distributive arrangement. Requirements of economic reciprocity always operate on the foundation of a prior distribution of external assets that calls for moral justification. It is misleading to characterize our moral intuitions on how to deal with distributive claims *on those assets* in terms of reciprocity.

3.6. THE LIBERTY-BASED ARGUMENT FOR WEALTH SHARING

My argument in defense of wealth sharing has sought to remove certain obstacles for the acceptance of unconditional shares of resources. I will examine the positive foundations of that view and how it may be specified under contemporary conditions in part 2 of this book. To prepare the ground for this exploration, however, I will now defend one further argument for the relevance and attractiveness of this notion, relative to a reciprocity-based conception of social justice.

This final section defends the following claim. There is a tension between a reciprocity-based justification of universal social rights and certain basic liberties to which Rawls and other liberal-egalitarians ascribe moral priority. In contrast, staking out a firm place for the notion of wealth sharing promises to provide a foundation to justify and specify the egalitarian objectives of countering morally arbitrary inequalities with a solid protection of those liberties.

In order to explain this point, we may distinguish between two models for specifying the basis of taxation to cover a basic set of universally provided (possibly needs-adjusted) set of social rights in a liberal-egalitarian regime. (A) *Egalitarian reciprocity*: Tax contributions to the social product in a talent-differentiated way, which tracks people's potential income, in order to enforce a duty of reciprocity to contribute according to one's productive ability. (B) *Wealth sharing*: Tax a set of reciprocity-free resources in order to equalize people's access to external assets to which nobody has a justified prior claim.

Let us first approach option A and what is arguably the most systematic and carefully elaborated attempt to defend a reciprocity-based way of specifying (broadly) Rawlsian ideals. White's egalitarian conception of reciprocity requires everyone who willingly benefits from the social product to make a proportional contribution in return, *based on her ability to do so*, that is, from each according to her productivity or potential earning power (White 1997, 318; 2003a, 114).

Now, it is worth noticing that for reciprocity to play a key role in this argument we need to hold that *reciprocity*-based duties along the lines of option A arise because the person in question has received certain weighty benefits from the cooperative scheme in question.[5] If I grow up in a liberal-egalitarian system of cooperation and I am, thus, provided with a wide range of opportunities, educational resources, and economic security through the cooperative efforts of others, adherents of egalitarian reciprocity would claim that I am therefore obliged to reciprocate. After all, I would not have been able to develop any of my talents and capacities without a great amount of support from family and society at large.

An important component in the *egalitarian* account of this idea is that an obligation of contribution must not require people to produce an output just as valuable as the share of resources they have received from their fellow citizens. Rather, such a requirement must remain sensitive to morally arbitrary (essentially undeserved) brute-luck inequalities in people's productive capacities. The underlying intuition is that producing a given output might be impossible, or require extreme sacrifices, for some while others could do it very easily.

Applying this idea to contemporary labor markets, those with great marketable talents may access highly productive jobs, assessed by identifying the pretax wages they *could* earn, that less fortunate individuals can only dream of. In White's view, then, this talent advantage must be reflected in the ideal scheme of taxation to meet egalitarian objectives. In a society guided by fair reciprocity, "citizens ought to take jobs at or above some minimum percentage of their peak-ability wage-rate" (White 2003a, 114). White specifies a scheme for ideal taxes and subsidies, based on people's earning potential, that incorporates the requirement that the size of people's taxes must track *earnings capacity* rather than their actual earnings (White 2003a, 78–85).

However, the idea of such a talent-based scheme of taxation is vulnerable to the objection that it seems to conflict with basic liberties to which liberalism attaches moral priority. In the Rawlsian ideal, redistributive arrangements must remain consistent with the requirement that people who are bound by the institutions and policies of the just society are economically free to do what they like with their own abilities. As far as society's public laws and rules for taxes and transfers are concerned, people can use their skills in the way they see fit, even if their choices may be far from socially optimal (Rawls 2001a, 64, 157–158; for a more demanding, libertarian version of the restriction against talent taxation, see Vallentyne 2003).

As a matter of principle, people (however talented they may be) have the right to choose freely—and, arguably, without economic sanctions—among the (high or low productivity) occupations that may be available to them at any particular stage of their lives. Attaching moral priority to the right to control one's self and labor and, thereby, what to do with one's own talents gives a strong presumption in favor of leaving people unconstrained by the ideal scheme of income taxation in that respect.

There are several reasons for liberals to feel uncomfortable about linking the enjoyment of universal social rights to talent-based taxation. First, the idea of deriving *enforceable* duties from this view clearly poses well-known and probably insurmountable practical difficulties. Under such a system, people with above-average marketable abilities would have a clear incentive to hide them from the public authorities. Even if one could come up with some mechanism that enabled people to truthfully reveal their talents, it seems likely that the enforcement of any such scheme would be too intrusive to be defensible, all things considered. This, of course, need not be a major problem for those who accept the guiding principles of this view, for they may still think this is an ideal we should aim to approximate, *insofar as practicable and reasonable* (also taking other values into account).

This suggestion, however, runs into the second, more fundamental difficulty that potential earning power is not fixed to our personal talents. A person's marketable talent is not independent or identifiable in isolation from the broader environment and social connections through which these "talents" can be used under specific conditions (Rawls 1974/1999, 253; Van Parijs 2003b, 206–207). It does not make much sense to say that a given talent is a relevant privilege if it does not fit into a beneficial economic slot in the economy and, thus, *actually* gives access to certain valuable assets at any particular time.

In contrast to the objectively verifiable categories of external wealth or job income, "potential income" is, thus, a moving and highly unstable target.[6] The ability to earn money with given talents not only depends on a variety of social conditions (many of which have more to do with connections and the fit between talents, personalities, and circumstances rather than talents *as such*), but it is also susceptible to sudden changes in market demand and social circumstances. Potential income is, therefore, often impossible to assess, even to ourselves (a point to which I will return in ch. 5).[7]

Third, even if we would assume that such problems of assessing the privilege of a particular talent are not deep enough to reject this project, there would remain important moral reasons not to ascribe a fundamental role to the idea of talent-based taxation, that is, that the difficulties to track potential income for purposes of taxation is not an obstacle we should regret. Such instruments imply that a person's relatively beneficial talent, or internal endowment more generally, could be turned into a burden in ways that would often seem unfair (Rawls 2001a, 157–158; Van Parijs 1995, 64).

Consider Judith, a brilliant pianist. She has successfully spent a substantial part of her childhood to develop this talent. This would have been impossible without the support of her parents, schooling, and the supporting social structure of society. Due to the huge market demand for the services that her talent enables her to perform, she is now able to earn an exceptionally high pretax wage using that musical gift by touring the world. However, she gradually realizes that she has only lived this kind of life because her parents wanted her to do so. One day, she finally decides to refuse any new offers, and to look for an occupation as a part-time gardener, a task she finds much more enjoyable. Considering her amazing skills as a pianist, it is indisputable that her internal endowment is highly favorable relative to that of the average member of this society in terms of "potential income."

But then the following question arises. Should Judith's access to this high-productive option she detests (that most other people lack) have *any* weight or relevance when specifying the ideal tax rates she would be obligated to pay at a job far below her "peak-ability wage rate"? Would justice ideally require her to pay a much higher tax at this job (and thereby affect her opportunity to accept it) than a person who works at her maximum ability at this job and, thus, lacks the (former) pianist's lucrative options?[8]

These three remarks should suffice to illuminate the relevance and force of liberal intuitions against the idea of linking the justification of resource rights tightly to the idea of talent-tracing taxation.[9] If we are provisionally committed both to a strong liberal notion of basic liberties *and* egalitarian requirements of the difference principle (or similar demands), our ways of justifying particular taxes and benefits must be consistent with both. Taxes based on people's potential income, such as those justified by egalitarian reciprocity principles, generate a clear tension in relation to this requirement.

In contrast, option B, that is, funding universal resource rights through assets covered by the principle of wealth sharing, avoids such tensions between liberal and egalitarian commitments. As argued above, the claim to a share of external resources does not trigger duties of economic reciprocity. Hence, the justification of such a source of taxation does not interfere with people's freedom to use their talents or to choose occupation in any way they please (regardless of the options they might face at any particular time).

This is why the concern for basic liberties protected in the liberal tradition, and the quest for a reflective equilibrium between liberal and egalitarian convictions, provides us with an additional and independent reason for attaching relevance and interest to the notion of wealth sharing. The presence of given external wealth, and an inclusive interpretation of such a category of resources, promises to provide us with a liberty-friendly source of taxation.

I should stress that the idea of linking substantial resource rights to the notion of universal wealth sharing does not depend on the *libertarian* view that we are never under noncontractual obligations to contribute with labor income, or that such obligations never vary depending on our ability to do so. Of course, applying a principle of wealth sharing to a substantial set of resources is not to claim that principles of economic reciprocity have *no* role to play in a plausible moral conception. It does suggest, however, that their scope and relative importance with respect to basic resource rights may be more limited than suggested by reciprocity-based critics of unconditional schemes.[10]

It is generally much clearer that principles of economic reciprocity are applicable in situations where people *choose* to be part of and, thus, receive benefits from a given cooperative arrangement, that is, that each citizen who (as stated in White's formulation quoted earlier) *willingly* shares its social product has an obligation to make a productive contribution in return. And it is more obvious that people can be said to make genuinely voluntary choices, for example, with regard to the household or associations they wish to be part of, or which of their capacities they wish to employ, if they have a reciprocity-free (i.e., with no debts attached) and independence-preserving set of resource rights to rely on.

The argument of this section suggests the following attractive possibility. In a sufficiently wealthy society, where the principle of unconditional wealth sharing applies to a substantial set of resources, people (like our pianist above) may be free to grow up in an egalitarian community that offers a rich set of social rights (such as education, health care, and basic income) *without automatically becoming indebted through ability-based duties of reciprocity*. Hence, the possession or development of any particular talent would not generate any constraints on their freedom to choose an occupation freely among the options available to them at any particular time. All advantages, natural or social, do not come with strings attached. I conclude that principles of wealth sharing have clear intuitive appeal and relevance to the normative commitments expressed in the Rawlsian framework.

The Exploitation Objection against Basic Income: Equality of Opportunity, Luck, and Responsibility

CHAPTER 4

Why Unconditional Transfers
Are Not Exploitative

4.1. Basic Income and the Exploitation Objection: The Challenge

In order to define and introduce the central task of part II, I will begin this chapter by placing some of the most important claims of part I in a broader perspective. Chapter 2 identified a number of reasons for why the demands of equality of status and, more specifically, basic autonomy offer important grounds for why a basic income solution would be preferable to its conditional rivals. Up until now, I have assumed that there may be a broad compatibility between the objectives of promoting equality of status, on the one hand, and counteracting the impact of brute luck on people's economic life prospects (i.e., equality of opportunity), on the other.

Arrangements for continuously moderating economic inequalities in systematic and unconditional ways may be required both in order to protect people's status as social and political equals at every stage of their lives and to counteract the impact of brute luck on their economic opportunity to pursue their conception of the good life. It is, however, far too early to conclude that we may generally expect a harmonious relationship between the demands of these two dimensions of the egalitarian ideal, or that any sensible way of addressing a trade-off between them would lead us to support universal and unconditional transfers.

Our arguments on the importance of a firm socioeconomic foundation for personal independence and meaningful work—established in chapter 2—certainly provide us with a powerful basis for preferring a society in which people can always rely on a basic income, to a society in which they cannot (for this type of argument, see also Casassas 2007; Pettit 2007; Raventós 2007). However, once the demands of *individual responsibility* are brought to our attention, it seems that we can actually mount a rather powerful argument for the opposite claim, that is, that equality of status and equality of opportunity would *both* offer weighty objections to the option of unconditional payments.

Why? First, once we spell out the specific links between contribution and recognition more rigorously, the notion of "recognitional bases of self-respect" can actually become something of a Trojan horse to the justification of basic income. The possibility of such an internal attack, that is, formulated from within the notion of equality of status, can be explained as follows. Suppose I would like to pursue a conception of the good life that attaches a very important role to advanced multiplayer online games. Other participants of these games are really impressed by my skills and appreciate the contribution I make to this community.

Does it follow from the priority of self-respect that our political conception of justice should—insofar as the basic income is concerned—regard this way of life as a sufficient contribution; that is, that "anything goes" as long as people are law-abiding, and as long as people are able to gain a sense of recognition for what they are doing within at least some group or association? An important piece seems to be missing here. A political community cannot reasonably ask its members to affirm a conception of justice according to which a life fully devoted to these games is held consistent with justice, solely on the grounds that the least advantaged would thereby be given more favorable prospects for confidence in the value of their abilities and projects, or their sense of self-worth.

We also need an account of contribution and responsibility that gives an argument for why the projects and attitudes of nonworking beneficiaries of this scheme are consistent with the fulfillment of their duties of justice and their expression of respect for their fellow citizens. Without such an argument, the self-respect-based argument for basic income will seem hollow in an important respect. Now, it may be true that it is devastating for self-respect to identify as a parasite, but could not the feeling of shame with which this is linked sometimes be "appropriate"? (White 2004, 274–275; cf. 2007, 96). If I consistently take without giving, even when I am capable of giving, this can be seen to express disrespect for those who have produced the resources I claim and, in turn, make it difficult for them to respect me as an equal (Schweickart 2002, 101, 76).

It can be argued, then, that such patterns of one-way taking may be harmful to the self-respect of both nonworkers and workers. There seems to be something disrespectful about the attitude of a person that expects others to contribute productively to secure the foundation of her (and other people's) opportunities, without feeling that she has any obligation to contribute something in return. These are not, the objection goes, the attitudes of symmetry and mutuality we would expect to see in a society of equals, and the public acceptance of such attitudes as consistent with justice would fail to provide a solid "bases" of self-respect. From this point of view, formalized work expectations are something we may have an important reason to *embrace* in order to protect people's equality of status.[1]

Second, the responsibility-based objection against basic income can be independently formulated (or specified) with the help of a luck-egalitarian account of equality of opportunity. The argument of chapter 2 implicitly assumed that any resources that could be used for improving the prospects of the least advantaged would be legitimate to tax in a sustainable and efficiency-sensitive manner. This assumption may seem reasonable on luck-egalitarian grounds *if* we hold that the distribution of talents and goods is mainly due to differences in class background, or natural talents, beyond our control (see section 1.6 in ch. 1).

However, the motivation behind Rawls's suggestion to include leisure in the relevant set of primary goods and his tendency to link the difference principle to the life prospects associated with the least advantaged occupations or "social positions" (see section 2.2 in ch. 2) point in a different and more responsibility-sensitive direction. This path can be given a straightforward, luck-egalitarian justification. "Voluntary" inequalities of economic outcome—reflecting different *choices and priorities* made under conditions of equal opportunity rather than "undeserved" inequality of opportunity—should not be equalized. So, the basic income regime may now seem to legitimize an institutionalized form of exploitation, which allows the voluntarily unproductive—who choose not to work (as distinct from those who do not work because they are *unable* to)—to drain the resources and energies of their hardworking fellow citizens.

Defenders of the basic income proposal have two main options for addressing the exploitation objection. One is to say: Yes, it is true that the basic income would allow some forms of exploitation avoided by existing, conditional schemes. Nevertheless, this problem is not likely to be serious enough to outweigh its many benefits in our attempts to satisfy *other* important requirements of justice, especially considering that it would also attack important obstacles to labor market participation (section 2.4 in ch. 2) and sources of objectionable free riding in current arrangements (section 3.3 in ch. 3). As Carole Pateman puts it, "If the cost of improving democratic freedom for all citizens is the existence of some drones, then, I submit, it is a cost worth paying" (Pateman 2006, 117; see also Barry 1997). This is what Stuart White has called a "balance of fairness" response to the exploitation objection (White 2006a).

However, chapter 3 has also prepared the ground for a more direct and fundamental response, which disconnects an important part of the justification of equality of opportunity from economic reciprocity and contributive obligations. This second reply runs as follows: No, the exploitation objection is unjustified. The basic income is funded with resources to which nobody has a justified prior claim (or, as some would say, to which *all* have an *equal* claim). It simply endows people with a fair share of gifts or "manna-like assets." Rightly interpreted and specified, then, such a scheme does not redistribute incomes to which some individuals have rightful, responsibility-based claims (e.g., based on desert, ambition, or reciprocity).

One of the most interesting aspects of Philippe Van Parijs's so-called real-libertarian justification of basic income is that it offers a powerful way of substantiating this second line of argument (Van Parijs 1995). Van Parijs is not the first to formulate the general idea that certain resources should be regarded as gifts to which nobody has a prior claim, or that those resources should be used in part to finance a universal and unconditional scheme. He is, however, the first to offer a comprehensive argument for why the relative importance of this element of justice is significant enough to fund a very substantial basic income (covering basic needs or more).

Chapters 4–5 are primarily devoted to the exploration of this argument and the debate it has sparked. The remainder of this chapter offers a close reconstruction and tentative defense of Van Parijs's argument for basic income and its account of equality of opportunity. Sections 4.2–4.5 provide an introduction to real-libertarian justice and seek to bring forth what seems particularly relevant and attractive about this theory from the point of view of our general, Rawlsian starting points. This is followed, in sections 4.6–4.8, by an exploration of the so-called restriction objection, which states that only those who are *involuntarily* unemployed should be entitled to payments. I identify a strong and a weak version of this objection and defend Van Parijs's theory against the strong version (the weaker version will be subjected to closer scrutiny in ch. 5).

At the same time, however, this analysis also argues that even Van Parijs's own account of gift equalization needs to incorporate certain important qualifications to unconditional payments, based on the long-term sustainability of justice (section 4.8). Fleshing out the requirements of these demands, such as the importance of certain cooperative virtues and forms of behavior for stabilizing justice, suggests that the normative status of basic income in this "gift distribution" framework is weaker and depends more heavily on the consequences of such a reform than *Real Freedom* indicates.

4.2. LIBERAL EQUALITY, BRUTE LUCK, AND RESPONSIBILITY

One way of realizing our Meade-Rawls plea for a property-owning democracy, which serves to endow people equally from the start, is to put a radical opportunity-equalizing politics of wealth sharing into place. Within the context of a thin, political account of a "fair system of social cooperation" (or in a conception that is untied from cooperative justice altogether), this suggests a path for dramatically reducing the relative importance of conditional transfers and welfare dependency, that is, the type of "ex post" measures that Rawls associated with welfare state capitalism (see section 2.4 in ch. 2).

By providing all with an equal (or maximin), individual share of the forms of wealth (in the widest sense) to which nobody has a justified prior claim, we could make sure that all have a workplace-independent source of security to rely on. This is clearly a promising path to address the exploitation objection. The "re"-distribution that a basic income achieves now appears, instead, as a form of *pre*-distribution, in the sense that it provides people with their rightful share of a set of resources to which all are equally entitled, thereby attacking ex ante inequalities at the root.[2] Hence, there is no objectionable free riding or parasitism involved in equalizing such assets in an unconditional way, and our initial worries about self-respect-harming, one-way-taking are misplaced.

These are, however, strong and controversial claims. On what grounds, more exactly, could this general idea justify universal and unconditional transfers? Historically, this type of argument has often been linked to the idea that we are equally entitled to the value of the earth in its "unimproved" state, which may for instance, be operationalized as an equal share of the current *rental value* of the relevant assets (Cunliffe and Erreygers 2004; Vallentyne and Steiner 2000a; 2000b). An early example is Thomas Paine's argument in *Agrarian*

Justice (1796) for why every proprietor owes the community a ground rent that would endow every person with a share of resources on an unconditional basis. There is also an interesting contemporary scheme in place, which can easily be interpreted and justified by appealing to the intuition that all are entitled to an individual share of natural resources. The Alaska Permanent Fund, established in 1976, provides every permanent resident of Alaska with substantial, equal annual dividends from the investments of *revenue from minerals on state land*, mainly oil income (see www.apfc.org).

Another relevant type of resources is that of inherited capital (as argued, for instance, by Knut Wicksell (1905) in his plea for a universal right to a share of certain inherited assets). Recently, such an idea of universalizing access to inherited resources played a role in the debate on the British Child Trust Fund, which served to guarantee a small capital endowment for each newborn child between 2005 and 2010 (e.g., Dowding, De Wispelaere, and White 2003; Paxton and White 2006).[3]

However, several contemporary theorists such as Bruce Ackerman and Anne Alstott, left-libertarians such as Hillel Steiner (who emphasizes the equalization of land-values and descendents' estates), or "real-libertarians" such as Philippe Van Parijs hold that a principle of wealth sharing (or "gift equalization" as Van Parijs prefers to call it) should be specified in a way that will justify universal (re)distribution of greater magnitude (Ackerman and Alstott 1999; Ackerman and Alstott 2006; Steiner 1994; Van Parijs 1995).

It is fair to say that Van Parijs's *Real Freedom for All* makes more ground than any other theory of justice to bring these intuitions and principles in defense of basic income into a coherent whole. Van Parijs's radical conclusion is that justice ideally requires the highest sustainable basic income and that its justified level will be "very substantial." His claim is not that this holds under any circumstances, but "under contemporary conditions in the advanced capitalist world" (Van Parijs 1995, 106). Under those conditions, he argues, the ideal (just) level of basic income may be expected to exceed what is "unanimously considered as belonging to the bare necessities" (1995, 84).[4]

4.3. THE STRUCTURE OF REAL-LIBERTARIANISM: BASIC CONVICTIONS

Van Parijs's theory of justice requires a specification of resource equality that respects self-ownership and liberal neutrality. In contrast to the mere "formal freedom" offered by right-libertarians, real-libertarianism requires not only that there are no legal restrictions for pursuing one's conception of the good life, but also that one has the means to do it (Van Parijs 1995, 4). More specifically, real-libertarians demand a securely enforced structure of rights that incorporates self-ownership, but also a maximin-guided distribution of the resources—opportunities in the widest sense—that form the basis of the real freedom to do whatever one might want to do. This means that the resource-endowment of the least advantaged should ideally be as high as possible (Van Parijs 1995, 25). The more resources that formally free individuals can access and use—for whatever purposes they might have—the more real freedom they enjoy.

Whether we should prefer formal-freedom-respecting forms of private or collective ownership of (the bulk of) the means of production (i.e., capitalism or socialism) depends, roughly, on which alternative is more likely to generate the highest sustainable basic income. Van Parijs defends the view that efficiency-based arguments give a strong presumption in favor of capitalism (Van Parijs 1995, ch. 6).

However, such reasons still leave us with the question why some should provide the relevant means (i.e., the basis of real freedom) to others. More specifically, we must, along with Philippe Van Parijs (1995, ch. 4), ask why a work- and income-oriented person, Crazy, should be obliged to provide the material basis of "real freedom" to a leisure-oriented person, Lazy, *if* Lazy is equally capable to seize the relevant resources and *if* Crazy and Lazy start off with equal resource endowments (they are, in other words, equally talented and equally wealthy).

Or, as Ronald Dworkin puts it: "Forced transfers from the ant to the grasshopper are inherently unfair" (Dworkin 2000, 329). So, what kind of response is available from within the real-libertarian framework to this argument and, thus, to substantiate and specify our "wealth sharing reply" to the exploitation objection? *Real Freedom* is a rich, complex, and dense philosophical work, but I will offer an interpretive account (to be expanded and defended below) in which the following core ideas constitute the fundamental building blocks in the real-libertarian case for basic income:

1. *Counteracting brute luck.* The funding of a universal basic income from the taxation of a restricted set of external assets is a way of correcting for spontaneous "brute-luck" inequalities of scarce external assets to which nobody has a prior claim.
2. *Sharing technological inheritance.* Basic income is a measure to reap and spread historical productivity gains equitably. It will tap off inherited wealth and distribute amongst all the value of assets otherwise monopolized by a few.

3. *Respecting neutrality.* 1 and 2 are satisfied in a way that respects the ideal of nonperfectionism. Every individual is given a fair share of society's wealth-generating capacity in a form that is maximally sensitive to different conceptions of the good, whether income- or leisure-oriented (thereby equalizing not only the opportunity to consume or access the means of production, but to do "whatever they might want to do").

In addition, I also think that one of the attractions of generalized gift-taxation, and unconditional distribution in cash, is that it provides a normative basis for meeting objectives 1, 2, and 3 in a way that firmly respects the liberal protection of unconstrained freedom of occupational choice, that is, no coercive or economic restrictions are imposed on people's freedom to use their talents on the labor market in any way they please.

Real Freedom relies on taxation of given external resources to equalize opportunities, rather than head taxes or—more mildly—talent-tracking ideals of taxation (linking ideal taxes to *potential income* of one's talents rather than actual resource endowments). It may thereby allow us to avoid a trade-off between liberal concerns of providing a tax-and-transfer scheme that respects economically unconstrained freedom of occupational choice and egalitarian objectives of brute-luck equalization. Since I have already defended the relevance and attractiveness of such a view (in relation to reciprocity-based rivals) in chapter 3, I shall here leave aside such liberty-based reasons for the notion of wealth sharing.

Van Parijs's strategy to deal with the exploitation objection is basically to argue that the underlying conditions of equality of external assets assumed in the Crazy-Lazy example do not obtain under real-world circumstances. The funding of an unconditional basic income does *not* imply that we should tax Crazy's work income in order to finance Lazy's unconditional basic income. Van Parijs would agree with Dworkin's position that such transfers are "inherently unfair." Universal and unconditional distribution is only justified as first-best justice insofar as it will address an underlying inequality of the shares of external resources that we receive throughout our lives (i.e., gifts, broadly conceived), thereby responding to requirements 1 and 2:

> In order to generate the level of income she wants to reach, it is safe to assume and crucial to notice, Crazy needs certain assets external to her talents, say a plot of land. Endowing (identically talented) Crazy and Lazy with equal plots of land certainly constitutes one

non-discriminatory allocation of real freedom between them. But if this endowment is not tradable, if they are both stuck with it, this allocation cannot be optimal from a real-libertarian standpoint. It will not give either Crazy or Lazy the highest attainable real freedom. Crazy may be desperate to use more than her plot of land, while Lazy would not mind being deprived of some or even all of his in exchange of part of what Crazy would produce with it. This directly yields the following suggestion. There is a non-arbitrary and generally positive legitimate level of basic income that is determined by the per capita value of society's external assets and must be entirely financed by those who appropriate these assets. (Van Parijs 1995, 99)

Even if we may be entitled to the result of our work efforts, this does not mean that we are also entitled to the value of whatever scarce assets we are given and on which our activities operate. Using this argument for equality of external assets, the justification of unconditional basic income depends on the presence of persistent and adjustable inequalities of external resources in the form of gifts. This argument for basic income as an individual right departs from the empirical fact that people receive exclusive access to valuable external resources very unequally, and the normative claim that a fair cooperation on an equal footing demands an initial opportunity-equalizing distribution of such resources among all.

This, in turn, relies on the conviction, inspired by Rawls, that it is unjust to allow distributive arrangements in which the actual opportunities for formally free individuals to lead a satisfying life (i.e., having the means for *real* freedom) depend crucially on circumstances of brute luck. The opportunity set at one's disposal should not depend in a fundamental way on conditions such as whether or not one happens to be in a position to receive such assets by way of spontaneous transactions through family, friends, informal networks or other equally arbitrary contingencies. The problem, from the point of view of justice, is not that there *are* opportunity-expanding gifts or gift-like resources in our economies. The problem is that they are so very unequally distributed.[5]

4.4. FROM VALUE EQUALIZATION TO BASIC INCOME

What does this principle of value equalization mean more exactly, and what are its practical implications? Van Parijs's principle of value equalization of gifts claims that we ought to equalize access to a set of external resources or, more precisely, subject them to efficiency-sensitive, maximin-guided redistribution. The notion of *value*, in this context, is specified by a conception of opportunity costs, that is, how costly it is to others not being able to use or consume them. It is "the object's having a value, rather than its sheer existence, that provides a potential for cash redistribution" (Van Parijs 2003b, 208).

This means that the idea of an ideal market plays a constitutive role to this conception of equality in the sense that appropriate market prices, reflecting opportunity costs, help define the requirements of justice. This commitment to the idea of the market helps incorporate the demands of responsibility, since this form of assessment intends to make people "pay the true cost of what they appropriate" (Van Parijs 2009a, 160).

Like Ronald Dworkin's version of resource-egalitarianism, real-libertarianism holds that this process of equalizing access to (the value of) external wealth must be constrained by the prior satisfaction of a principle that calls for equality of *personal* resources (addressing disadvantages due to personal handicaps, inequality of marketable talents, and other aspects of our internal endowments). Clearly, the case for universal equality of external endowments would not make much sense as an interpretation of equality if we did not first address the fact that some people are handicapped or have other weighty special needs (Van Parijs 1995, ch. 3, revised in Van Parijs 2009a, 159).

It is important to note the moral priority ascribed by Van Parijs to cover selective compensation to persons with particularly disadvantageous internal endowments (or, where possible, actions to prevent that special needs are turned into disadvantages in the first place). Hence, equality demands that part of the external wealth of people with more advantageous personal endowments is used for these objectives.[6] For present purposes, however, I will set aside Van Parijs's views on how best to meet this objective, since such requirements are not directly relevant to his justification of basic income. In the following, then, I will simply assume that this morally prioritized concern has been properly addressed and that we are thus free to focus entirely on inequality of *external* assets.

What valuable resources should (under present conditions) be included in the category of external assets to which the principle of value equalization of gifts applies? It is wrong to say that the "real-libertarian" right derives from the right to external assets that were not "created by any agent" (Vallentyne 2003, 34) or (less restrictively) that "no one alive created" (Widerquist 2006b, 445). On Van Parijs's view, natural resources, inherited wealth, and donations should generally be included in the set of valuable resources to which each person has an equal claim (Van Parijs 1995, 101).[7] When there is systematic and significant inequality of such brute-luck "gifts," whether natural or produced, and whether inherited or generated by people presently alive, they are subject to sustainable, revenue maximizing taxation and redistribution.

In *Real Freedom*, however, Van Parijs holds that redistributing the value of resources such as natural assets, gifts, and bequests would be radically insufficient to fund a substantial basic income. For that reason, he takes the case for the highest sustainable basic income to depend crucially on the idea that this categorization of gifts has overlooked a hugely important category of assets, namely, the value of unequal *job assets* (Van Parijs 1995, 106–30).

According to Van Parijs, well-paid and meaningful jobs presently incorporate a large gift component in the form of a "scarcity rent" that must be equalized when we apply the requirement of value equalization to contemporary job societies. People who are given the privilege to *benefit systematically and substantially from having exclusive access to assets in scarce supply* are favorably endowed relative to those that do not access any share of scarcity rents (assuming they are equally situated in other respects).

In this context, scarcity refers to situations in which, at the going price (i.e., wages in the case of jobs), there is more than one person willing to buy or control the relevant set of assets. Van Parijs emphasizes that actual labor markets work very differently from those of so-called Walrasian models, where the equilibrium wage is also the market-clearing wage and, thus, no involuntary unemployment exists.

As long as job rents exist on top of this hypothetical market-clearing wage, as they arguably do on a massive scale in every actual labor market (whether under capitalism or market socialism), favorable jobs should be viewed as "taps fitted onto a pool of scarce external assets to which all have an equal claim" (Van Parijs 1995, 129; see also Van Parijs 2009a; 2009b).[8] In the absence of redistribution, the group that happens to be in a position to seize much more than an equal share of this rent (i.e., the income exceeding the market-clearing equilibrium) monopolizes an asset in scarce supply (Van Parijs 1995, 108).

Van Parijs stresses the existence of mechanisms, such as those described by "insider-outsider," and "efficiency wage" theories of unemployment, which would tend to drive the wages well above the hypothetical market clearing equilibrium even under perfectly competitive circumstances.[9] It is, however, very important to see (and easy to overlook) that his way of specifying this account of employ-ment rents for real-world conditions expresses a broad notion of job inequality, according to which it is a sufficient condition for job rents to exist that *many people could point to attractive jobs and honestly claim that they would be more than happy to perform those tasks for a wage very far below actual wages.*

The existence of job rents in this wide sense is, of course, particu-larly visible in times of persistent and high levels of involuntary unem-ployment. However, the key criterion is not job scarcity in the form of high unemployment, but the existence of substantial and systematic inequality in the value of the various job assets that people access. According to Van Parijs's way of specifying the notion of job rents for real-world conditions, massive gifts may thus be incorporated in people's wages even under conditions of full employment (Van Parijs 1995, e.g., 109, 113). How, then, should we deal with this source of brute-luck injustice?

> In the case of scarce jobs, let us give each member of the society con-cerned a tradable entitlement to an equal share of those jobs. The endowment-equalizing level of the (additional) basic income will then...be given by the per capita competitive value of the available jobs. (Van Parijs 1995, 108)

As Van Parijs explains, taxing such scarcity rents is not (morally speaking) a tax on someone's earned income but "a fee on the use of lucky opportunities by relatively well-paid workers" (Van Parijs 2001c, 123). Basic income will thus help counteract distributive brute-luck consequences of inequalities in "a complex set of opportu-nities...which enable people to tap—very unequally—society's tre-mendous income-generating power" (Van Parijs 2003b, 206–207).

Rather than arranging job auctions, which would be highly imprac-ticable for all sorts of reasons, Van Parijs's solution for nonarbitrary and just taxation of employment rents is to tax wages in a stable and predictable way and to insist on the gradual implementation of the basic income scheme (Van Parijs 1995, 124). This, he argues, would allow people to adapt to the new conditions of the real-libertarian arrangement and, thus, respect legitimate expectations formed under established institutional arrangements. Given that taxation does not take people by surprise, the fact that they choose to hold on to their jobs and keep doing so when having the real option not to (thanks to predictability and the existence of a basic income) will ensure that their share of employment rents is not negative.

That a person holds on to her job under this distributive scheme shows that the actual wage is not lower than the hypothetical market-clearing wage (I will identify some problems with this argument in ch. 6). Van Parijs also argues that income of the self-employed could be taxed for analogous reasons, and "given that even an optimal taxation of material gifts and labour income would leave people's external endowments highly unequal, interests and dividends too can legitimately be subjected to [predictable] maximum-yield taxation" (Van Parijs 1995, 119).

To appreciate Van Parijs's argument on job assets, we should also observe that the intuition about technological inheritance appears in an indirect way in *Real Freedom*. The fundamental importance of technological inheritance to the social product of today should be evident by considering what a particular individual or cooperative venture would produce if the stock of tools, infrastructure, social institutions, culture, traditions, knowledge, and so on inherited from previous generations were unavailable to us (Alperovitz 1994; Fitzpatrick 1999, 58–60; Le Grand and Nissan 2003, 34; Simon 2001).

On the other hand, as long as this inheritance is already freely available to all (say skills universally obtained through normal socialization and schools or social and material infrastructure that is fully accessible to everyone), it may be viewed as a basic income *in kind*. Under those conditions, the fact that one person uses this technological inheritance for productive purposes does not prevent others from doing the same thing. It is therefore far from obvious why its presence generates any need for redistribution (Van Parijs 1995, 113; White 2003a, 161–162).

The argument for generalized maximin distribution of gifts (as extended to scarcity rents) provides a link between intuitions on technological inheritance and the injustice of job inequality. Locating the source of injustice to the latter does not beg similar objections, since access to the value of attractive jobs *is* exclusive to those that control them. Clearly, people are able to access the benefits of that inheritance very unequally depending on which slot (if any) in the labor market they occupy.[10]

On the "real-libertarian" view, unconditional access to equal market value of the relevant set of given external resources is the ideal way of equalizing such privileges from a liberal-neutralist point of view. In sum, Van Parijs's case for generalized maximin distribution of gifts not only promises to offer a "formal freedom" respecting and responsibility-sensitive account of resource equality, it also presents a way of bringing intuitions on real freedom, brute-luck inequality, technological inheritance, and liberal neutrality into a coherent whole.

Before moving on to examine objections to this position, we should pause for a moment to reflect on how Van Parijs's theory offers a possible way to link our general notion of wealth sharing from chapter 3 to our initial Rawlsian arguments on economic prospects in sections 2.2–2.3. First, if it is justified to say that the relevant set of gifts constitutes a very substantial part of the assets people control, an argument that seeks to maximize the sustainable basic income of the least advantaged (through efficiency-sensitive, maximin distribution of *any* resources available) and an argument for why we should maximize the share of *gifts* of those that have the smallest share of them will be similar in their practical implications.[11]

Second, it should be emphasized that Van Parijs's theory is clearly not an outcome-egalitarian position of the kind I argued that Rawls sought to reject (i.e., by focusing on the life prospects linked to the least advantaged social positions rather than continuously equalizing people's economic condition). It is based on the idea that we should seek to "maximin" people's lifetime *opportunities*, in the form of the real freedom to do "whatever one might want to do," not to equalize the *outcome* of people's choices (Van Parijs 1995, 47–48, 248, n.30, 281, n.88).

Nevertheless, since Van Parijs includes job rents in the category of resources that must be subject to maximin-guided equalization (in order to generate the highest "lifetime basic income," see Van Parijs, 1995, 245, n12) *and* defends (for "mildly paternalistic" reasons) a regular stream of smaller payments rather than a large wealth endowment at the start of our adult life, the political requirements of his opportunity-equalizing view may be very similar to those of outcome-egalitarian alternatives.[12]

Third, our initial analysis of Rawlsian arguments for the advantages of basic income relative to conditional options were partly based on an account of primary goods and economic prospects, stressing why Rawlsians need to attach moral importance to leisure. Van Parijs's "Dworkinian" account of universal wealth sharing offers a way of accommodating this concern by opting for the more general category of external resources as the central currency of justice. An equal share of external resources (in the form of a freely disposable, individual share of wealth) provides not only purchasing power but also—because of its unconditional nature—access to discretionary time.

In this context, however, Van Parijs's option has the advantage of avoiding the need for weighting leisure and income in order to spell out the requirements of equality of opportunity. As we have already observed in chapter 2, the need to do so would make the policy implications of our Rawlsian theory highly indeterminate (Van Parijs 2009b, 6). Moreover, it can be difficult to make political judgments about the right balance between rival goods while at the same time staying out of controversial assumptions about the nature of a good life (Birnbaum 2010a, 18–19). It seems, then, that this notion of value equalization of gifts provides us with a powerful way of conceptualizing economic inequality and of specifying an important element of our Rawlsian starting points for practical purposes.

4.5. RESOURCES AS THE CURRENCY OF SOCIAL JUSTICE

For any (broadly) luck-egalitarian claims for compensation or redistribution to get off the ground, we need to know not only whether a particular condition is the outcome of choices for which we should be held economically responsible, or if they are relevantly undeserved. We also need to know whether or not that condition should count as a *relevant* disadvantage from the point of view of a political conception of justice. One basis of resistance against the idea of providing resource bundles of *equal value* to all is the view that such a criterion rests on a failure to take into account (undeserved) inequality of the opportunity to turn assets into actual states of welfare or well-being (Arneson 2003).

Perhaps access to *un*equal value would often be required to achieve equal (opportunity) for welfare simply because people may need very different amounts of resources, and different kinds of resources, to access (roughly) the same level of welfare. Like other so-called resource-egalitarians, such as John Rawls and Ronald Dworkin, Van Parijs shares the view that social justice does not incorporate the commitment to distribute (the opportunity for) welfare. Instead, the *politically relevant* objective is to provide people with fair shares of some general set of valuable and publicly identifiable "resources," or "all-purpose" means, with which they can pursue their particular ends according to their own ethical convictions.

From a nonperfectionist and responsibility-sensitive view, it is important that they should be able to do so in ways that do not jeopardize crucial liberty interests and take into account the costs that individual preferences and choices impose on others (i.e., reflecting conditions of relative scarcity and the preferences of others in the relevant community). In order to specify what set of "arbitrary" inequalities may be relevant to social justice, we need an objective and workable basis for sorting advantaged individuals from disadvantaged individuals for purposes of redistribution, thereby allowing interpersonal comparisons. The notion of equal value and similar preference-based suggestions for determining what resource claims and habits are expensive or not to others offer obvious candidates to achieve this (for a left-libertarian version of this view, see Steiner 1994, 271–272).

However, as *welfare-egalitarians* (and other critics of resources as the relevant currency of social justice) are quick to point out, resources are only instrumentally valuable. To use the words of Amartya Sen, income and wealth are valuable only insofar as they can be converted into "capabilities to function" and thereby provide us with the real freedom to actually access valuable experiences and objectives (Sen 1992, 110; 2009, ch. 12; see also Cohen 2004). As argued by Sen, then, the case for equality of resources may seem to rest on a form of commodity fetishism. Is it not morally misguided to focus on resources instead of *what they enable us to do*; that is, the particular valuable beings and doings to which they give access?

I will not try to provide a full defense of "equal value" against this type of objection here (and I will return later to some reasons for why I find Van Parijs's resourcism insufficient, see section 5.6). However, in order to appreciate the strength and relevance of the resource-egalitarian orientation in seeking to work out an applicable ideal of justice, I find it important to stress three things. First, this view is part of a liberal theory of social justice that starts out from the assumption that reasonable people disagree fundamentally about *what particular beings and doings* may have intrinsic value and, indeed, about the *relative importance of various capabilities or forms of welfare* to a good life (Browne and Stears 2005; Dworkin 2011, ch. 16; cf. White 2007, 87–89). In this context, resource-egalitarianism provides us with tools for how to address the difficult and important task of weighing relevant disadvantages for arriving at practical decisions.

Second, it would certainly be misleading to say that the concept of resources (as employed by theorists such as Dworkin and Van Parijs) only covers external wealth and simply ignores unequal capabilities for happiness, or the possibility to reach some objectively valuable set of human experiences (say friendship, work, or art), or whatever metric for welfare we may prefer. As we have seen, it would capture, prevent, and compensate for fundamental welfare (and other capability) disadvantages arising from unequal *personal* endowments (which are an important component of our resources), if those disadvantages are of a kind that fully-informed people in our ethically diverse communities would generally find troubling enough to require special attention.

Dworkin's innovative way of addressing this problem is guided by a thought experiment about hypothetical insurance behind a veil of ignorance, in which we have full information about the distribution of internal endowments in our society but do *not* yet know our own place in that distribution, that is, whether we will turn out lucky or unlucky (cf. Dworkin 2000; 2002; 2004). One possible way of interpreting this approach in the present context would be to ask what level of insurance premium to accept in this experiment—for example, how much of our external wealth endowment (i.e., the basic income) we should set aside—to afford compensation in case we would end up with the capability disadvantages in question (Van Parijs 2009a, 159–160).

Third, resource-egalitarians have advanced powerful arguments for why ethical integrity and individual responsibility for one's life projects are of fundamental importance to a good life (Dworkin 2000, 267–74; Dworkin 2004). In the words of Dworkin, "my life cannot be better for me in virtue of some feature or component I think has no value" (Dworkin 2000, 268). Imposing on people—against their will—some particular conception of objective welfare will not give a better life for those who do not identify with that account of welfare, or who subordinate such dimensions of welfare to other concerns.[13] Hence, resource-egalitarianism does not reject that welfare matters in crucial ways to morality and the good life. However, on grounds of respect for reasonable disagreement, individual responsibility, and ethical integrity, it rejects the view that a *concrete, fleshed out, ethically thick interpretation of what welfare consists in* should be used as the starting point for defining the requirements of social justice.[14]

4.6. THE RESTRICTION OBJECTION

There are, however, several reasons voiced in the literature on *Real Freedom for All* for why liberal-egalitarians may have good reasons to feel uncomfortable about Van Parijs's way of dealing with resource inequalities in general and job assets in particular. Even if we accept that inequality of jobs—or scarcity rents more broadly—is a relevant dimension of social injustice in our world, several authors would now deny that job-poor Lazy, who is *willingly* unemployed, is unequally endowed compared to job-rich Crazy (see, e.g., Van Donselaar 2009; White 1997; Williams 2003).

The category of criticism I have in mind accepts that social justice requires equalization of external resources in some form, and that job inequality must be addressed in this context. However, it holds that access to such assets should be restricted to those who are involuntarily unemployed and, thus, willing to work, rather than being indiscriminately distributed amongst all. This is the claim of Andrew Williams's *restriction objection.*

Williams's objection, however, is just one of several views in defense of restriction, and I will not discuss his particular argument until chapter 5. We may usefully distinguish between strong and weak versions of the restriction objection. Strong versions claim that our reasons for restriction apply to *all* assets placed in the category of gifts, including natural resources, inherited assets, and job rents. Weak versions of the objection accept the presumption in favor of unconditional and universal distribution for some resources (such as the former two). However, it denies that *job assets* should be included in the set of resources to which all have an equal claim.

One reason in defense of restriction (whether in strong or weak forms) can be referred to as *the unjust preference argument.* This is based on the suspicion that there must be a crucial moral difference between preferences with regard to work and other aspects of our conception of the good life (say, our religious convictions, or the leisure activities, and the kinds of food we prefer). Brian Barry and Stuart White have expressed such intuitions as follows.

> We do not believe that people with antisocial traits (strong dispositions towards, say rape or pedophilia) should have as much chance to fulfill their desires as others, and if the wish to live at others' expense is an antisocial trait there is no reason for making special efforts to indulge in it. (Barry 2001, 68)

> Liberal neutrality is not absolute neutrality: some preferences can only be satisfied by violating the demands of justice, and it is not objectionable to define rights in ways that disadvantage people with such preferences. According to justice as fair reciprocity...work preferences are implicated in the demands of justice. (White 2003a, 159)

Liberal neutralists who are convinced that an unconditional stake or basic income would be just under present conditions often hold that distributive arrangements of actual societies are ethically biased in favor of a set of productivist lifestyles narrowly focused on the world of employment and consumerism. Such a social state of affairs may be said to leave a comparably limited space for various cultural activities, nonmarket-based forms of economic interaction, democratic participation, or family and friends.

Real freedom is not only a matter of choosing between different bundles of goods or services. It is a matter of choosing between different ways of life—whether market oriented or not (Ackerman 2003; Ackerman and Alstott 1999; Van Parijs 1995, 33; Wright 2010). Why should those who wish to settle for a life devoted to, say, art, religion, or nature, and therefore prefer to stay out of employment, not be able to use a fair share of society's inherited income-generating capacity for such purposes? The real-libertarian conception of justice, and its way of specifying our idea of wealth sharing, provides them with a normative basis to justify such a neutrality-based claim.

Nevertheless, if Barry and White are on the right track, we may have reasons to reject this argument. The liberal state is not, in its distributive arrangements, required to be neutral between workers and nonworkers. The unjust nature of the latter's attitude to society and cooperation—the fact that she violates a duty of justice—seems to disqualify her preference from having any weight in the liberal account of resource equality.

On one simple interpretation of Barry's claim, it seems clear that the objection fails. The reason is that it puts Lazy's attitude to work and society on a par with preferences that violate other people's fundamental rights. But we do not object to those that retire early or settle for a leisure-oriented life *as long as they do so with resources they rightly own or control.*

I do not object to the idea that social justice may demand us to internalize certain norms of contribution (defined broadly) and that this may have implications for the projects and intentions of both Crazy and Lazy, an issue to which I will return in chapter 6. However, beyond a certain point, a relevantly neutral state arguably has no right to interfere with or moralize about such work-leisure decisions. Surely, the fact that people may wish to act upon ethical views that require them to minimize their time spent in employment does not make their attitude to their fellow citizens comparable to that of rapists!

But the underlying concern of this argument for restriction is, perhaps, not whether people should be free to use resources to which they are entitled for very different purposes, including nonproductive options. It is one thing to claim that the state ought to be neutral with respect to competing ethical views on paid work, quite another to say that those who can work but choose not to *should be entitled to redistributive transfers.* The objection could thus be reformulated as follows: "We respect your way of life and the right to pursue your objectives with the resources that you've earned. However, it would be unfair of you to quit work *and* expect your fellow citizens to provide you with an income that you are equally capable of earning, that is, 'to live at others' expense.'"

It should be clear by now, however, that if the case for value equalization of gifts rests on solid foundations, no one has a prior claim to the resources in question. Van Parijs seems to have a strong liberal argument for why Crazy has no justified complaint against Lazy's case for universal distribution of *the gift-part* of the income flow that Crazy controls. Indeed, the situation is very similar to that of the following example used by Barry himself in another context:

> If I have stolen what is rightfully someone else's property, or if I have borrowed from him and refuse to repay the debt when it is due, and as a result he is destitute, it would be unbecoming on my part to dole out some of the money that should belong to him, with various strings attached as to the way in which he should spend it, and then go around posing as a great humanitarian. (Barry 1982/1997, 539)

So, is there a way of specifying the argument about unjust preferences that would break down this strong connection between resource equality, liberal neutrality, and basic income? This brings us to Gijs van Donselaar's original and sophisticated way of characterizing the nature of exploitation (Van Donselaar 1997; 2003; 2009; White 2006a). With our above distinction, Van Donselaar offers a *strong* version of the restriction objection. His view is that "access to work itself, like access to resources, should . . . depend on a person's willingness to work" (Van Donselaar 2009, 11). It seems, then, that Lazy's claim is *always* unjust, whether we are speaking of jobs or any other resources.

This challenge involves a wholesale rejection of the Dworkinian framework—and its notion of value and opportunity cost—on which Van Parijs's argument depends. Van Donselaar argues that access to any set of resources to which nobody has a prior claim should be restricted to those who have an "independent interest" to use them, that is, independent of whether *other* people have an interest in the relevant asset. On Van Donselaar's account of this idea, this typically means that an individual wants to use the asset productively. It is an interest in "an opportunity to supply herself with an income." This is contrasted with a person's interest in claiming scarce assets as merchandise for the sole purpose of "selling them to others" (Van Donselaar 2009, 10).

Returning to the Crazy-Lazy scene, the basic idea can be clearly illustrated as follows. Given her leisure-oriented preferences, Lazy has no independent interest in more than a modest piece of land. In the absence of Crazy, she would not use more. Crazy, on the other hand, who is keen to work and has an income-oriented conception of the good, has an independent interest in using more than an equal share (Van Donselaar 1997, 125ff.; 2003, 100). The idea of providing equal *tradable* shares of resources to Lazy and Crazy in this situation is objectionable. It means that Lazy is made better off than she would have been in the absence of Crazy, whereas Crazy is made worse off than she would have been in the absence of Lazy. To Van Donselaar, the appropriate word to describe this economic relation is *parasitism*.

From the viewpoint of this David Gauthier-inspired position, the Dworkin-Van Parijs line of argument allows some persons to take advantage of others' efforts in an exploitative way by first standing in the way of people with independent interest to use resources, and then offering to step aside in return for income (Van Donselaar 2003, 98, 100). "The ancients [views expressed in Jewish, Christian and Muslim scriptures] were basically right: there ought to be conditions to inheriting the earth" (Van Donselaar 2003, 95). Hence, there is no need for Crazies to compensate the Lazies when appropriating more than an equal share of resources.

4.7. Against Restriction. A Real-Libertarian Reply

This section provides an indirect response to the strong version of the restriction objection. It intends to highlight some of the ways in which Van Parijs's theory may accommodate intuitions that support this objection, while also generating recommendations that seem more promising in other respects. A fuller discussion of the independent interest criterion, and a more direct reply, will be offered in chapter 5.

At this point it is important to notice that the narrow focus in much of this debate on the abstract story about dividing plots of land between Crazy and Lazy can easily give the misleading impression that the real-libertarian case for unconditional basic income is more fundamental and less historically contingent than it actually is. After all, the real-libertarian claim—when all the theory's complexities and qualifications are taken into account—is not, as I have emphasized, that basic income is justified in *any* social world but only given that certain conditions obtain.

Let us explore, then, some of the normative resources available to real-libertarians for responding to the restriction objection in its strong version, once the argument is resituated in its broader historical and theoretical context. One underlying reason for why it may seem fair or reasonable only to admit resources to those who intend to use them productively can be traced to the concern that Lazy's resource claim must not be allowed to block the process of setting up a flourishing and complex economy, ensuring economic and social progress (Van Donselaar 2003, 102ff.).

To be more precise, an important reason for why Lazy's right to claim resources for nonproductive purposes may seem problematic rests on the worry that allowing substantial unconditional shares of resources might threaten the satisfaction of other, far weightier moral claims. Leaving people free to receive and simply consume a share of "gifts" may jeopardize commitments of fundamental moral importance. To exemplify, this may include the satisfaction of special needs of individuals who are unable to work and/or seriously disadvantaged in other ways, or of securing the conditions of social justice for future generations, or, if applied domestically in economically advanced nation-states, international duties to address urgent *global* poverty (see section 1.6 in ch. 1).[15]

Obviously, we need work to cover the costs of doing so. We might, therefore, want to hold Lazy obliged to use her share of resources productively. She would, for example, be required to do her bit of the collective obligation to leave the next generation "a sufficiently generous level of resources and collective opportunity" (White 2003b, 85). All this rightly points to the observation that there must be strong reasons to impose justice-based restrictions on the expansion of unconditional distribution *if* admitting unproductive options would be unacceptably costly in these respects.

Still, few of those who defend a substantial basic income (and certainly not Van Parijs) hold that such a policy should be accepted under circumstances where it may be incompatible with morally prior objectives of this kind (e.g., Baker 1992, 107, 118–119, 123, Van der Veen and Van Parijs 1986/2006, 12; Van Parijs 1995, 76, 84, 86–87). Basic income proponents tend to hold the view that the case for unconditional distribution must be sensitive to conditions of wealth, health, and productivity in the society under consideration:

This idea was at the core of Thomas Paine's claim (in his Agrarian Justice, 1796) that, as a matter of "Justice, not Charity," we should all be given an unconditional endowment when coming of age, in recognition of our equal ownership of the Earth. *Whatever force this line of argument might have had in Paine's time, it is bound to have far more in our own.* (Van Parijs 1998/1999)[16]

Intuitively, it looks as mistaken to suggest that unconditional distribution is justified under *no* conditions as to suggest that it is justified under *all* conditions. In the question of intergenerational justice, *Real Freedom* (like Rawls's justice as fairness) supports the view that social justice must include a just savings principle to protect the interests of future generations. Van Parijs's criterion for intergenerational justice holds, roughly, that the opportunities for future generations must not be made worse than those enjoyed by present generations (Van Parijs 1995, 39–40).

As noticed before, *Real Freedom* also holds that some have prior moral claims to any such assets before the case for universal and unconditional distribution comes into play, namely, those with certain "handicaps," or disadvantageous internal endowments more generally. It admits that the volume of relevant gifts may sometimes be insufficient, for such reasons, to allow substantial universal and unconditional transfers (even though there are also, of course, many arguments for why basic income strategies can be very helpful instruments to *facilitate* sustainable, economic development, see, e.g., Standing and Samson 2003).

Unless the conditions are such that a full basic income can be introduced in a way that is consistent with *sustainable* maximin distribution of "real freedom" for all (including future generations), and with meeting the morally prior concern of satisfying special needs, real-libertarian justice may require that a means-test and a work-test be attached to the social minimum (Van Parijs 1995, 76, 86–87). Since a full basic income would presumably not be sustainable, in the broad sense suggested, *if* people choose to opt out of the labor market on a massive scale, it would not be just even on real-libertarian (or similar) standards of justice.

On the other hand, it is certainly implausible to hold that intergenerational justice demands eternal material expansion (Rawls 1971, 284–293).[17] And surely, anyone who accepts that justice-based restrictions—along the lines suggested—must be imposed on the freedom to use gift-like assets would agree that such restrictions will not seem equally fair or relevant regardless of the level of accumulated wealth or economic productivity. The technological inheritance argument suggests something plausible, namely, that any obligation to work attached to resource rights cannot be unaffected by the general level of productivity and accumulated wealth in the society to which our principles of justice apply (see also sections 3.4. and 7.4, in chs 3 and 7.).

Now, when specified in this context, the source of the unjust preference argument for restriction is not only that the expansion of "real freedom" might jeopardize certain weighty justice requirements. The objection is also based on the (alleged) *unfairness* that some would need to carry the burden of meeting such collective obligations whereas others simply choose not to. Thus stated, however, the objection tends to rely on a one-sided characterization of work as a burden, and its normative force is weakened once we take steps to concede the core point of Van Parijs's case for job rents as a form of gifts to which all may have an equal claim.

Many of those who are presently involuntarily unemployed, or who remain stuck in a lower segment of the labor market, would be more than happy to carry the benefits and burdens of work at wage rates far below those presently offered to those in privileged forms of employment (for further arguments on the inequalities of access to privileged jobs, see Attas and de-Shalit (2004) and Wolff (2004)). In this sense, there are massive brute-luck inequalities in access to valuable—that is, meaningful and/or well-paid—jobs.

Van Parijsian job rents exist (by definition) only as long as many people are willing to perform existing jobs at wages below the actual wage levels. Of course, the presence of job rents does not mean that jobs do not involve toil or "pains." It means that many people—on balance—find the relevant jobs so attractive that they would be prepared to accept them for wages below actual market levels, either because of the intrinsic satisfaction of work or for the monetary (and other) material rewards it brings.

According to *Real Freedom for All*, it is only under such conditions of job inequality that job rents exist and must be added to the pool of gifts that fund the universal and unconditional basic income.[18] For the sake of argument, suppose (along with Van Parijs) that society is affluent enough to afford offering everyone the material basis of "real freedom" in the form of a basic income that covers basic needs, by correcting for spontaneous brute-luck inequality of scarce gift-like external assets (such as jobs and the exclusive access to technological inheritance they incorporate), without thereby jeopardizing the satisfaction of morally prioritized special needs or protecting the justice interests of future generations.

When situated in this context—which is, after all the only context that Van Parijs addresses in *Real Freedom*—the strong version of the restriction objection, according to which people could *never* claim or use a share of society's gift-like resources for whatever purposes they like (whether productive or not), appears difficult to sustain. Whether or not ancient scriptures were "essentially right" in associating conditions to inheriting the earth, it would be difficult to defend a productivity- or wealth-insensitive application of justice, according to which policy prescriptions with respect to work conditions in ancient times would be equally relevant today and 100 years from now (assuming economic and social progress). To consistently describe people who do not (wish to) use the gift-like assets they claim *for productive purposes* as parasites, standing in the way of those who want to work on them, does not fit well into a conception of justice that seeks to provide all with equal opportunity not only to access the means of production but to do whatever they might want to.

If one subscribes to a perfectionist policy, incorporating a protestant work ethic or, more broadly, civic-humanist ideas on participation and work as key components of the good life, work or activity requirements may be perfectly in order *regardless* of social and material conditions. However, from a neutrality-based point of view, interpreted for and applied to "contemporary conditions in the advanced capitalist world" (Van Parijs 1995, 106), attaching such conditions to the use of all of society's gift-like assets seems objectionably restrictive. A view according to which only "independent interests" tied to work-based objectives are allowed to escape the charge of exploitation is difficult to combine with the liberal commitment to nonperfectionism (cf. Ackerman 2003, 180). By contrast, Van Parijs's account of value equalization can accommodate this intuition in a natural way.

4.8. Can Restriction be Justified on *Real-Libertarian* Grounds?

I shall now argue, however, that a further challenge against the justification of basic income in *Real Freedom* arises from internal requirements of the real-libertarian framework. Van Parijs's discussion on neutrality and basic income largely evolves as if preferences for work and leisure were just like any personal preferences. However, bringing considerations on intergenerational justice and the moral priority of special needs into attention demonstrates that job-preferences are not quite like any other tastes even in the real-libertarian framework.

Taking sustainability into account, the requirements under consideration may clearly drive the legitimate basic income down to zero even from the real-libertarian standpoint (Van Parijs 1995, 84, 86–87, 259, n.44), and a broad commitment to productive contribution seems crucial to avoid that outcome. Furthermore, the arguments for the viability *of the basic income scheme itself* clearly depends heavily on the assumption that people would not turn into Lazies on a massive scale under such an arrangement, that most people would perform socially and economically useful tasks, and that it would nourish the sense of solidarity on which its stable realization depends.[19]

With this in mind, it seems that our "unjust preference" argument is reintroduced in a milder form. Suppose that we go along with Van Parijs's argument that basic income would be justified under certain specified conditions. If many people in this society would have no intention to contribute productively *in any way at all* to the maintenance of a just society (i.e., on real-libertarian standards), whether in the labor market or elsewhere, this would clearly jeopardize the future prospects for our real freedom.

When we attend to the question of societal ethos and cooperative virtues, I can see two different (and potentially complementary) ways of specifying how noncontributive lifestyles would be problematic from a real-libertarian standpoint. First, one possible basis of a general moral requirement to contribute productively in some form is the Rawlsian *individual* duty to further just arrangements under circumstances when they are not yet in place and contribute to the maintenance of just arrangements once they have been realized (Rawls 1971, 334ff.).

Now, it may be true that the content of justice is partly defined by the requirement of gift equalization and that these (and other) demands of justice should be primarily directed to the main institutions and social arrangements (i.e., the "basic structure") of society, rather than individual agents. Nevertheless, the notion of an individual duty to further and maintain justice suggests something more demanding than *mere passive compliance* with public rules.

For any egalitarian conception of justice, including real-libertarianism, to become and remain feasible, it would seem important that people seek to make at least some nontrivial contributions to support the various conditions on which its realization and sustainability depend. As discussed in chapter 3, such conditions are, of course, highly diverse and may include much more than the activities performed in the formal labor market. Specifying the demands of the individual duty of justice may, thus, provide us with a basis for why many informal social contributions (such as those discussed in chs 2 and 3) ought to be recognized and why people's commitment to social contribution (in a wide sense) matters greatly also to real-libertarian standards of justice.

Second, even if radically noncontributive options would not (contrary to the above argument) violate any individual duties of justice, they would still be problematic from the real-libertarian viewpoint in a different, weaker sense. *Real Freedom* includes a number of suggestions about the institutions and attitudes that may be required to make the realization of real-libertarian justice feasible (Van Parijs 1995, 226–233), that is, how to move from here to there. Van Parijs does not say much, however, about the attitudes and dispositions that the public acceptance of such a conception of justice—and the particular policy of basic income—would *generate* once in place. Considerations of *stability*, which play an important role in Rawls's writings, address the conditions required for a shared, public conception of justice to remain feasible, and the propensity of such a conception to generate its own support, once it has been realized.

When incorporating such concerns, it should be clear that even a strongly neutralist conception of justice should see no objectionable ethical bias in the claim that state institutions must officially encourage and recognize various cooperative virtues and forms of behavior that help support and stabilize the relevant background requirements (indeed, they would seem seriously defective if they fail to do so) (cf. Rawls 2001a, 86, 116–118, 125–126).[20] Hence, a plausible account of liberal neutrality does not imply that the state should remain indifferent to people's attitudes with regard to participation and contribution.

The crucial condition for the compatibility of a justification of such commitments with a neutrality-based point of view is that it does not appeal to the supposed superiority of any particular conception of the good life. Neither the argument for an individual duty to further and maintain justice nor the argument for the importance of cooperative virtues of contribution and participation to the stability of justice (sometimes referred to as "instrumental republicanism") violates this condition.

As for the possible impact of real-libertarian justice on the relevant feasibility conditions, the probability of competing empirical scenarios of sustainability (in this broad sense) to materialize would clearly depend strongly on the broader policy framework in which the basic income is implemented, as well as the technical details of the basic income scheme in question. Robert van der Veen has argued that linking a basic income to an "infrastructure of participation," with supporting norms of contribution and a set of publicly financed opportunities and social structures to mobilize and channel people's efforts in constructive directions, provides a promising "compromise model" between real freedom for all and egalitarian reciprocity (Van der Veen 1998, 160). If my argument in this section is correct, however, such a broader agenda—introduced in section 2.7 in chapter 2—would be required even by the ideal application of purely real-libertarian standards.

In contrast to various reciprocity-based views (like those expressed by Stuart White), this interpretation of real-libertarian justice may still leave the Malibu surfer entitled to an unconditional share of external assets. At the same time, however, such an institutional ideal would include norms and participatory opportunities to ensure that people would not typically use one's opportunity set for pursuing radically individualist or unproductive purposes. Taking dynamic consequences into account, then, is likely to generate important qualifications to the strong conclusions of *Real Freedom*.

This step makes the status of the neutrality-based, first-best justification of basic income weaker and more sensitive to considerations on the practical effects of basic income than Van Parijs's justification of basic income to "Lazies" may indicate. This need not imply that real-libertarianism must endorse restrictions in some form. It will, however, require close attention to the impact of unconditionality on the various virtues and forms of behavior—participation, contribution, and solidarity—that are likely to be crucial for such a conception of justice to generate its own support (see also sections 6.7 and 7.2 in chs 6 and 7).

CHAPTER 5

Jobs as Gifts: A Reconstruction and a Qualified Defense

5.1. THE PROBLEM: ARE JOBS GIFTS AND, IF SO, DO ALL HAVE AN EQUAL CLAIM TO THEIR VALUE?

This chapter continues our exploration of how best to specify luck-egalitarian commitments to equality of opportunity and, thus, complement the status-egalitarian demands discussed in chapter 2. Philippe Van Parijs's way of arriving at his radical conclusion that justice requires "the highest sustainable" basic income rests heavily on one interesting and controversial argument, namely, that the so-called employment rents, accessed through favorable jobs, belong to the category of resources to which all have an equal claim.

Several authors who accept the intuitive force of gift equalization for some assets, such as scarce natural resources, inherited wealth, and/or donations of various kinds (see also section 7.4 in ch. 7), deny that this principle should be extended to job assets. With the distinction introduced in chapter 4, they advance weak versions of the restriction objection. Universal and unconditional access may be suitable for some assets, but only individuals who are willing to work are entitled to share in the value of jobs.

In order to analyze this version of the objection, I will here identify and examine a number of arguments—which are stated in, or derivable from, works of Andrew Williams, Stuart White, Gijs van Donselaar, and Robert van der Veen—that may potentially break down the analogy between jobs and (other) gifts. The objections of which I will focus most of my attention are based on the (alleged) failure of the job assets argument to meet criteria of (1) *envy-elimination* or (2) *independent interests*, and for (3) not being sufficiently sensitive to the *talent-dependency* of jobs, or the demands of (4) *ambition-sensitivity*.

Competing views will be assessed by testing them against our convictions of justice in particular cases and the requirements for an institutional ideal to be applicable (introduced in section 1.5 of ch. 1). Drawing on Van Parijs's works, I will seek to identify the best available replies to these objections, but I will also point to some of the ways in which the job assets argument may be vulnerable to criticism. I will argue that Van Parijs's view remains a very powerful candidate for specifying our opportunity-equalizing objectives for political purposes in present-day societies. However, I will also suggest that it is not able to fully accommodate or explain our intuitions of social justice, or the advantages of the basic income policy, unless combined with (and sometimes weighed against) considerations that address, more directly, demands of equality of status, and self-respect.

5.2. WILLIAMS'S ARGUMENT FOR RESTRICTION: ENVY-ELIMINATION VERSUS VALUE EQUALIZATION

Perhaps the most obvious basis for questioning the relevance of job assets to the principle of gift equalization derives from the fact that their value (i.e., the scarcity rent) cannot be cashed in, in the way of other scarce assets that are *realistically* tradable. According to such a tradability criterion, only assets that are actually tradable can be relevant for universal value equalization.

Consider the simple case in which two individuals are equally situated with respect to capital endowments. Now, one of them, Crazy, comes to benefit systematically and substantially from controlling a job that offers a wage well above the competitive market-clearing equilibrium, whereas the other, Lazy, is not in possession of any such asset. For what reason should we not include the scarcity rent at Crazy's disposal among the gifts that call for universal and unconditional equalization?

When exploring what types of resources that may be included in the primary good of wealth, John Rawls discusses the status of nontradable assets as follows: "Mill provisionally defines wealth as signifying…the whole sum of things possessed by individuals or communities that are means for the attainment of their ends." But, he observes, Mill thinks that this definition "while philosophically correct, departs from common usage and is not suitable for economics;

and so Mill limits wealth to those things that normally have an exchange value" (Rawls 1975b/1999, 271).

Rawls decides to agree, but he does not present us with any additional arguments for doing so. When placing such a restrictive notion of wealth in relation to our present purposes, this would mean that disregarding scarce goods that do not "normally have an exchange value" would amount to sacrificing what is accurate, indeed "philosophically correct," for what is practicable and convenient, and conforms to common usage.

Of course, not all the things we find valuable may always be suitable for market-based assessment (Satz 2010). In general, however, an account of resource inequality that manages to include components of scarce external wealth that fall beyond the scope of Mill's narrow definition—such as the value accessed by renting a flat for several years at a price far below competitive equilibrium prices, or the value accessed by controlling a job with very substantial job rents—must surely count as an unambiguous improvement relative to a notion that does not.

Suppose there are nontradable components of scarce external assets that we receive and benefit from very unequally. Suppose, further, that it would be possible to measure and seize such privileges in a nonarbitrary way. Does not the empirical fact of nontradability present us with a reason to equalize hypothetical market value, instead of acting as if such inequalities did not exist, or as if they remain irrelevant to concerns of social justice?

However, accepting the *relevance* of nontradable assets to our assessment of resource inequality does not automatically lead to the conclusion that such elements of wealth should be (re)distributed in the form of unconditional payments. Using Andrew Williams's interpretation of resource-egalitarianism, the fundamental criterion for assessing whether our individual bundles of external resources are fairly distributed is that of *envy-freeness* rather than access to equal value.

Williams argues that the former does not necessarily require everyone to be endowed with resource bundles of equal value. Instead, the relevant criterion is that—among efficient distributions—"there is no individual who prefers some other individual's endowment to her own" (Williams 2003, 113). This distinction is often overlooked since the demands of envy-elimination and value equalization tend to coincide. Williams helpfully shows that this is not always the case, and he holds that the former is, ultimately, the relevant criterion (2003, 116).[1]

This step does not block the principled case for unconditional payments as such, but it presents a forceful challenge to the inclusion of job assets in the set of resources that would fund the basic income. If a person with leisure-oriented preferences is voluntarily unemployed and, thus, would not want a privileged job (however attractive *others* may find it), she does not envy the jobholder's bundle of resources.

More specifically, if job resources are characterized realistically as nontradable, and if we take into consideration the fact that jobs are liability-involving and therefore burdensome in ways that require asset holders to forgo leisure, no relevant source of envy between job-poor Lazy and job-rich Crazy seems to remain (Williams 2003, 122–121). Accepting envy-elimination as the resource-egalitarian objective thereby confirms the intuition that the only justice-relevant inequality in the case of job endowments is the one between the job-rich and those who are *involuntarily* job-poor.

This observation about the liability-involving nature of jobs captures one way in which job assets are different from *some* other external resources. It is also true that such liabilities are often burdensome (Williams 2003, 116–117, 122–123). This is a reason why not every unemployed or "job-poor" individual envies the "job-rich" even in the absence of redistribution. In response, however, we should first observe that such or similar liabilities are attached to other external assets than jobs. That quality itself does not trigger the intuition that only those who envy those particular bundles are disadvantaged relative to holders of those resources (i.e., in the absence of equalization). In our economies, owning objects or having use-rights to assets is often conditional on actively performing certain tasks.

To take a simple example, a person is generally not allowed to keep an animal if he or she mistreats it, and this minimally requires that the animal is fed and provided with acceptable living conditions. This may obviously require a lot of work. In other examples, nonactivity is not permissible because failure to care for resources may impose negative externalities on others. More broadly, whether or not *formal* liabilities are associated with particular resources, many assets share the general quality that they require activities (and thus forgoing leisure) in order to remain useful (say for maintenance and repairing). In any such case, those who voluntarily buy, rent, or bid for liability or activity involving assets do so because they find the price worth paying, all things considered.

Starting from the notion of value equalization, it is correct to say—as we normally do in market-based economies—that someone who has a very expensive cat or a cellar filled with a huge collection of the most excellent wines, is, in the politically relevant sense, more favorably endowed—richer—than a person who lacks those resources, *even if the latter does not like cats or does not drink alcohol* (assuming they are relevantly equal in every other respect). And if that is the sensible thing to do in our attempt to assess people's resources in plurality-respecting and responsibility-sensitive ways, it would also be plausible to say that someone who receives and willingly holds on to a very attractive job (i.e., with substantial employment rents) is also richer than someone who does not, even if the latter prefers not to work.

Whether or not liabilities are involved, the intuition behind our notions of value equalization and opportunity cost remains the same. In cases where A receives an asset that is scarce (in the sense that many others would like to have it at given prices, taking any activity-demanding liabilities into account), whereas B does not, A is privileged in relation to B (whether or not B *herself* has a taste for the particular asset in question). What matters is that many would find it highly attractive to hold on to the resource at given prices, in spite of, or sometimes *because of,* any requirements to forgo leisure (to care for a dog can be demanding and time consuming but also, of course, highly rewarding).

Apart from the case of jobs, however, value equalization and envy-elimination are not likely to diverge in the assessments of inequality they generate for such cases. Defenders of envy-elimination can go along with the conclusion that the presence or absence of liabilities does not *itself* produce a morally compelling or workable distinction for separating valuable jobs from other external assets and explain why the restriction objection may apply to the former but not to the latter.

In considering how and why the requirements of equal value and envy-freeness may diverge, and what criterion we should opt for in the case of conflict, consider a gift in the form of a castle at a highly attractive location (which is extremely valuable if "value" and "attractiveness" are assessed in terms of opportunity costs) to which nobody has a prior claim. Is B's right to a share of that type of asset affected by whether she would like to stay there or not? Her preferences are very modest and she prefers a small cottage in the forest.

It seems that Williams's account of envy-elimination may support B's claim to an equal share of the castle's value *as long as our castle is tradable.* In such a case, in which an individual—given her set of preferences—has no personal interest in using the asset in question, she can typically trade such resources (like the cat or the wine cellar above) for resources she finds useful in pursuing *her own* objectives (Williams 2003, 122–123). In a market framework, then, the possibility to do so will normally generate envy over resource bundles in the absence of access to equal competitive value.

But then the following question arises. It so happens that our castle "gift" does not come in the form of a property that can be sold in exchange for other goods. Instead, this particular (non-Walrasian) market operates in such a way that it offers the privilege for some people, in this case A, to rent the castle at the same price as B's cottage, which is just a small share of the price it would fetch in a fully competitive market. Because of a long family tradition, and the conservative views of many inhabitants of the local community, those in control of the property prefer that the castle remains in the hands of people with a particular family connection (i.e., many feel that their projects benefit greatly from this family's presence). Hence, A, who has this connection, is enabled to access the castle under exceptionally favorable terms. Even with this price structure, however, B still prefers her modest cottage to the castle and, so, does not envy A's resource bundle.[2]

Does this new (nontradable) form of the castle gift mean that B suddenly loses every rightful justice-based claim to a share of its value whereas everyone who shares A's preferences, and can think of no more attractive place to stay, remain entitled to share in the asset (i.e., if gift taxation, in some form, is possible)? Is cottage-holding B, with her modest preferences, and castle-holding A, who prefers something more glamorous, no longer unequally endowed?

This is indeed the outcome of generalizing Williams's treatment of envy-elimination in the case of job assets, that is, of characterizing resources "by means of the rights and liabilities actually associated" with holding them in the relevant society. It seems, then, that anyone who finds this implication implausible will need to conclude that the objection from envy-elimination fails to drain the criterion of value equalization of independent normative force.

So, we are back to where we started. Why would the case for value equalization—that we normally apply in assessing and comparing people's share of external wealth—cease to make sense simply because the resources in question are not actually or realistically tradable (as in the case of our castle, or, more realistically, centrally located flats with rents far below competitive equilibrium rates, or jobs offering massive shares of employment rents)? Generalized value equalization of gifts can consistently accommodate that intuition while "envy-freeness"—as applied to resources in their real-world form—cannot.

5.3. "Independent Interests" Revisited

I will now turn to a different path for justifying a weak version of the restriction objection. As argued in chapter 4, the unjust preference argument for restriction cannot easily invalidate or marginalize demands for the equalization (or "pre-distribution") of gifts. Perhaps the most important argument against unconditional access to resources is based on the demands of reciprocity. To claim unconditional benefits is to exploit the cooperative efforts of our fellow citizens to generate the resources on which our claims are made.

As we have seen, however, our fellow citizens (presently alive) did not produce all the assets in our economy. The observation that not all resources may be sensibly characterized as *fruits of the cooperative efforts* of our contemporaries has led even a reciprocity-oriented theorist, Stuart White, to suggest that *some* assets (such as land and inherited wealth)—or their financial equivalent—may offer the basis for a modest basic income and/or basic capital (White 1997; 2003a, 162–166, 192–196).

According to one version of this argument, the cooperation-criterion is bound to drive a wedge between the pre-social goods of natural resources and inherited assets, on the one hand, and job assets, on the other. In contrast to the former, where some elements of unconditionality may be accepted, the privileges accessed through jobs *are* the fruits of the cooperative efforts of one's contemporary fellow citizens, and, so, principles of reciprocity (and, thus, demands of work conditionality) applies to them (White 1997). In response to this argument, however, Van Parijs has made an important remark. Clearly, the *value* of assets that are not produced through the cooperative efforts of one's contemporary fellow citizens, and the size of the unequal privileges they provide, also depends completely on the complex forms of social cooperation, effort, and technology in which a demand for them arises (and, in general, no less—and sometimes more so—than job rents).

In other words: whether we are talking about natural assets in their unimproved state or the products of people's cooperative efforts (e.g. buildings or jobs)—past or present—the competitive value of all of them *is* the result of the cooperative efforts of one's fellow citizens. They are valuable and, thus, relevant for redistribution only to the extent that many people in our existing societies currently (want to) make use of them in one way or another. It seems, then, that the cooperation-based criterion cuts across these types of assets and fails to deliver a workable tool to place them into different categories (Van Parijs 1997, 328–329).

This leaves us with the question why we should not, instead, apply universal value equalization to any "scarce" gift-like external assets, whatever their origin or nature. So, a powerful real-libertarian response to this version of the "unjust preference argument," in line with the conclusions of chapter 3, suggests the following. Any reciprocity-based requirements of contribution must operate against the background of a prior unconditional scheme, ensuring that people's rights to fair shares of scarce gifts—whether natural or produced, whether inherited or generated today—are firmly in place (Van Parijs 1997).

But this is not the end of the story. Those drawn to the conclusions of White may now wish to consider whether a reinterpreted version of Van Donselaar's criterion of independent interests could offer a better route for justifying a weak version of the restriction objection. As emphasized by Stuart White (2003a, 94–95, 162–166) and Karl Widerquist (2006b), people can have independent interests in external assets that are not reducible to productive interests. Following this track, White suggested more recently that while a person's *use value* of job assets is "narrowly productive," someone may have an independent interest (a personal, direct interest) in using other types of assets, such as a plot of land, for many different objectives (White 2006a, 12–13).

Following White, we may consider a person who wants to use a share of land for spiritual contemplation rather than (mainly) productive purposes. Surely, he argues, it would be unreasonable to deny this person the right to claim a share. According to White, then, this suggests that "unconditional" distribution makes sense in the case of land assets and other types of resources *in which people may have a great variety of independent interests* (productive or not). On the other hand, Van Donselaar's "labourist" distribution, making access to resources conditional on people's willingness to work, appears to be the fair option in the case of jobs. It is, after all, difficult to see how people can have independent interests in *these* assets unless they are willing to work.

This is a forceful argument, which offers a more sensible interpretation of the independent interest criterion—and one that is more consistent with neutrality-based premises—than the strong version of the restriction objection examined in chapter 4. However, it is not clear to me that this broader notion of independent interests offers a solid basis for the kind of unconditional/conditional distinction that White is looking for. More fundamentally, the plausibility of this argument depends, of course, entirely on the acceptability of the independent interest criterion itself. If the latter falls, this objection against the job assets argument falls with it. I will make no attempt to reject this powerful and complex theory here, but I will point to a number of cases in which I find its implications counterintuitive.

White defines unconditional division as a division where people are given an equal "tradable" or "marketable" share of the relevant assets (White 2006a, 11). But how can the universal right to claim and use certain assets, in which one has an independent interest of *some* kind, generate a universal and equal right to a tradable share of the relevant resources? It is plausible that the best interpretation of the independent interest criterion requires that some resources should be made available even to people without narrowly productive interests. It is less clear, however, that the best practical approximation of this view demands that *everyone* should be free to receive an equal share of the market value of these assets. This option would offer opportunities for everyone (whether or not they have any independent interests of relevance) to use the market value of assets *for any purpose* (whether or not it has got anything to do with the independent interests that might be relevant for the type of asset in question).

To illustrate this point and explain why I find value equalization more consistent with powerful moral intuitions, we may return to the example of oil-rich natural resources. Considering this type of assets, supporters of White's version of the independent interest argument and supporters of universal value equalization both seem to have confidence in the conviction that unconditional distribution is justified. It seems to me, however, that only the latter will actually provide a strong basis for this conclusion.

To see why, suppose that two groups in our society have very different views on the practice of oil drilling. Our first group, the *Ewings*, have a strong independent interest in oil reservoirs and all the natural assets from which oil can be extracted. They can't wait to access and use them for productive purposes and, thus, "supply themselves with an income" (Van Donselaar 2009, 10) by applying their work to these resources. By contrast, our second group, the *ecocentrics*, have no independent interest in using these assets in any way. They are guided by the view that oil drilling tends to violate the integrity of the earth, but they respect that others act on different views in this matter. If the Ewings did not exist, the ecocentrics would simply leave these resources where they are.

So, if the ideal distribution of assets should trace people's independent interests, there would be no need for brute-luck redistribution from the Ewings to the ecocentrics when the former claim these resources and massive inequalities arise in the values accessed by these groups. I find this implication difficult to accept. More broadly, I find it hard to maintain—if guided by a norm of equal concern and respect—that Alaskans, in setting up the Alaska Permanent Fund, got things wrong when making its firm commitment to give *all* members of the community an equal, annual share of income from the relevant natural resources, rather than trying to direct shares of those assets exclusively to those with a taste for making direct use of them (productively or otherwise).

To give an additional example, accepting the idea of people's independent interest to use particular resources as the core basis for identifying justified claims to the relevant set of gifts gives rise to objections similar to those addressed in relation to envy-elimination. In our example about the castle and the cottage, it seems clear that the independent interest criterion will always reject calls for value redistribution from our castle-holders to people with cottage-preferences.

Giving the latter a claim to a(n equal) share of our castle gift—in which she has no independent interest (she does not want to use it for productive purposes or live there, given her modest preferences)—would impose an unfair burden on people with castle-preferences. In Van Donselaar's words, access to equal value would provide people with cottage-preferences resources "in excess of their satiation levels" (Van Donselaar 2009, 171). Hence, the independent interest criterion fails to accommodate the intuition that there *is* an objectionable inequality between cottage-holding B and castle-holding A in the absence of redistribution.[3]

If, when considering how to distribute a given set of assets, it does not make sense to divide and distribute equal and nontradable volumes of trees, oil, or masterpieces from a personal art collection to every individual *in kind*, neither should it make sense to try distribute an equal volume of attractive jobs to all, thus disregarding the relative importance ascribed to such resources by different individuals with their various conceptions of the good (cf. Van Parijs 2003b, 205–209). At the same time, we should attach equal moral importance to the interests of all persons and their economic opportunity to pursue their projects. That is the real-libertarian basis for why it would seem objectionably discriminatory to deny anyone the cash equivalent of an *equally valuable* bundle of resources.

5.4. Job Assets and Inequality
of Marketable Talent

There is, however, another important argument for why the requirements of egalitarian justice may lead us to ascribe far greater importance to differentiated and targeted payments instead of universal resource shares of equal value. One possible route for specifying the source of intuitions in support of this view is to claim that Van Parijs's way of categorizing inequalities rests on an empirical mistake.

Job inequalities seem to reflect, at least in part, more fundamental, underlying inequalities of marketable talent (i.e., internal endowments). Is it not *these* inequalities, rather than the job inequalities to which they lead, that we should seek to address? Once we take into account that the chance of receiving and holding on to attractive jobs depends crucially on whether or not one has a certain marketable talent, it can be argued that the right way of capturing and correcting for the relevant inequality consists, essentially, in *selective* compensation for inequality of talents.

Should we not distribute resources from individuals whose talents are in demand on the labor market to those whose talents provide very limited labor market prospects in the absence of redistribution? Would not this be preferable to giving everybody ("talent rich" or "talent poor") an equal share of job rents? I have argued, in section 3.6 in chapter 3, that the protection of weighty liberal interests supports the attractiveness of seeking a way of avoiding reliance on talent-based taxation in addressing brute-luck inequalities. Taking external assets as the most fundamental component of economic injustice allows us to do so. Focusing on inequality of external assets rather than personal endowments will also have the effect of shifting attention from targeted compensation for unequal talents to universal (re)distribution of external wealth as the main objective of distributive justice (cf. Van Parijs 1992a, 22–23).

As we have now seen, however, the fact that the spontaneous distribution of job assets places individuals in unequal positions, in part, due to an underlying inequality of internal endowments—inequalities of marketable talents—leaves real-libertarians vulnerable to the charge of locating the real source of inequality in the wrong place. It may thereby allow resources to slip into the wrong pockets (i.e., those of people who are job-poor but talent-rich) and fail to hold people responsible in a way that is sensitive to the unequal abilities with which they are endowed.[4] Such a claim on the nature of job inequalities finds support in the following remark by Robert van der Veen:

> To obtain benefit from various favorable circumstances that enable you to cash in on the rent of a particular job asset, you must first spend time and effort in positioning yourself for the job in question and then perform work on the job itself. This shows that the "gifts" that cause unequal access to the rent of job assets are relevantly similar to internal endowments which determine productivity and relevantly different from the external endowments of wealth, which do not. (Van der Veen 2004, 175)

If Van der Veen's classification is correct, the distribution of job rents cannot plausibly be placed in the same category of inequality as the distribution of external wealth in the form of gifts and bequests of the standard kind. The former is now revealed as a case of inequality of marketable talent whereas the latter is a case of inequality of external assets. Since the extension (beyond normal gifts) of the set of external resources to which the principle of value equalization applies is crucial to Van Parijs's argument for a *substantial* basic income, this factual mistake may, thus, be fatal to that position. Accuracy in empirical assumptions demands that luck-egalitarians stick to some kind of targeted talent equalization as the core component of social justice after all.

What can be said in response to this objection? It is clear that taxing and redistributing the job rents involve implicit talent taxation, since talent is, indisputably, one important element of all the complex and often unstructured conditions that enable or prevent people from finding and holding on to valuable jobs. Obviously, people cannot come to receive or hold on to such assets unless they have certain talents. These assets are, we may say, *talent dependent*, and talents are part of our internal endowments.

Van Parijs has never denied this fact, and *Real Freedom* is certainly incompatible with any notion of "self-ownership" or "basic liberties" that would prohibit taxation of *any economic return to talents*. Indeed, it was emphasized in *Real Freedom* that this indirect taxation of privileged internal endowments would be a highly welcome implication of the argument: "If the wealth stocked on top of a cupboard is to be shared among all, it makes no sense to restrict it to those tall enough to reach it" (Van Parijs 1995, 123–124). Does our present objection indicate that he was wrong not to be troubled by this observation?

First, on closer inspection, the distinction assumed by Van der Veen between job assets and normal gifts within the dimension of talent-dependency is less sharp than the above quote indicates. The different sets of external resources are not categorically different within this dimension. The interaction between internal (talent-dependent) and environmental (talent-independent) conditions could be stated just as well in connection with gifts and bequests as an argument not to regard them as a common asset for all to share equally.

As Peter Vallentyne puts it in another context: "An attentive daughter may receive more gifts from her parents than her neglectful brother" (Vallentyne 2003, 39). Vallentyne, along with thinkers such as Eric Rakowski, thinks this may give reasons to allow the attentive daughter to keep the part of the gift that is attributable to her choices (Rakowski 1991). My point here is another. The fact that people receive external gifts unequally is, no doubt, partly due to the fact that some have certain abilities that others lack.

Some people may be very attractive and have a particular social ability to get along well with others, to make people around them feel comfortable and happy, and so on. Social abilities, physical attractiveness, or any other relevant part of our internal endowments belong to all the contingencies that may put people in highly unequal positions to receive gifts and bequests.

To exemplify, internal inequalities such as these are part of the likely explanation for why some people end up with a wealthy husband or wife, why some may become favorite children, or why some may fail to please a new partner of a divorced parent, or manage to access networks of wealthy friends that enable them to enjoy various material benefits. Surely, those who are endowed with the relevant dispositions will, due to that fact, have a greater propensity to receive gifts and bequests than those who lack such abilities.

Hence, taxing gifts of the usual kind for the purpose of universal redistribution *also* implies indirect taxation of internal endowments. If there is a difference between job assets and gifts in the form of donations and bequests within the dimension of talent dependency, it is a matter of degree. In view of these complications, however, it is far from obvious that the best way to consistently address these inequalities of external assets would consist in the expansion of targeted, selective redistribution from the talented to the less talented (in the relevant sense). According to the suggestion at hand, we should ideally make a clean separation between one set of "external" (talent independent) conditions and the "internal" (talent dependent) conditions. Once we manage to deal adequately with the underlying causes of unequal external assets, a significant part of external gifts in our societies, both of the ordinary kind and of the "scarcity rents" kind, should perhaps be expelled from the category of external assets to which all (including the most talented) have an equal claim.

At this point, however, we realize that such a suggestion faces overwhelming practical difficulties. Arguably, the objection—thus construed—relies on a misrepresentation of the conditions for the choice we are to make. That choice must of course rely on accurate facts. But the argument proceeds from the questionable premise that all the relevant facts that are needed to apply such a distinction can in principle be found or known, and that they could thus be turned into an operational set of principles to guide policymakers.

In this case, there are strong reasons to doubt that we can ever hope to make such a clean cut between causes based on external and internal conditions. Since these features of our world will not simply go away, political theorists would leave the stage too early if claiming to have found the correct criteria for making the distinctions, and leave the rest of the job to empirical social scientists and politicians.

Our effort to work out an institutional ideal is motivated by a concern to find morally acceptable principles *and broadly applicable guidelines* for addressing the most central resource inequalities in the kinds of societies we address. We need principles and action-guiding considerations, whose informational demands do not make the required distinctions impossible to apply. Inevitably, this demands certain stylized assumptions about the nature of the economy and how best to conceptualize and assess the inequalities we seek to address. This is the case for any theory of justice that seeks to provide guidance for practical purposes.

Of course, no argument about consistency or applicability succeeds in removing the intuitive basis of the above objection at the root if it is shown that the observation of talent-dependency is *essentially* true in the case of jobs and *essentially* false in the case of other external assets. Thus, some may suggest that the reasons for why people receive job assets unequally can (at least roughly) be traced back to their unequal internal endowments (rather than talent-independent factors), and suggest that the path forward is to look for a way to identify those internal inequalities and seize them for purposes of equalization in some other feasible and generally attractive way.[5]

Considering this possibility, however, it seems that it is the notion of inequality of marketable talent rather than the rival view of jobs as external assets that rests on problematic empirical assumptions. As Van Parijs explains when examining the relationship between talents and jobs,

> How much a person, with given talents, will manage to earn is heavily
> dependent on what productive slots her connections, her training, her

citizenship, her place of residence, her mother tongue, the fluctuations of her temper, and sheer luck will enable her to occupy, and on how well she fits in, in that slot, with co-workers, bosses, and clients as well as local culture and technology. Consequently, it is wrong to imagine that one could address the growing inequality of earning power by identifying and correcting inequalities in people's internal endowments. (Van Parijs 2003b, 204–205; see also 2001a, section 7; 2009a; 2009b; Van der Veen and Van Parijs 2006, 9–10)

Some of the problems with a theory of justice that builds its account of labor market inequalities on the notion of unequal internal endowments were identified in dialogue with Rawls and White in section 3.6 in chapter 3. Rawls accepted the arguments against taking people's marketable talents (their *potential* income) as the focal point of the political analysis of resource inequalities and the identification of tax-and-transfer schemes to address them. His own views can be interpreted in different ways, but, as discussed in section 2.2 in chapter 2, it seems that his preferred—practically minded—way of avoiding these difficulties was to connect the maximin objectives of his theory to the unequal life prospects of different types of occupations, or social positions (i.e., regardless of the marketable talents and, thus, potential income that the *holders* of different positions might have).

One of the most important points in Van Parijs's more recent writings on distributive justice is, however, that it looks increasingly untenable to characterize the most central inequalities of our economies as consisting in (or flowing from) unequal internal endowments *or* inequalities linked to social positions.[6]

As we have seen, a person's productivity or "potential income" cannot be assessed through stable, identifiable internal endowments. The privileges that a person can access depend in full on what she can do with her present abilities in a particular social and technological context, and to which slot in the economy these abilities may help—through a wide range of contingencies—give her access at any particular stage of her life.

There is no clear economic advantage in having a particular talent in the absence of such a context. Job inequalities are not reducible to talent-inequalities. Considering the internal endowments of people within the normal range, it is difficult to say in the abstract that someone is more favorably endowed than another in terms of marketable talent if her set of talents has not actually provided access to valuable external assets. By contrast, it makes perfect sense to say that an *actual holder of a privileged job* is more favorably endowed, in terms of the value she has received, compared to someone whose job contains a far less valuable share of employment rents (assuming they are equally wealthy in other respects).

It also makes perfect sense to say that it would be unfair of those who have been lucky enough to gain access to these beneficial slots in the economy to deny those who have been less fortunate a maximin share of the opportunity, bargaining power, and sense of security that they themselves may take for granted. And it would be unfair of them to rely on their greater share of external wealth to, as Van Parijs puts it, "bend the weakest to their will by compelling them to do what they themselves would never dream of doing" (2003b, 209).

Under conditions where the talents or skills required for existing *social positions* are constantly changing, where labor markets are increasingly flexible, and its agents more mobile, fewer can also expect to be able to choose and hold on to stable occupations throughout their working lives (and, thus, with clearly identifiable and comparable life prospects linked to them) (Van der Veen and Van Parijs 2006, 9; Van Parijs 2009a, 156–161; 2009b, 13–15). Whenever there is long-term unemployment and careers are interrupted, where time and effort are invested in nonformalized contributions, and transfers of private wealth play an important role in the distribution of life prospects, a Rawlsian social positions-centered framework (i.e., focusing narrowly on inequalities between positions rather than *external endowments of individuals*) will also fail to register inequalities and disadvantages of fundamental importance.

Considering these competing ways of conceptualizing labor market inequalities for the political purposes of social justice and to provide adequate guidance on how to address growing inequalities, I conclude that the argument about the talent dependency of jobs fails to reject Van Parijs's broad account of external gifts.

5.5. Jobs and Ambition-Sensitivity: The Choice-Circumstance Distinction

The last objection I wish to identify and examine rests on the view that extending the reach of gift equalization to cover job assets fails to meet the criterion of ambition-sensitivity in a satisfactory way. While inequalities that arise from conditions of good or bad "brute luck" may be arbitrary from a moral point of view, the case for equalization does not apply with the same force to inequalities in the category of good or bad "option luck," that is, the economic outcome of voluntary and avoidable risk-taking. The fact that people need to bear the good or bad consequences of choosing to accept (or reject) the option of buying a lottery ticket they are all equally free to buy looks intuitively different to a clear case of brute-luck inequality, say, that some of us are born into this world with certain handicaps while others are not.

As we have seen, Van Parijs's theory holds that work-oriented Crazy *is* entitled to a larger income than leisure-oriented Lazy, since Crazy works but Lazy does not. In this sense, it is fully consistent with the requirement that justice must be sensitive to ambition. The crucial real-libertarian argument is, of course, that this does not deprive Lazy of the right to an equally valuable share of the external assets ("gifts") upon which Crazy's productive activities operate.

Why, then, may this be insufficient? I think the most straightforward way of criticizing *Real Freedom* from this angle goes like this.[7]

The notion of job rents as gifts does not take Crazy's efforts or Lazy's nonefforts *to stay or become available for* a job into account (Birnbaum 2001). Hence, this scheme may seem insensitive to differences in the willingness of different people to take risks, and the time people are prepared to devote to make themselves available for a good job.

Assessing and redistributing job rents in the way Van Parijs proposes will capture and equalize job advantages, whether they are attributable to chance (being in the right place at the right time to get the job) or choice (being available for a job after 10 or 20 years of demanding education). Those who are guided by the intuition that gift equalization does not give sufficient room for justified, choice-based inequalities are thereby provided with a foundation from which to complain that such a generalized maximin treatment of gifts would seriously overtax Crazy.

This is clearly a relevant objection to Van Parijs's inclusive account of gifts, but it is not, I think, a *decisive* one. Its emphasis on choice, responsibility, and the freedom to take risks does, however, alert us to an important basis for questioning that real-libertarianism would justify a *monthly* income stream rather than lump-sum payments in some form (I develop this point in section 5.6).

Van Parijs's way of dealing with jobs can be said to express the idea that a person's place in the (class) structure of job endowments is not voluntary (Van Parijs 1987). In addressing the practical relevance and application of the distinction between choice ("ambition") and circumstances ("endowments"), it is clear that both chance and deliberate (employability affecting) choices play a role for explaining the labor market options that a person faces. In making a nonarbitrary and practicable distinction between choice and circumstances in the context of an institutional ideal, our criteria need to be sufficiently general to offer a path for applicable policy implications while also being sensitive to the general conditions of the economies we address.

Now, just as a part of what is taxed under Van Parijs's scheme of generalized gift taxation is a return to talent (section 5.4), another part is attributable to the choices made, and activities undertaken, to get hold of valuable external assets (Van Parijs 1995, 121–124). But again, like talent-dependency, this broader quality of *choice-dependency* is present both in the case of jobs and in the case of standard gifts. In the absence of redistribution of the assets under consideration, our share of job rents may result from the fact that we apply energetically for jobs (or fail to do so) or make the right (or wrong) choices of education and career path. But it is also true that *receiving an inheritance may be the result of paying regular visits, and getting on well with, an old and rich relative of ours* (Van Parijs 2003b, 206).

Real-libertarians deny that this fact should make us bear the economic consequences for failure or success to receive a job or inheritance for other than maximin (i.e., efficiency-based) reasons. A wide range of unstructured background inequalities and contingencies are materialized in the job inequalities we face. Considering the rapid changes in talents in demand, the economic and educational opportunities where one happens to be born, the untraceable interaction of social conditions and talent, the role models, friends, and social connections we happen to access, the fit (or lack of it) between one's abilities, language skills, and technologies in use, if one gets along well with potential employers and colleagues and so on to be in a position to seize job rents, it insists that great inequalities in the amount of valuable external assets that people command should not be ascribed to choice.

Instead, these rents should gradually (to allow for adaptation) be subject to predictable and sustainable yield-maximizing taxation, also taking the long-term *impact on skill acquisition* into account, to ensure that people hold on to their assets voluntarily and that everyone is endowed with a fair share of gifts (Van Parijs 1995, 121–122, 168, 281, n.86). One crucial observation that guides this broad interpretation of gifts is, then, that in the type of societies we address, cases of inequality that may often, at first glance, be ascribed to option luck and ambition actually "operate on the background of very unequally distributed brute luck" (Van Parijs 2003b, 206; 2009a, 158).

Arguments on option luck in the labor market may have significant force under conditions where endowments were fully equalized (or spontaneously distributed more or less equally). However, as observed by Nicholas Barry, people face "hugely unequal starts in life" in any market-based and liberty-respecting economy (Barry 2006, 101–102). Access to capital resources, beneficial social networks, privileged slots in the economy, and so on, are likely to remain highly unequal even under far-reaching, maximin-guided policies operating within limits fixed by the protection of fundamental liberties (accepting, for example, that the family provides an important part of our socialization). These underlying inequalities are, thus, bound to structure people's choices and to shape, in fundamental ways, the outcome of these choices.

Even in welfare state capitalism, most people must take risks in order to make a living (spend money on courses, start their own company, opt for one career rather than another, choose one partner rather than another, etc.). They have no option but to do so from positions that are highly unequal with respect to the particular skills or access to the slots in the economy that are rich or poor in terms of technological inheritance or social capital.

Surely, the requirement that those whose choices were successful must be allowed to keep their economic advantages (the result of good "option luck") for other than efficiency-based reasons (i.e., to help sustainably maximize the minimum) seems to lose much of its relevance in a world in which people lack the freedom not to gamble, and where people inevitably make their choices from radically unequal starting points.[8] This observation about the unequal brute-luck foundation for the choices people make under real-world conditions supports the case for ascribing a relatively limited practical role for principles of ambition-sensitivity. These considerations provide us with a basis for rejecting a tighter link between the choices people make to become available to spontaneously receive valuable resources (whether an inheritance, a job, or something else) and their rightful claims.[9]

5.6. Basic Capital or Basic Income? Luck, Responsibility, and Equality of Status

However, the above remarks do not explain why this project of brute-luck equalization of external assets should justify a policy of monthly cash payments as the best way to distribute opportunities to do whatever one might want to do (Pateman 2003, 134–135). Under the basic income policy favored by Van Parijs, everyone will always—throughout their entire lives—be entitled to a permanent, regular (nonmortgageable) income stream.

Why should not real-libertarian principles lead us, instead, to opt for fewer but larger lump-sum payments? The arrangement favored by

Van Parijs denies people the option of accessing greater portions of the total resource share to which they are entitled and, thus, more room for using those means in very different ways. Van Parijs justifies his commitment to monthly payments by defending an argument for "mild paternalism," which assumes that people "in their right minds" would wish to protect their real-freedom "at later stages of their lives against the weakness of their will at younger ages" (Van Parijs 1995, 47).

However, if the guiding luck-egalitarian idea is to address brute-luck inequalities of *opportunity* (rather than outcome), this restriction on the access to resources seems too far-reaching to be described as mild. Indeed, considering that this responsibility-sensitive, opportunity-equalizing agenda is based on liberal (and, in some respects, even libertarian) commitments, we actually have important reasons to find the option of lump-sum payments superior. Yes, the latter would provide more room for squandering one's endowment, but it would also give much greater opportunity and flexibility to realize valuable projects that require costly, long-term investments (Ackerman and Alstott 1999; 2006).

True, a "weakness of will" argument would give us weighty reasons against concentrating all resources into one basic capital. However, if we were solely motivated by the principles offered in support of *real-libertarian* commitments, I find it difficult to see why a monthly basic income would be preferable to, say, annual or biannual payments. After all, the latter may be combined with some form of conditional safety net to protect us against the most disastrous effects of risky choices and temptations of wasteful consumption we may find difficult to resist.

If we share Van Parijs's objective to achieve the highest sustainable average level of freely disposable assets throughout a lifetime, it would also be natural to consider additional deviations from the principle of monthly uniform payments. It is, for example, likely that different choices with respect to the level, form, timing, and frequency of payments (e.g., small regular payments vs. lump-sum payments, cash vs. in-kind transfers) would have different outcomes for people's economic behavior. This, in turn, would be likely to affect the expected long-term, average level of the basic income.

With this in mind, one could suggest that some resources should be distributed in the form of in-kind transfers and/or mildly conditional investment-oriented capital endowments to young adults (e.g., educational resources, wage subsidies) instead of generous monthly cash transfers. The guiding thought is that mild conditionality may sometimes be acceptable even for real-libertarians *if* that would significantly improve life prospects, in this case by strengthening people's typical labor market attachment and work effort.[10] Another idea would be to offer a higher basic income for the elderly or other age groups for which work supply is likely to be relatively insensitive to the existence of a basic income. These are considerations that a reasonable political attempt to turn this luck-egalitarian agenda into practice needs to take into account.

The central point I wish to make, however, is that this choice must also be informed by our response to a more fundamental normative question. What is the relation between the requirements of these resource-based, luck-egalitarian criteria for equality of opportunity and our arguments on the socioeconomic conditions for equality of status defended in chapter 2? The category of thinkers I have referred to broadly as relational egalitarians have stressed the limitations of the luck-egalitarian choice-circumstance distinction. This family of views holds that luck-egalitarianism fails to take on board the conviction that people may have justice-based claims for resources *even if one's situation of urgent need is essentially traceable to one's own choices rather than bad brute luck* (Anderson 1999, 296–300; Scheffler 2003, 18–19; Satz 2010, 74–76).

The driving force behind this alternative interpretation of egalitarian justice is an attempt to achieve a society in which all of its members can interact as social and political equals, and, thus, people are not required to "grovel or demean themselves before others as a condition of laying claim to their share of goods" (Anderson 1999, 314). From this point of view, liberal-egalitarian justice, and the guidelines for the division of responsibility between individual and society, does not primarily rest on a choice/circumstance distinction.

Instead, the guiding ideal for policies of egalitarian justice must be to reach a society in which people are—irrespective of whatever (reckless, imprudent, or unwise) choices they have made in the past—enabled to take part as full participants of society with equal standing. This is, then, a society in which the relations between citizens are free from (the worst and most obvious sources of) domination, oppression, and abuse.

Consider someone who begins her adult life with plenty of wealth and who has completed an excellent education (i.e., she has been offered a fair share of resources). Under the influence of a charismatic entrepreneur she decides to invest all of her money in a risky business endeavor in which she has great confidence. Contrary to her expectations, however, this turns out to be a complete failure and all of her wealth is lost. As a consequence, her deliberate choices (rather than her bad brute luck) have led her into desperate need and, hence, exploitable dependency.

Should not a just society, based on equal concern and respect, universally protect the conditions for a person's equal status and, thus, offer social protection against the need to accept roles of servility or degrading activities at any stage of her life? And, as illustrated by our example, should it not do so regardless of whether a person's condition of need can be traced to choices or circumstances?

Following the argument in chapter 2, I would respond to this in the affirmative. It seems to me, however, that real-libertarianism is incapable of accommodating this powerful egalitarian intuition. One possibility is, of course, to suggest that the concern to avoid these situations is sufficiently universal and uncontroversial to explain and guide Van Parijs's paternalistic argument for why we must provide people with fresh starts at regular intervals (i.e., monthly payments) instead of embracing some version of a basic capital scheme.[11]

However, it is not clear to me that such a theory holds normative resources to explain *why* there would be anything fundamentally objectionable about the conditions of humiliation and subservience with which status-egalitarians are rightly concerned (cf. Wolff 2010, 346).

As we have seen, the central objective of real-libertarianism is, after all, to provide (formally free) individuals with equal shares of resources to do whatever they might want to do, and, thus, presumably *even to pursue personal relationships systematically structured by domination and servility* (a point I will spell out more fully in chapter 6). The above remarks suggest that the real-libertarian, resource-based account of disadvantage cannot be plausible as a *full* theory of social justice and needs to be combined with (or balanced against) considerations that also address, more directly, the requirements of respect and self-respect.

In the absence of such considerations, this conception of social justice also appears insufficient to accommodate and explain some of the key arguments for why a basic income is such a promising idea from an egalitarian viewpoint. In this context, the arguments on equality of status provide us with a foundation for arguing that a plausible, responsibility-sensitive account of resource-egalitarian standards need to build on (and not replace) the (often) prioritized requirement of basic autonomy. Such a pluralistic account of social justice incorporates an additional, normative foundation from which to defend that the social and economic conditions for every person's basic autonomy should be consistently secured at each stage of her life.

I argued in part I that this requirement offers a number of independent arguments in defense of an unconditional basic income.[12]

Placing these concerns in relation to Van Parijs's resource-egalitarian argument above, it is worth noticing that this distinct, status-egalitarian idea also provides a different kind of argument for why the idea of a regular unconditional income seems like a far more interesting option than a basic capital.

In contrast to the real-libertarian view, this argument is not based on paternalism (in relation the endowments to which individuals may be entitled). Instead, it rests primarily on considerations of bargaining power and personal independence (see also sections 2.3–2.4 in ch. 2). It is difficult to see how a basic capital policy, which may allow very substantial economic inequalities to arise and structure people's relationships, could offer similar advantages as the basic income *for continuously addressing the fundamental power imbalances and dependencies* that block the realization of status-egalitarian aims (cf. Wright 2006; 2010). This line of argument rests on an assessment of the transformative potential of competing policy tools to systematically protect people from vulnerability to abuse, and from situations in which they—as Lovett puts it—have no option but to "trade away their freedom from domination" in order to meet their most fundamental needs (e.g., Lovett 2010, 199–200).

Some may think that attaching an important role to these status-egalitarian considerations would make luck-egalitarian and resourcist views redundant to the idea of justice and the justification of basic income. Instead, I think this offers a richer set of reasons to express and explain the most important (and sometimes conflicting) values at stake (Birnbaum 2010b). Let me close this section by offering two brief observations to support this claim. First, relational egalitarians who present their view as an *alternative* to luck-egalitarianism suggest that we should not be too bothered by resource inequalities if people have all reached a standard of living that is *sufficient* for them to interact "as equals" in social, political, and economic life (Anderson 1999). However, I see no compelling reason for why brute-luck equalization of assets to which nobody has a prior claim (i.e., gifts, in our broad sense) ceases to be relevant (though it may certainly be less *urgent*) once everyone has reached a certain critical sufficiency threshold.

To be sure, "first come, first served" is no less arbitrary as a principle to guide the distribution of such resources above a sufficiency threshold than below it (even if it is a case of inequality where the least advantaged is a dollar millionaire). This example illustrates that the problem with very substantial brute-luck inequalities is not reducible to their potentially harmful impact on people's social and political status as equals.

Second, luck-egalitarian views helpfully explain why our reaction to a state of need that results from irresponsible and wasteful choices, made against the background of fair shares, tends to be different to a state of need that results from a clear case of bad brute luck. However, an institutional response to the former situation that is unforgiving, and/or fail to maintain the social bases of self-respect, is inconsistent with core convictions that guide the liberal-egalitarian project. The pluralist position I have sketched allows us to hold on to both of these convictions and explain the nuances of that reaction.[13]

5.7. Basic Income, Exploitation, and Self-Respect: Concluding Remarks

Based on the above analysis, it seems, then, that the position from which part II of this book started, and against which the exploitation objection was directed, may be justified after all. Taken together, the demands of equality of status and equality of opportunity provide powerful *and complementary* arguments for why the basic income proposal is attractive from the point of view of social justice.

Of course, the political conclusions of these two elements of the egalitarian ideal with respect to basic income may not always coincide. I argued that a purely real-libertarian standard of fairness, based on equalization of opportunity (rather than outcome) and the freedom to pursue (and bear the consequences of) very different objectives, squares uneasily with the far-reaching paternalist argument for monthly, unconditional payments. I also mentioned a number of other deviations from the policy of frequent cash payments that would be natural to consider from such a viewpoint. Hence, there may well be situations in which the best practical fine-tuning of this responsibility-sensitive, resource-egalitarian agenda would fail to satisfy weighty requirements of equality of status.

What I have just said is not that this agenda is unjustified, but that it is one-eyed and insufficient on its own. Accepting this pluralism may present us with a trade-off between opportunity-equalizing and equal-status-protecting requirements that are *both* justified but sometimes in conflict. In my earlier analysis of equality of status, I briefly discussed the possibility of a trade-off between the enforcement of responsibility and the protection of self-respect, and why Rawlsians have reasons to ascribe special importance to the latter. Provided that our link between status-egalitarian objectives and unconditional transfers is firm, we may thus have a robust foundation for the argument in defense of unconditional distribution even if the taxation needed to fund such a scheme would sometimes seize assets that do not plausibly fall into the category of "brute-luck" advantages, that is, that this may—all things considered—be a moral cost worth accepting.

However, our exploration of Van Parijs's work has now left us with the conclusion that considerations of equality of opportunity, luck, and responsibility generally provide us with a powerful, additional basis *in support* of unconditional transfers. If this is all correct, then, any remaining tensions between the enforcement of responsibility and the protection of self-respect in conditional elements of the welfare state (e.g., schemes that rest on an insurance-based or humanitarian rationale) would become far less dramatic.

Other arrangements for income security (to the extent they are needed) would now operate against the background of a prior, unconditional "gift-equalizing" scheme, which has endowed people with a firm economic basis to cover their basic needs and to secure their personal independence in a non-stigmatizing way. Behavioral requirements in conditional schemes would now become far less worrying since these conditions no longer imply a "work or starve" condition.

I now hope to have said enough to provide a satisfactory defense of the general notion of wealth sharing and to support the attractions of the real-libertarian way of specifying such an idea in the light of the exploitation objection. With respect to the latter, I do not claim to have provided a decisive rejection of the responsibility-based objections that were articulated against the real-libertarian version of wealth sharing. Indeed, one of my aims in these chapters has been to identify and help specify some of the most important ways in which it may be vulnerable to such objections.

However, I have sought to show how a forceful response can be formulated and that this alliance between Rawlsian justice and wealth sharing (or "gift equalization") has weighty advantages from liberal-egalitarian starting points relative to some of its main rivals. I conclude that the core idea of *Real Freedom for All*—once tied to qualifications based on the broader ethos needed to maintain justice and the requirement of basic autonomy—stands as a very powerful candidate for specifying the demands of a radical-liberal interpretation of Rawlsian objectives.

The Feasibility of Basic Income: Social Ethos, Work, and the Politics of Universalism

Why Do People Work If They Don't Have To? Basic Income, Liberal Neutrality, and the Work Ethos

6.1. Basic Income and the Work Ethos: Exploring an Unexpected Alliance

We have now reviewed a number of arguments for why schemes that provide unconditional payments to every member of society, irrespective of their willingness to work, may be superior to the work-tested minimum income programs of traditional welfare states. As discussed in the last two chapters, Philippe Van Parijs's powerful neutrality-based justification of basic income argues that a universal arrangement of that kind serves to equalize access to certain external resources in a way that will expand people's "real freedom" to do whatever they might want to do.

The problem I wish to examine in this chapter arises from the challenge of feasibility that this liberal justification of unconditional distribution needs to face. By offering everybody the opportunity of not working, a basic income at subsistence level or higher might erode the economic foundations on which its sustainable realization depends. An interesting way of responding to this challenge—briefly defended by Van Parijs—is to add a strong egalitarian work ethos (along the lines of Joseph Carens and G. A. Cohen) to this ideal (Carens 1981; 1986; Cohen 2000; 2008). Van Parijs has suggested that this kind of ethos might be justified on instrumental grounds, given its obvious potential for boosting the volume of paid work at a given net wage and, thus, the level of the highest sustainable basic income.[1]

My exploration in this chapter is guided by the observation that there is an apparent tension between the endorsement of a strict work ethos and the liberal, neutrality-based motivation for unconditional transfers. As we have seen in part II, the notion of gift equalization regards the view that resource claims must always be linked to work requirements as illiberal. A conception that respects neutrality must provide freedom for people to use these resources for whatever purposes they might have, whether to earn a high income, to seek an inherently rewarding job, or to engage in projects beyond the world of employment. A strong work ethos could improve the feasibility of a substantial basic income, but it would seem to do so only if it were also to reduce significantly the set of options and ways of life that would be generally perceived as legitimate in such a society. Would this strategy for making the basic income feasible not thereby neutralize the liberal gains upon which its justification depends?

These general remarks indicate: (1) that it may be difficult for the basic income to survive unless most people are firmly committed to contributing productively to their societies, but also (2) that the neutrality-based case for basic income would be difficult to reconcile with a strong work ethos. It seems clear, then, that specifying the role of the work ethos in the liberal egalitarian justification of basic income is important in understanding the implications of such an ideal as well as in assessing its feasibility and consistency with our considered moral convictions.

However, despite the centrality of liberal neutrality and exploitation in the basic income debate, the preoccupation of the literature with formal work requirements has left the moral status of the work ethos surprisingly unexplored. This chapter attends to this gap. I hope to demonstrate that no account of liberal egalitarian justice and basic income will be complete without having paid close attention to the complications and trade-offs brought to light by considering the role of the work ethos in this type of ideal.

The argument is organized as follows. In section 6.2 I recapitulate the key elements of Van Parijs's liberal egalitarian argument for basic income and introduce the challenge of defending full universality while also satisfying feasibility and neutrality-based objectives. Sections 6.3 and 6.4 state my neutrality objection to the alliance of basic income and the work ethos in the context of Van Parijs's *Real Freedom for All* and identify a set of possible escape routes. Neutralists may find it promising to relax the ethos by making its requirements nonobligatory. Section 6.5, however, argues that this option runs into other difficulties, revealed by my structural exploitation objection.

Sections 6.6 and 6.7 develop a set of arguments for why the most promising path to save our alliance against both objections should retain a firm, feasibility-supporting, and exploitation-resisting ethos but that this needs to take the form of a broad ethos of contribution, not a productivist ethos of work.

6.2. The Challenge: Can Basic Income Be At the Same Time Universal, Feasible, and Neutral?

In their inspiring and seminal piece "A Capitalist Road to Communism" (1986), Robert van der Veen and Philippe Van Parijs linked their case for (a gradually expanding) basic income to the cause of promoting a Marxian realm of freedom (as opposed to a realm of necessity) in which people are free from alienation. In this kind of ideal society, people would work mainly because of the satisfaction they derive from their activities rather than monetary gain: "The content of work, its organization, and the human relations associated with it could and should be so altered that extrinsic rewards, whether material or not, would be less and less necessary to prompt a sufficient supply of labor. Work, to use Marx's phrase, could and should become 'life's prime want'" (Van der Veen and Van Parijs 1986/2006, 5).

The typical liberal objection to such Marxian accounts of freedom as nonalienation is quite familiar. To be sure, everyone prefers inherently rewarding activities to soul-destroying toil. However, many people may be willing to spend significant amounts of time on work they find tedious if the additional purchasing power gained through this (alienated) work helps to increase their opportunities to access *other* experiences to which they ascribe great value (Kymlicka 2002, 191–95). In response to the plurality of ethical convictions with regard to work and competing activities, egalitarian liberals tend to grant a central role to the idea of nonperfectionism in fundamental matters of distributive justice.

Fortunately, the most sophisticated argument for the expansion of comprehensive, unconditional schemes sets out to avoid reliance on this kind of controversial Marxian conception of the good life. Philippe Van Parijs's subsequent "real-libertarian" justification of the highest sustainable basic income (the most thorough and widely known plea for such a reform) attaches considerable moral weight to the idea of *state neutrality* in relation to different ethical ideals. Specifically, it sets out to be fair to, and respectful of, both the consumerist objectives of Crazy, who wants to earn a high income and is prepared to forgo much leisure time in doing so, and Lazy, who wants to minimize paid work and prefers, say, spending more time surfing along the beaches of Malibu.

What the unconditional scheme is supposed to achieve is not the promotion of any particular conception of the good life. On the contrary, the idea of liberal gift equalization attempts to correct an (alleged) illiberal bias in existing, work-tested safety nets. While the preferences of Crazy and Lazy should be respected and while they both need to take economic responsibility for their choices (implying that Crazy will end up with a higher income than Lazy), liberal egalitarians must consider them both to be entitled to an equal (or, taking efficiency into account, "maximin") share of certain gifts to which neither has a justified prior claim. Assuming that people are equal in other respects, it would be unfair to allow only some to benefit from the value of inherited or other gift-like external assets, and it would be illiberal to require people to use them only for work-oriented purposes, hence Van Parijs's famous conclusion that even the Malibu surfers should be fed (Van Parijs 1991; 1995).

Against this backdrop, we are now prepared to address our challenge. How should we describe the status of paid work in a liberal basic income regime committed to: (a) accepting basic income as a universal right (in the strong sense of being offered to each and every citizen), (b) guaranteeing that such an arrangement is feasible, and, yet, (c) remaining respectful of neutrality in the sense described by liberal gift equalization? One possible view combines basic income with a strong work ethos along the following lines. A basic income society does not make the obligation to work redundant. It merely offers another and, perhaps, more humane means of enforcing it. John Baker rightly emphasizes that it is one thing to oblige people to work and quite another to say that those who fail to live up to this obligation should be left to private charity or starvation (Baker 1992, 123).

Even if we drop the idea of attaching a formal work requirement to the social minimum, this still leaves open the question of whether the state could or should legitimately maintain the normative super-structure of such a policy. Indeed, we might have good reasons to strengthen any existing work ethos by requiring everyone to act in accordance with norms to work as much and as productively as they can in order to counterbalance any reduction of work incentives that might result from dropping formal work requirements. One might even argue that a basic income becomes a relevant option, consistent with both equality and efficiency, only when most people can be presupposed and trusted to internalize the work ethos to such an extent that no work-test would be necessary in order to enforce the relevant obligations.

By way of illustration, consider Peter Kropotkin's view in *Conquest of Bread* (1905). Kropotkin held that under conditions of anarchist communism, resource claims of people that refuse to produce anything useful would be responded to as follows: "If we are rich enough to give you the necessities of life we shall be delighted to give them to you…You are a man, and you have a right to live. But as you wish to live under special conditions, and leave the ranks, it is more than probable that you will suffer for it in your daily relations with other citizens. You will be looked upon as a ghost of bourgeois society."

For Kropotkin, then, a person leading such a life has the right to an income but will "live like an isolated man" (Quoted in Woodcock 2004, 172). Similarly, Joseph Carens, in his argument for moral work incentives in *Equality, Moral Incentives, and the Market* observes that "the stronger the social disapproval associated with nonconformity, the more likely individuals are to conform" and "in the egalitarian system the social disapproval for refusing to earn any pre-tax income would be extreme" (Carens 1981, 133).

In line with contemporary radical egalitarian versions of a strong work ethos, we may characterize this ethos as *productivist* in the sense (described by Stuart White et al.) that it is intended to support "a very high level of participation in formal employment" (Pearce, Paxton, and White 2006, 179). The internalization of requirements to work unselfishly (possibly to one's best ability) could, thus, be included in a set of duties officially mandated by the state. As illustrated by these examples, a strong work ethos may be fully compatible with, and supportive of, a universal basic income policy. Denying subsistence income to those who do not work (or who do not express a willingness to do so) is one way of enforcing work obligations. Other ways include ostracizing such individuals, leaving them in "social isolation" (Kropotkin), and expressing "extreme social disapproval" (Carens).

However, whether or not we think there is something appealing about an alliance between basic income and a strict productivist ethos in this respect, this option clearly does not square well with the neutrality-based argument for gift equalization. The latter holds that a basic income would be justified, at least in part, as a kind of (expanded) universal inheritance scheme. It is an unconditional payment to which everyone is firmly entitled, whether we wish to use it for productive or nonproductive purposes. Hence, while such an alliance may offer a feasible route for offering every person a guaranteed income, thereby achieving both (a) universality and (b) feasibility, an

account of justice of this kind would radically constrain the real freedom associated with (c) neutrality and, thus, contradict our nonperfectionist rationale for basic income.

6.3. The Neutrality Objection against *Real Freedom for All*

I will now situate and specify my *neutrality objection* more fully in the
context of Van Parijs's *Real Freedom for All*. On a resource-egalitarian
view, ideal markets reflect how valuable resources are to others and,
thus, how costly not being able to use some particular asset is to others. Building on Ronald Dworkin's work and his account of opportunity costs, Van Parijs relies on a market framework to assess the
value of people's gift-like resource endowments. His principle of gift
equalization would cover gifts and bequests but also (more contro-
versially) the undeserved brute-luck privileges that Van Parijs believes
constitute a very significant proportion of the wages of attractive jobs
in present-day economies.

He lists a wide range of mechanisms that explain why some people can enduringly lay claim to significantly more than the reservation wage for a given job (as revealed by the fact that many people
would be happy to take available jobs at wages far below actual wage
rates). The part of the actual wage that exceeds a hypothetical market
clearing level—at which at least someone is prepared to take the job
in question—is a "job rent" that is up for maximin redistribution,
thereby providing everyone with an equal share of the value unless
greater rent shares for some help boost the size of the least favored
person's share (Van Parijs 1995, ch. 4, esp. 107–109).

For my present argument, the important thing to observe is that
it is only when there are many people who envy present jobholders at
current wages that job rents exist. As Van Parijs explains, "The more
other people care about one particular resource and the less of it there
is—shortly, the more precious it is in the society concerned—the higher
its competitive price will be" (Van Parijs 1995, 51). However, the following question then arises: How are we to specify the social conditions
under which preferences to work are formed? As we have seen, these
preferences play a crucial role in defining the size of the job rent to
which all have an equal claim. I will discuss the issue of neutrality and
the conditions of preference formation more fully, as well as some of my
own positive views on this, in section 6.6. In this section I restrict my
attention to the critical task of spelling out the tension between neutrality and the work ethos in Van Parijs's argument about job rents.

In some of his writings, including *Real Freedom*, Van Parijs affirms various kinds of "solidaristic patriotism" or "motivation-conscious institutional engineering" as instruments required for promoting the most ideal conditions for realizing his egalitarian objectives (Van Parijs 1995, 230–231; 2003a, 230). In *Real Freedom*, he is not very articulate about what this patriotism might require with respect to work.[2] In a later exploration of Rawls's difference principle, however, Van Parijs explicitly defends an ethos of work and thrift and the view that institutions must not abstain from "promoting the work ethic of the more skilled and affluent." Within the constraints of basic liberties, such a regime

> must not shy away from resolutely designing institutions that foster an ethos of solidarity, *of work*, indeed of patriotism, not of course because of the intrinsic goodness of a life inspired by such an ethos, but because of its crucial instrumental value in the service of boosting the lifelong prospects of the incumbents of society's worst position. (Van Parijs 2003a, 231)

If this kind of public endorsement of a firm work ethos is now part of the requirements of solidaristic patriotism (and Van Parijs confirmed his commitment to this view in a reply to an earlier version of my argument),[3] the real-libertarian—that is, neutralist—justification of basic income runs into several internal difficulties.

Requiring people to conform to an ethos of work *at the same time* as one builds the case for basic income on the empirical existence of large "employment rents" seems illiberal. In such a context, work preferences and, thus, the valuation of job resources do not merely reflect the spontaneous ethical convictions and priorities that may flourish in a pluralistic liberal egalitarian community. The aim, after all, is to find a conception of justice based on equal respect for income-oriented Crazies and leisure-oriented Lazies.

Now, Crazy, with his income-oriented conception of the good, can reasonably complain about the alliance of gift equality and the work ethos in the following way: on Van Parijs's definition of job rents, the privilege of having a particular job *is* a privilege only because so many people express a preference for holding Crazy's job at the going wage. But, clearly, it is no surprise that people express very firm work preferences if they are *morally required* to do so by the official and publicly expressed norms of their political community.

Adding the work ethos will lead to the size of the job rents Crazy commands and, thus, to his debts to society greatly and artificially increasing relative to a society with no obligatory work ethos. Furthermore, a strict, state-induced egalitarian work ethos in this vein would provide limited opportunity for Crazies to actually pursue their income-intensive (and inequality-generating) conception of the good without confronting public moral condemnation. Thus, this context of preference formation seems to preclude much of the social space and the economic opportunity needed to live by Crazy's consumption-oriented ideals.

Interestingly, *Lazy* can also complain about the lack of a meaningful form of neutrality in this scheme. The "real freedom" for Lazies to spend their entire days surfing, offered by liberal gift equalization, is now greatly reduced by the work ethos. The genuine freedom to engage in nonmarket activities of all kinds is given by one hand (liberal gift equalization), but is it not then taken back by the other (the work ethos)? True, even the surfer would actually be entitled to a steady flow of income in this world. Nevertheless, with a strict work ethos in place, the official morality of this political community would radically constrain people's freedom to actually *make use* of those means for leisure or other alternatives to employment. How much is gained for the Malibu surfers by moving from a view that consistently attaches work obligations to resource claims to a view that offers everyone a basic income but leads to extreme disapproval of people that actually lead such a leisure-oriented life?

If we are convinced by the view that there would be something fundamentally illiberal about denying resource transfers to surfers, how could we feel comfortable about ostracizing them as a means of achieving a higher basic income? It is important to see that my neutrality objection is not directed against the work ethos as such. The objection is directed against adding the work ethos to liberal gift equalization. Clearly, the case for such an ethos itself need not (and usually does not) appeal to the ethical superiority of a work-based conception of the good. But even if the work ethos is justified on Van Parijs's strictly instrumental grounds and, thus, serves only to boost the "real freedom" of the least fortunate (itself a neutrality-based objective), the point is that adding it may largely neutralize the liberal gains of unconditional cash transfers.

To see the force of this objection, it is worth emphasizing that Van Parijs's theory seeks to offer a normative platform from which to claim that unconditional distribution will be more respectful of non-consumerist and nonmarket lifestyles—that is, more liberal—than work-test schemes. As explained by Van Parijs, the point is not to discourage waged work or a "career dominated existence" but "to do as much as can be done in order to provide everyone with *a genuine opportunity to make different choices*" between different kinds of lives and activities (Van Parijs 1995, 33–34, emphasis added).

To sharpen our objection, consider the most radical work ethos that can contribute to feasibility under which every individual should be prepared to work full time (if able) without any significant inequality-generating net gains on the grounds that this would maximize the "real freedom" of the least advantaged (through the highest sustainable basic income). This view is compatible with the surprising conclusion that a neutrality-based respect for both Crazy (with a strong taste for money) and Lazy (with a strong taste for leisure) may in fact suggest a regime in which the ethical views and behavior of neither of them is consistent with the requirements of justice. Both may be legitimately ostracized *in the name of real freedom*!

It is debatable whether this implication would constitute grounds for rejecting this type of work ethos if justified by the Marxian perfectionist objective of making work "life's prime want" and, thus, making material rewards redundant for motivating work effort.[4] In our framework of liberal gift equalization, however, I fail to see how such a view could be said to respect the ethical convictions and aspirations of Crazy and Lazy in a meaningful way and to reasonably address their competing claims, unless it were also to allow some space for their conceptions to be legitimately affirmed and pursued.

Hence, while liberal in form, our alliance would actually seem to offer a distribution of resources and a public ethos ideal for those valuing and identifying with their work for noninstrumental reasons while rendering the freedom of Crazy or Lazy to pursue their objectives formal rather than real. My tentative conclusion, then, is that if the liberal egalitarian case for gift equalization wishes to (1) remain consistent with liberal conditions for preference formation, (2) deliver the liberal advantages (relative to work-test schemes) with respect to leisure and nonmarket options, and (3) avoid reintroducing any perfectionist bias in favor of inherently rewarding activities, it needs to reject this type of work ethos.

6.4. Saving Neutrality by Redefining the Work Ethos? Three Ways Out

In order to avoid the neutrality objection, we may seek to interpret the requirements of our informal work ethos differently. Before relevant options are identified, it should be emphasized that it is not unnatural for us to accept the strong interpretation of what an ethos requires of us—that is, that it presents us with a moral *obligation* of justice. For G. A. Cohen, whose arguments have sparked and inspired much of the present debate about justice and the work ethos, it is clear that deviations from an "ethos" of justice, once in place, are nothing less than instances of injustice. As he explains: "We might have good reason to exonerate the perpetrators of injustice, but we should not deny, or apologize for, the injustice itself" (Cohen 2000, 143). If that is indeed what the concept of an ethos of justice implies in the present context, the neutrality objection holds.

How, then, could an alternative to this work ethos be characterized in order to avoid the neutrality objection? First of all, I think it would be absurd to suggest that the liberal effort to respect different conceptions of the good demands that we remain indifferent between (a) a set of policies that would actively promote the activities, projects, and motives that support the realization of justice and (b) policies that would be likely to erode the conditions upon which the feasibility of social justice depends. Even if we accept liberal gift equalization, there is no objectionable ethical bias in the claim that we must support the social infrastructure and recognize the instrumental virtues and forms of behavior that are indispensable conditions for liberal egalitarian justice to obtain.[5]

Unless gift equalization is tied to some form of public ethos of contribution that helps generate and reinforce the complex economic, social, and cultural conditions for such a conception of justice to remain workable and attractive, those conditions may well collapse. If the neutrality objection to the alliance between basic income and the work ethos is sound, the important thing to observe is that the justification for and the measures relied upon to support such instrumental requirements must not remove the social space or economic opportunity to actually make use of the freedom offered in a wide range of "crazy" and "lazy" directions without official moral condemnation.

Against this background, we may consider two deviations from the strong work ethos in order to achieve consistency with neutrality-based objectives. First, it is clear that the relevant ethos must require conditions under which radically noncontributive choices (likely to harm the feasibility conditions of justice) are not typical. They may, nonetheless, still be held morally permissible. In other words, we may characterize contributive dispositions as virtues rather than as obligations. Under this *relaxed* version of the work ethos, there is no doubt that people do good if they identify with and act upon the ethos. However, while it is clear that those who do not live up to these demands are less virtuous than those who do, the former do not violate their duties of justice. This strategy leads to the conclusion that people are genuinely free to shape and act upon preferences in ways that deviate from the demands of the ethos without thereby failing to perform their duties.

A second, independent strategy for achieving consistency with liberal objectives is to decouple the work ethos from productivism. In other words, we may *broaden* our ethos so that relevantly contributive activities need not be exclusively performed within the formal sector of the economy (or, indirectly, by seeking to become employable by retraining, or by preparing to start one's own firm, etc.). Clearly, many of the activities beyond the labor contract are no less important than paid work to the long-term sustainability of justice.

This broader type of ethos may cover the unpaid efforts performed by people who devote a lot of time to caring for children or elderly relatives or who volunteer for good causes, invest a significant share of their energies in environmental protection, or act to make the relations of their families, neighborhoods, and associations—from church choirs to sports organizations, political parties, reading groups, and so on—deeper, more sustainable, and more well-functioning. No doubt, such efforts in support of the social infrastructure and the social and human capital of one's society are crucial to the maintenance of a productive and sustainable community of justice. Even "nonworkers" may be contributors, a point to which I will return in the final section of this chapter.[6]

These ways of adjusting the strength and the scope of the ethos generate four possibilities, of which only one was considered above. We have seen that the neutrality objection easily becomes fatal *if* the work ethos takes the form of a strict duty to work. However, we have now identified three additional possibilities: (1) a wider duty of *contribution*, (2) a lax (but narrowly productivist) *virtue* of work, and, finally, (3) a lax and broader virtue of contribution.

The safest way to save liberal gift equalization from the neutrality objection is to opt for option 3. A weaker (from duty to virtue) *and* nonproductivist (from paid work to a broader notion of contribution) ethos of this kind would not involve rejecting the ethical objectives of either money-oriented Crazy or leisure-oriented surfers as unjust or unworthy of respect. A broader ethos would imply fewer activities and lifestyles in violation of its precepts. And even though deviating from the relevant virtues must clearly be discouraged by such a view (say the attitudes of a very greedy Crazy or a very passive Lazy), the step from obligation to virtue allows us to say that even nonvirtuous attitudes and behavior can be compatible with justice. Hence, this view does not create any tension with the concern for finding a metric of resources that is meaningfully neutral between (and that seeks to respect) their conceptions of the good and their genuine freedom to pursue them.

However, avoiding the claws of the neutrality objection is not the only thing that a compelling and feasible alliance between gift equalization and the work ethos needs to achieve. I will now consider the strategy of relaxing the ethos (options 2 and 3) and argue that there are strong arguments against this due to its failure to meet *the structural exploitation objection*. This will eventually lead us in the direction of option 1.

6.5. THE STRUCTURAL EXPLOITATION OBJECTION

One of the attractive implications of gift equalization is that such an idea, if given a significant role, may support the opportunity for people to abstain from activities they strongly dislike. Having an independent material foundation to rely on allows people to say no to unattractive jobs, and, under the lax option now being considered, there is no obligatory work ethos to chase them back. People can opt for more flexible working patterns and can devote more time to non-market activities or lifelong learning or take sabbatical leaves.

Dropping requirements that one must be willing to work means that those who are unmotivated are perfectly free to voluntarily cut down on working hours, whereas those who are involuntarily unemployed or underemployed may find a wider range of working opportunities available.[7] However, bringing feasibility and the concern for stimulating a sufficient volume of paid work and other useful activities into the picture reveals my objection. Any view according to which work becomes voluntary for everybody—through the basic income—and a sufficient amount of taxable work and necessary toil is brought about only through morally nonbinding, informal pressure will often seem morally tainted for the following reason.

Such a move is not merely an innocuous, liberal demoralization of the labor market that does away with any official endorsement of Protestant work moralism and ultimately allows personal convictions with regard to the good to guide the distribution of work and employment. In contrast to a scheme under which an obligation to work is consistently applied to everyone (whether through a work-test, a contribution test, or a morally binding ethos), this scheme relies on informal expectations. Sensitivity to informal pressure is likely to differ widely among individuals in any community for a great number of reasons that should, arguably, not affect our conception of the just society. The basic income regime under consideration is open to the objection that it introduces, or strengthens, the exploitation of the responsible by the irresponsible. It offers greater freedom from toil for one category *only because another category "voluntarily" chooses to carry a burden to which both have the same aversion.*

It must be emphasized that my structural exploitation objection is distinct from and less fundamental than other versions of the exploitation objection to basic income found in the literature (e.g., Elster 1986; Van Donselaar 2009; White 2003a). It does not hold that a scheme offering "something for nothing" is inherently exploitative by violating some fundamental principle of reciprocity or ambition-sensitivity.

It does not reject the idea of providing everyone with an equally valuable share of society's gift-like assets, whether those resources are natural or produced. And it does not reject Van Parijs's case for including job assets in the category of resources to which the norm of gift equalization must be applied. It arises from the more limited, yet vitally important, concern for guaranteeing that the work preferences helping to define our resource-egalitarian requirements are genuine and that the conditions under which they are shaped and expressed are consistent with other requirements of justice.

Once again, let me explain my concern in the context of real-libertarianism and demonstrate why *Real Freedom* seems unable to accommodate this objection. First, suppose that two individuals, Christian and Hedonist, have the same kind of unfavorable job (on every objective indicator of what a good job consists of). Christian and Hedonist have the same negative attitude toward this job, and they would both prefer minimizing the time devoted to paid work (Christian may seek greater freedom to pursue spiritual interests, while Hedonist wants as much time as possible for more worldly pleasures). They are different, however, in one crucial respect: Christian is highly sensitive to moral pressure whereas Hedonist has no qualms about putting personal interests and needs first.

The political community accepts that the spontaneous distribution of job assets is highly unjust. It accepts the moral desirability of connecting a maximin brute-luck-countering distribution of such gifts to the liberal objective of equalizing people's freedom to do whatever they might want to do. Now, Van Parijs offers a useful way of protecting jobholders from unjust taxation under real-world conditions. Given the existence of a basic income and time for adapting to the new scheme (taxation must not take anybody by surprise, so the scheme is, thus, implemented gradually), jobholders are not only formally but genuinely free to make the same choice as someone who chooses not to work (Van Parijs 1995, 115, 121, 123–124). In Van Parijs's view, the fact that a person actually holds on to her job under these conditions demonstrates that her new posttax wage does not fall below the hypothetical market-clearing wage under which jobholders would cease to be privileged in this way.

This protection against overtaxation, that is, against capturing more than the *rent* portion of their wages, certainly seems to be helpful as long as we can plausibly assume that people continue to work because they genuinely prefer to do so, or work less because they genuinely prefer to do that. But would that always, or even typically, be the case? At first sight, the step toward a basic income regime would seem highly beneficial for both Christian and Hedonist. They belong to the job-poor prior to redistribution, and their freedom to reduce their working hours is strengthened.

Hedonist, our pleasure-seeking individualist, happily drops out of the world of paid work as soon as possible. However, despite a fairly long phase of gradual transition toward predictable job rents taxation and basic income (leaving plenty of time and opportunity for adaptation), Christian *still* stubbornly holds on to the same job. In fact, Christian is prepared to continue toiling for almost any (posttax) wage at all, not because the job is enjoyable or well-compensated but because Christian acts on a strong moral conviction—fuelled by the virtues of contribution—that in a decent society someone has to perform those tasks. And Christian is prepared to do so.

To be sure, there are good reasons for claiming that Hedonist is allowed to systematically exploit Christian under this distributive arrangement. The presence of many Christians contributes, no doubt, to the feasibility of a generous basic income. Feasibility, though, is purchased at the cost of injustice. However, self-sacrificing Christian is clearly *not* relevantly worse off than Hedonist in any sense captured by Van Parijs's metric of equality.

In the real-libertarian framework, the fact that Christian "voluntarily" holds on to his job, while having a genuine option not to, shows that he does not prefer Hedonist's endowment to his own at the going posttax wage. This means that we can legitimately keep taxing Christian at ever higher levels in order to help boost Hedonist's basic income, knowing that the existence of the option not to work guarantees that this taxation will not eat its way into the hypothetical market-clearing wage below which nobody is prepared to take the job. I, thus, submit that *Real Freedom* fails to accommodate the conviction that Hedonist exploits Christian in a way that has relevance for justice.

I now turn to a second type of case in which the structural exploitation objection is relevant. One obvious reason for why some people are more likely than others to express a preference for doing *less* paid work or for opting out of the world of employment altogether under this scheme is that they choose to assume a larger share of informal responsibilities for care and—more broadly—to do more societally important unpaid work. Considering the patterns of a shift of this kind and possible motives behind it, there is, once again, cause for caution before concluding that actual choices reflect genuine preferences formed under fair conditions.

This concern is closely connected to feminist reservations about basic income and the potential gender-conservative effect of some of these kinds of proposals, especially those regarding cash payments as part of an alternative to, or replacement for, universal access to high-quality professional care and those not overly worried about a gender-structured division of paid and unpaid work. In the context of care, it is sometimes argued on neutrality-based grounds that free money (basic income or basic capital) is preferable to distribution in kind, such as subsidized, high-quality day care, since this would enable people to make use of resources *according to their own preferences* (Ackerman and Alstott 2006).[8]

However, consider the case of our old friend Crazy and his wife *Christina*. Both are skilled, competitive entrepreneurs and have a strong preference for devoting most of their energies to market activities. As much as they may care for their families and neighborhoods, both have the same aversion to a life devoted primarily to necessary, unpaid efforts in the domestic sphere or civil society associations. However, Christina has a far greater moral sensitivity than Crazy.

With unconditional gift equalization in place (in the form of a basic income), linked to nonobligatory virtues of contribution, Christina may have considerable difficulties in resisting informal pressure to (partly) withdraw from the formal labor market, especially under arrangements in which access to affordable professional services for reducing the unpaid workload is limited. Again, we have a case in which respecting people's "voluntary" choices of activity under a basic income scheme (made in the absence of any obligation to accept the relevant tasks) means that those who are insensitive to our demands for (in this case, unpaid, informal) contribution (Crazy) are endowed with greater opportunity to pursue their personal projects only because others (Christina) are far more sensitive to—and prepared to subordinate their own, personal projects to—the demands of our virtues of contribution.

In the above scenario, the objection was directed against situations in which Christian (in the first example) and Christina (in the second) are wrongly interpreted as expressing personal tastes for certain activities but in which choices actually reflect self-sacrificing priorities that compensate for the absence of commitments to the required contributions on the part of others. However, there is also the important case in which some individuals identify with and actively affirm an inferior social role according to which they are expected to accept a mix of activities that most others reject (if they can) and for *that* reason would continue to do so with little or no pay.

To the extent that dropping universal and binding requirements to contribute leaves many more opportunities for selfish individuals to systematically exploit self-sacrificing choices and adaptive preferences, and to the extent that the feasibility of basic income is increased *because of the existence of the latter*, the case for liberal gift equalization is highly vulnerable to the structural exploitation objection. Hedonist is free to exploit Christian, and Crazy is free to exploit Christina.

Let us sum up: Relaxing the work ethos could save liberal gift equalization from the neutrality objection. However, while a lax ethos is more consistent with the liberal aspirations justifying the real-libertarian project, it now appears wide open to the structural exploitation objection. This is a world in which morally sensitive or manipulated Christians may "voluntarily" remain stuck in onerous forms of paid work. And it is a world in which morally sensitive or manipulated Christinas may be "voluntarily" stuck as full-time housewives with life projects and roles confined to family life, while their more individualistically inclined and morally insensitive fellow citizens *thereby* gain the freedom to give priority to their personal life projects.

If that is the implication of equalizing the real-libertarian "freedom to do whatever one might want to do" and, thus, respecting the great diversity of ethical views and choices, it is difficult to retain the view that this is the freedom liberal egalitarians should be fighting for. Let us, then, explore whether we can find a different, relevantly *exploitation-free* strategy to bring universality, feasibility, and neutrality back in line.

6.6. Interests, Preferences, and the Priority of Basic Autonomy

I shall work toward a solution by discussing first (in this section) how a different account of neutrality and the context of choice could make gift equalization more resistant to structural exploitation, and then by indicating (in the following section) the kind of work ethos that we should opt for and how the path I have identified could also counter the neutrality objection.

Anyone who makes a strong connection between justice and respect for people's ethical convictions has good reason to embrace nonperfectionism in fundamental decisions. Our liberal case for equalizing access to resources in a form that is useful, whatever specific purposes ("conceptions of the good") one might have, corresponds well with that requirement. I also believe—as is emphasized by "political" liberals (following Rawls's later writings) and libertarians—that a plausible account of liberalism should protect people's freedom to enter into social relations that *some* would find to involve objectionable forms of exploitation or subordination and should not stigmatize those who do so.

In response to the cases of Christian and Christina, those accepting this priority of liberty might claim that respect for a great diversity of ethical conceptions and individual choices entails that relations deemed exploitative by some but found to be valuable by others are bound to persist in a liberal society (a point stressed by Van Parijs, see, e.g., n.10 below). Are the outcomes explicated in section 6.5 a cost we must be prepared to accept if we ascribe fundamental importance to people's freedom to pursue very different ideals and engage in many different forms of relationships?

In response, my view is that there is, indeed, something flawed about a position that allows the liberal concern for respecting diverse conceptions of the good life to block efforts to prevent vulnerability to systematic patterns of the kind revealed by our objection. Liberalism seems radically deficient if solely concerned with providing everyone with opportunities that will be maximally sensitive to people's preferences, whatever they may consist in and, more fundamentally, whatever the background conditions of preference formation. I believe that one of the missing pieces in *Real Freedom* is that it pays too little attention to the broader context of choice.

It would seem that before it is plausible to place the liberal idea of respect for people's actual convictions and priorities at the center stage of justice, we need to ensure that everyone has access to the resources, capacities, and broader set of background conditions needed for them to identify, assess, and pursue intelligently a wide range of meaningful options. For the outcome of any resource-egalitarian view to be morally appealing, we need to identify material, psychological, and intellectual requirements for people's preferences to be considered authentic.

As argued in chapter 2, I hold, following Cécile Laborde, that whatever ethical weight we may wish to ascribe to any particular perfectionist values, all individuals share a fundamental interest in accessing the conditions of *basic* or (in Laborde's words) *minimal autonomy* from which they can approach such competing accounts of the good life (to recall, "minimal" is meant here to emphasize that it does not suggest the endorsement of "maximal" autonomy in the form of a liberal-perfectionist, autonomy-oriented conception of the good life, often associated with Mill (1859/1989)). The idea of basic autonomy remains impartial with respect to the various ends one might want to pursue. However, it serves to provide individuals with the means necessary to understand and to shape their own views about competing ideals and aims.

As argued by Laborde, "we do not have a (basic and universal) interest in pursuing a life of autonomous assertion, but we do have a (basic and universal) interest in avoiding ethical servility" (Laborde 2006, 371). In order to avoid a view according to which liberal respect for diverse conceptions of the good justifies the existence of structural exploitation (by failing to protect people from social oppression, denial of voice, manipulation, and indoctrination), it seems crucial that each individual—especially at a formative stage of her life—is provided with the ability to form and to articulate her own perspective.

To be autonomous in this basic or minimalist sense is, as I construe it, to access the basic conditions needed to approach *competently* and *confidently* the tasks and ways of life at one's disposal; to access the economic, social, and educational resources required to assess, shape, and pursue one's options as a well-informed equal. If people are born and socialized into accepting and perhaps identifying with highly constrained situations of subordination and servility, the notion of respect for people's expressed preferences would clearly fail to respect their interests (Pettit 1997, 96–97). Hence, every person needs to be endowed with the fundamental conditions of self-respect, one of them being (following Rawls) the ability to pursue projects with a lively sense of their moral worth and a nonsubservient self-conception, another condition being that they can access at least some association of shared ends in which they can seek social recognition (McKinnon 2003, 146; Rawls 1971, 440–445; for a fuller discussion and additional references, see chapter 2).

If the case for real freedom as the key metric of liberal equality is reinterpreted so as to operate on the basis of (or balanced in relation to) a prioritized requirement of this kind—a basic autonomy floor—this is likely to generate significant deviations from the real-libertarian view. This serves to emphasize the conditions of well-informed choice and to protect people from denial of voice and subjection to exploitable dependency in relation to other agents (and not only from perfectionist *state intervention* or morally arbitrary inequalities of *economic resources*).

For present purposes, I have two sources of protection against structural exploitation in mind. First, the requirement of well-informed choices suggests the need for a social environment in which everyone is provided with certain educational, deliberative, and time resources as well as some degree of freedom from family commitments that enables them to participate in public life. People must be provided with an awareness of the diverse set of ideals available and, thereby, some critical distance and independence in relation to the views they have been socialized into.

This concern for securing genuine opportunity for all to participate in public deliberation and social life, regardless of family conditions or care responsibilities, yields one reason for sometimes giving priority to distribution *in kind* over gift equalization in cash. Before we provide people with free money, with which they can do whatever they like, it seems crucial to offer high-quality education and universal access to affordable child and elderly care in order to provide everyone with a reasonable chance to examine their options in life.

Second, taking self-respect into account, social institutions and the broader societal ethos would need to help place individuals in a position to be able to identify, resist, and challenge norms of subservience and, thus, to form and to articulate their own views with firm confidence in their own moral worth, capacities, and projects. In many ways, a basic income contributes to meeting such a requirement, more so than work-test alternatives.[9] Clearly, however, access to a work-independent source of assets of this kind is not sufficient. In some respects it can also—as argued in section 6.5—be counterproductive in relation to the protection of the full range of conditions for basic autonomy, unless combined with, or restricted by, other policies and norms.

If the equalization of real freedom must operate within the bounds of a prior protection of basic autonomy that reshapes the conditions for preference formation, a just welfare regime must not only be concerned with making potential victims of exploitation more resistant to the imposition of ethical servility. If we are concerned with protecting basic social and psychological conditions for self-respect, political institutions would need to counter any social arrangements that systematically tend to reinforce the denial of voice, roles of submissiveness, and inferior status for the members of any particular social group (Okin 1989, 104–105).

Returning to the issue of basic income and its potential gender conservatism, it has been forcefully argued: (a) that men's equal involvement in child rearing and women's full participation in the social and economic life of the polity are needed to successfully target disrespect and objectification of, and violence against, women, and (b) that norms according to which parents are equally expected to combine nurturing activities and care responsibilities with work and civil society activities are particularly helpful in fostering and maintaining public-spirited, equal-status-respecting dispositions (Okin 1989, 99–100).

It is beyond the scope of this book to examine or to defend these familiar claims. However, if these assumptions are correct, they provide further grounds for why a basic autonomy-constrained account of gift equalization needs to attend to the difficulties for a civilizing ethos—supporting people's sense of equal worth and a nonsubservient self-conception—to grow strong in many social contexts heavily structured by rigid gender segregation and (more broadly) systematic lack of personal interaction across groups.

Hence, if such arguments on relevant norms and dispositions rest on solid empirical foundations, proposals providing incentives to break down a gendered division of labor and to influence people's individual choices in order to generate basic autonomy-protecting, collective outcomes are not—as *Real Freedom* and similar views suggest—objectionably illiberal restrictions on people's range of choices. On the contrary, they would be required in order to protect people's prior status as confident and well-informed choosers, empowered by the necessary capacities and social ethos to make valuable use of whatever options their (unconditional) payments provide them with.[10]

This generates an agenda in which the liberal egalitarian case for unconditionality is placed in a broader and more complex normative framework. It also indicates why and how supplementing the non-perfectionist justification of basic income with a component of this kind carries with it normative resources for criticizing gender conservative outcomes without abandoning broadly neutralist commitments. Adding this component and, thereby, basing liberal equality on slightly thicker ethical foundations do not entail the rejection of the liberal case for gift equalization. It merely emphasizes some of the broader conditions required to place every person in a position of basic independence from which they can assess their own convictions and more confidently stave off any unjust expectations on the part of others.[11]

Under these conditions it would be easier for Christian and Christina to reject conditions and relationships that seem exploitative. In the case of Christina, the availability of affordable services to lighten the necessary unpaid workload and other participation-enabling services would help to improve her bargaining position even more by providing a fuller account of the broader conditions for independent preference formation and participation in public life. However, I believe that this is only one part of the remedy needed.

6.7. Gift Equalization and the Ethos of Contribution: Toward Reconciliation

The central feature in our cases of structural exploitation was the existence of necessary tasks and burdens—paid or unpaid—to maintain justice. Moving contribution from the category of (obligatory) duty to (optional) virtue would enable selfish individuals to free ride systematically on the efforts of people with a far greater sense of duty, without any public condemnation. In contrast to other versions of the exploitation objection, most notably those of Stuart White and Gijs van Donselaar, nothing in my argument denies that justice might require liberal gift equalization, along the lines of Van Parijs's argument, if certain conditions are met.

One of those conditions is that the definition of gifts—broadly conceived so as to incorporate job rents—must be based on genuine preferences shaped under circumstances consistent with basic autonomy. A scheme of this kind must also be able to maintain the relevant feasibility conditions of justice in a fair way. In this final section, I examine the kind of ethos that could help meet these conditions. Can we avoid definitions of gifts or mechanisms of feasibility that are morally tainted while at the same time evading the neutrality objection?

It seems to me that an ethos able to satisfy these conditions needs to facilitate people to internalize (say, through educational institutions and public norms) nothing less than a civic duty of contribution (see also section 4.8 in ch. 4). By helping to temper incentive-based inequalities and to equalize necessary activities (paid or unpaid), this firm sense of obligation would serve to foster an arrangement that is consistent with basic autonomy and is economically feasible. Considering the field of options identified and itemized in section 6.4, I wish to suggest, then, that a broader duty of contribution (option 1), covering both paid work and a wide range of nonremu-nerated activities, appears to be more promising than its rivals, all things considered.

Our initial Van Parijsian reasons for linking gift equalization to a work ethos of some kind were strictly instrumental, based on the potential role of the latter in boosting the sustainability of higher unconditional payments. However, the difficulty in making Van Parijs's account of gift equalization, and the preferences helping to define its requirements, immune to the structural exploitation objec-tion is also an indication of a deeper moral connection between the ideal of (basic autonomy-constrained) rent sharing and an ethos of contribution. For the reasons explicated in section 6.5, it is difficult to see how the argument for job rents and the voluntary distribu-tion of work can provide sufficient protection against exploitation for Christians and Christinas unless most life projects chosen—employment-oriented or not—are shaped and pursued within such moral constraints.

I have argued that a strict productivist ethos is precluded by the neutrality objection and that a nonobligatory ethos (options 2 and 3) runs into other difficulties. However, once we accept that the justice-preserving ethos is based on a notion of contribution in accordance to which paid work may be sufficient but not necessary to the fulfill-ment of relevant duties, it seems both meaningful and sensible to hold that it is of moral importance to express equal respect for, and leave room to pursue, radically different ways of life that may sometimes ascribe limited importance to employment. Moreover, such a broad account of contribution is clearly needed in order to accommodate our intuitions about exploitation in cases like that of Christina, where the necessary tasks are mainly informal.

In order to spell out the arguments for this option more clearly, I will now confront it with two possible objections. The first objec-tion, presented to me by Stuart White, runs as follows: Would not this ethos be a nonstarter because of a mismatch between the needs of feasibility and the additional types of activities covered by the norms considered? After all, the feasibility of an unconditional scheme depends specifically on a large amount of *taxable income*. In response, however, it is plausible to assume that up to a point: (a) the size of the average market income would often shrink substantially if the quantity and quality of such informal activities—such as those listed in section 6.4—were reduced, and (b) the public expenditures needed to compensate for the direct and indirect consequences of the relative absence (or poor quality) of such activities—when possible at all—would often be very substantial.

More fundamentally, (c) the point of the ethos cannot only be to support conditions necessary to fund the particular policy of a basic income in a sustainable way but also to support the background conditions of the broader conception of justice in relation to which that policy plays a role. Bringing basic autonomy into the picture helps further highlight reasons why many informal, nonremunerated activities contribute to the maintenance of justice. This includes many independence-supporting educational and care activities as well as civil society activities, which open available paths for valuable contributions, social recognition, and, thus, the self-respect component of basic autonomy.

Arguably, it must also include the informal efforts needed to maintain the cultural structure on the basis of which people can meaningfully interpret and assess competing conceptions of the good life. The cultural structure, often relying heavily on the input of time-consuming, informal activities, helps provide a foundation— a language, traditions, skills, and artistic forms of expression—from which to approach, understand, and assess different ideals of life (cf. Dworkin 2000, 274). To say that such cultural activities should often be counted as contributions to the maintenance of justice is not to violate (a plausible account of) state neutrality. The case for recognizing their value is not rooted in the endorsement of any particular conception of the good life. The objective is merely to satisfy the preconditions for people to approach and to assess competently and confidently any competing options they might face.

Under the form of distributive justice considered, nonworkers who claim an equal share of gifts—for whatever purposes they might have—would not violate reciprocity or desert, since nobody has a justified prior moral claim to the resources in question. Nevertheless, we have identified a weaker sense in which the members of a gift-equalizing society that fail to contribute in *any* nontrivial way (in the labor market or elsewhere) to maintaining justice and its background conditions can be seen as acting unjustly.

Given our feasibility-oriented perspective, even real-libertarians— however neutrality-oriented they may be—cannot be politically *indifferent* between the projects of, say, a Red Cross volunteer and a "dope-smoking Play Station addict" (McKinnon 2003, 153). This holds as long as we can safely presuppose that the first contributes in an important way to preserving the conditions of justice while the second does not. The gift equalization scheme would cease to satisfy our criteria of justice if this type of free riding were to become systematic and widespread. Our ideal of gift equalization should, thus, actively and continuously renew and reaffirm a universal commitment to contribution in this broad sense and not take its existence for granted. In this kind of society, people would not have to work in order to receive a basic income but would be presumed, encouraged, and trusted to contribute in some way.

This, however, leads to our second objection. Would not such a duty-based option fail to provide a compelling response to the neutrality objection? More specifically, would not the endorsement of such an ethos lead us in the direction of a "participation income" rather than *unconditional* payments as the first-best option? The participation income, associated with Anthony Atkinson, is paid to employees, self-employed, involuntarily unemployed, people unable to work, students, caregivers, certain volunteers, and other contributing categories but *not* (as with the unconditional basic income) to those contributing nothing at all (Atkinson 1996).[12]

In response, my argument is not meant to suggest that this ethos would be difficult for those who tout the unconditional nature of the basic income to take on board. Indeed, I suspect that most people, including supporters of basic income, would find it absurd to propose that our educational institutions and shared public norms should not express *any* duty-based expectations to contribute (for instance, by remaining indifferent between contribution and noncontribution in the example just provided). As argued by Claus Offe, a viable and attractive basic income society is one in which those who might choose to work less under this arrangement would typically be involved in other useful activities.

Unlike the productivist ethos discussed in section 6.3, the broader ethos fits in well with the conviction of supporters of basic income that the unconditional scheme would and should (as recently defended by Van Parijs himself) provide greater opportunities for—in the words of André Gorz—"voluntary artistic, cultural, family and mutual aid activities" than any conditional scheme (Van Parijs 2009c, 7). As Offe points out, this requires close attention to the existence of available opportunities for contributing through "institutional alternatives to employed work" (Offe 1992, 76).

What about the surfers? It may not be too far-fetched to assume that in some societies a local application of our public ethos should hold that skilled surfers really do contribute in crucial ways, for instance, by helping to attract tourism and investment. Where this is not the case, however, it needs to be emphasized that the idea of maintaining a duty to contribute (implying that institutions should be arranged so that surfers are moved—by nonostracizing means—to contribute in other ways) is guided by a concern about the *distribution* of necessary contributions. For all of the reasons worked out in sections 6.3–6.4, there is no intention to imply that the sacrifices required by that duty would be overly demanding and, thus, leave only limited room for people to legitimately pursue their personal projects, whether in "crazy" or "lazy" directions.

Spelling out the more specific requirements of such an ethos and examining whether a basic income tied to it would actually meet the relevant criteria are demanding and complex tasks, which I cannot pursue here. In the present context, the implication of my argument is, though, clear enough. If the contributive dispositions necessary for achieving adequate levels of basic income (covering basic needs or more) would—at present levels of wealth, productivity, and work satisfaction—be possible only through the public threat of ostracizing large groups or by sacrificing the prior protection of basic autonomy, our response to the second objection would be: "yes," conditional options *would* seem to be preferable. The strategy of formalizing a greater part of our duties within a broadly universalistic context, for example, through some form of participation income or through a link between the basic income and some temporary but compulsory public service, would then be a natural option to consider.

However, there is a rich literature providing powerful arguments for why a well-designed basic income policy, linked to an infrastructure of participation and norms of contribution, would be particularly well-suited to foster economic initiative, meaningful work, and a rich associational life. To the extent that they prove to be correct, a feasible, neutrality-respecting, and exploitation-free account of gift equalization may be fully within reach in many economies, without taking the path through formalized contribution tests.[13]

I began this exploration by defending the notion that a difficult and important challenge is to spell out the case for a *universal* basic income in a way that satisfies *feasibility* while respecting *neutrality*. To this, I later added requirements of *nonexploitation*. I have gradually specified some of the constraints imposed by these desiderata as they were situated and fleshed out in the context of *Real Freedom*, tested in relation to the central convictions guiding the project of "gift equalization" and, later, in relation to our intuitions about exploitation. Feasibility, neutrality, and nonexploitation can clearly be specified in different ways in our search for reflective equilibrium. Supporters of unconditional schemes will be drawn to different ways of resolving the tensions I have tried to expose.

To some, the view we arrived at might seem to entail losing both neutrality *and* feasibility instead of achieving them. One option is to hold that we must accept any basic liberty-respecting ethos that will result in the highest sustainable basic income being higher than it otherwise would be. When Van Parijs defends a strong work ethos on instrumental grounds, he seems prepared to go quite far in this direction by denying that there is any conflict between neutrality—rightly interpreted—and a very strict ethos that would enable the feasibility of a high basic income. By contrast, other basic income adherents tend to take the opposite view. The neutrality objection seems to be decisive and, surely, the correct response must be to decouple the basic income from *any* such ethos: Be patient and settle for the level of basic income that is feasible at present without any state-induced ethos *even if* that basic income might fall far below subsistence.[14]

I want to take a third view, avoiding these two opposing, bullet-biting alternatives. There is a clear conflict between a strict productivist ethos and the neutralist justification for basic income. However, not every feasibility-promoting and exploitation-resisting ethos contradicts the neutrality-based rationale for basic income. It is true that the feasible basic income scheme operating within the constraints I identify would not be *as high* as under the strict ethos that was considered. And the menu of accessible and legitimate projects and lifestyles consistent with our duties of contribution would be more limited than some neutrality supporters might be comfortable with. This conclusion and its implications may be less pure and less determinate than those offered by the two alternatives mentioned. For all of the reasons stated, however, this is the path for gift equalization I find to be the most compelling.

CHAPTER 7

Social Justice in Practice: On the Political Implications of Radical Liberalism

7.1. Basic Income and the Real World: From Theory to Practice

In the preceding chapters I have sought to establish that there are many reasons to find the idea of a universal and unconditional stake attractive if one accepts certain liberal-egalitarian starting points associated with the Rawlsian project. An unconditional set of universal social rights can be justified as a way of supporting a brute-luck-countering (maximin-guided, i.e., efficiency-sensitive) equalization of the freedom to do whatever one might want to do.

By providing everybody with a fair share of external resources, it can ensure that the freedom people enjoy under liberal institutions is not only formal but would also give all members of society a material foundation of *real* freedom. A basic income could help counteract morally arbitrary inequalities in the opportunities for people to control their own time and to select freely what kind of employment and other activities they wish to pursue. It would, thus, distribute opportunities in a way that is less restricted to consumption or market activity than work-related schemes.

By taking the form of a regular basic income rather than, say, one payment of a large basic capital, it could also do so in a way that helps place individuals—at any stage of their lives—in a position of basic autonomy. Hence, it has a potentially crucial role to play in a policy agenda concerned with enabling people to pursue their projects without the need to live under conditions of degrading and/or exploitable forms of dependency (in relation to partners, families, bosses, or state officials).

The argument of this book is guided by the assumption that the general ideals set out by radical liberalism, and its universalist framework of property-owning democracy, are not only relevant under very distant, highly idealized conditions but may also serve as an important source of inspiration and guidance in real-world politics. If this is the case, however, we need to set up a close dialogue between such abstract standards and a broader set of social ideals and proposals that are more closely adapted to real-world conditions and political feasibility constraints. This is the explorative task to which I will turn in this final chapter.

To address this task I will examine the relationship between the ideal of radical liberalism that I have discussed in chapters 2–6, and three universalistic social models formulated in the more empirically oriented literature on the welfare state: the encompassing model (Korpi and Palme), postproductivism (Goodin), and the universal caregiver model (Fraser). Models of this kind often play a central role in typologies of different welfare states or regimes. While they are often introduced for descriptive or explanatory purposes, it is also clear that important, empirically situated arguments have been defended for the *desirability* of each of these models. They provide valuable concepts and insights for the guidance of welfare reform under current political circumstances, rooted within a normative framework of welfare universalism.

To place the ideals of radical liberalism in relation to these models is useful to our analytical purposes because the arguments in their defense respond to a number of different and complementary desiderata of great importance. Hence, they help alert us to an empirically richer set of considerations of relevance to any plausible attempt to contextualize and apply a given conception of justice. So, by moving back and forth between our abstract ideals and these three social models under conditions of noncompliance to justice, this analysis intends to connect ideal and nonideal forms of normative theory and, thus, to generate some tentative guidelines for the real-world application of radical liberalism.

Of course, it is impossible to predict the outcome—and political feasibility—of a gradual shift toward a basic income regime with certainty. Unavoidably, many of the remarks in this final chapter, drawing mainly on theoretical sources, will be rather speculative. A fuller and more complete view on these matters must be carefully guided by relevant empirical research. Consequence-based arguments will not be stronger than the empirical assumptions on which they rely. Nevertheless, a necessary and crucial part of the process of assessing arguments for and against a basic income regime is clearly to spell out with precision the particular mechanisms through which a basic income is expected—by its supporters and critics—to bring about certain outcomes. This is the theoretical project to which the chapter seeks to make a contribution.

Before turning to our three models, however, I will stay in the framework of ideal theory a bit longer in order to identify a set of important virtues and commitments on which an attractive and viable basic income regime seems to rely, once in place (section 7.2). Having characterized and specified some reasons in defense of the stability of such an ideal, I then take a step closer to real-world conditions in order to state and examine a series of challenges based on political legitimacy (section 7.3), environmental sustainability (section 7.4), and gender equity (sections 7.5–7.6) in nonideal theory.

Taking budgetary and other political feasibility constraints into account, an argument is needed on how best to understand the relationship between the basic proposal and the many schemes currently in place in contemporary welfare states. I will argue that the most fruitful response to that task seeks to combine a relatively modest basic income with social insurance arrangements and broad range of social services, rather than replacing the latter instruments with generous cash payments.

7.2. The Virtues of Radical Liberalism: Work Conditionality and the Stability of Justice

Before approaching our concerns of political feasibility and the application of our ideals to the real-world context, there is a more fundamental and politically important issue—arising in ideal theory—that requires closer attention. I have discussed in general terms the objections against liberal wealth sharing that are based on stability and the individual duties to maintain justice (see sections 4.8 and 6.7 in chs 4 and 6). More needs to be said, however, to spell out some of the relevant normative criteria and empirical mechanisms in light of our discussion about neutrality, the work ethos, and structural exploitation.

In approaching this matter, a useful starting point is Stuart White's case of Joe (White 2006a, 1–2). "Joe spends a fair amount of time in his apartment, watching TV or reading books. Sometimes he goes down to the pub or to the cinema. He is law-abiding, but he does not, apparently, contribute anything to his society. He produces no goods. He raises no children. He cares for no elderly dependents. He lives for himself and his own gratification."

For White, there is a strong case for holding that Joe is violating duties of reciprocity by making claims on resources without trying to make a productive contribution in return. As we have seen, neutrality-based arguments for an unconditional stake wish to reject such fairness-based objections by isolating a set of resources to which the principles of reciprocity (or similar moral requirements) do not apply. Hence, they have reasons to hold Joe's claim immune to such objections as long as nobody has a justified prior claim to the set of resources of which Joe claims a share.

However, arguments for the moral importance of an active commitment to contribution and solidarity may be defended and reshaped on the grounds of a duty to promote and maintain just arrangements and, more broadly, considerations about the stability of a given institutional ideal. So, even if it is perfectly consistent with, or required by, justice to distribute some set of resources unconditionally and, preferably, in the form of direct cash payments, this will not reject the relevance of arguments for attaching great importance to the willingness to contribute.

It seems, then, that in order to remain attractive and internally feasible, a liberal-egalitarian ideal of this kind must generate a required threshold level of "republican" dispositions and virtues upon which such arrangements (and social justice, more broadly) depend (Dagger 1997; 2006; Kymlicka 2002, 299–312; Laborde 2008). Some critics may now fear that a basic income would breed an atomistic, private society in which people tend to withdraw from communal attachments to lead individualistic lives like Joe's. Such objections are guided by the worry that the members of a basic income society would enjoy a sense of "freedom without responsibility," that is, that this would become a society in which many do not contribute to their communities and in which they lack a lively sense of solidarity and social interdependence (see, e.g., Anderson 2001, 72).

While relevant and important, this ethos-based argument against basic income looks less troubling once the relevant forms of work, and the full set of civic virtues with which we are concerned, are not narrowly specified in terms of an ethos of productivism, exclusively tied to the aim of supporting a very firm universal commitment to full-time employment. If, instead, the set of activities and virtues is specified by (1) a more broadly defined ethos of contribution, (2) a commitment to identify and act upon the common good (in Rawlsian

terms, a strong and active "sense of justice"), and, finally, (3) supporting the independence and participation-enabling social structure
on which the sustainable satisfaction of basic autonomy depends, the
stability objection seems less worrying.

Of course, even when related to such a broader picture, defenders of liberal wealth sharing (or "gift equalization") have reasons to
be troubled by Joe's attitude if it would become widespread. Now,
before discussing the relevant mechanisms, we must first observe that
it would be incorrect to say that there is no empirical evidence on
the labor market effects of a substantial basic income guarantee. In
fact, no less than five large-scale experiments were conducted with a
negative income tax (NIT) system (offering an unconditional income
guarantee to low-income families, which is gradually reduced as the
household's income from other sources increases) in USA and Canada
between 1968 and 1980 (see, e.g., Munnell 1986; Hum and Simpson
1993; Robins et al. 1980).

The results of those experiments have been widely debated and
new results still keep emerging from the analysis of this rich empirical
material (Forget 2011). Supporters of basic income-type schemes have
grounds for concluding that the results provide valuable evidence for
their claim that a basic income guarantee would be economically feasible and have a number of beneficial effects on health and well-being.
At the same time, critics of such a reform have grounds for concluding that this research supports that such a scheme would reduce work
hours somewhat, and that the size of this reduction is nonnegligible
(for a helpful overview and discussion of the vast literature on these
experiments, see Widerquist 2005).

Notwithstanding the complexity of the results and the debate on
how to interpret the outcomes of the experiments, it is, of course, not
obvious that the conclusions from North American experiments with
a negative income tax in the 1970s can teach us very much about the
implications of implementing an individual, universal basic income
today, especially when such a proposal is considered for other parts of
the world and for institutional and social circumstances very different
from those in which these experiments were conducted.

In particular, one clear limitation of the NIT experiments for our
current purposes is that they seem to have little to say about the possible effect of moving from a conditional to an unconditional program.
Since the plans tested were, on average, more generous than existing conditional schemes, we do not know to what extent differences
between control groups (and the lower payments most of them were
entitled to) and experimental groups (eligible for NIT payments) are

attributable to the greater benefit generosity of these programs or to their unconditional nature (Widerquist 2005, 57).

There is, however, one conclusion from these experiments that is very important to the objection we are presently considering. While the experiments suggest that a (relatively modest) reduction in work hours may result from the implementation of the NIT plans tested, they give no support whatsoever for the hypothesis that a basic income guarantee would lead to a massive *withdrawal* from the labor market, that is, that many people might quit the labor force altogether (Widerquist 2005, 56; see also Hum and Simpson 1993).

In addition, Widerquist argues that no support is given for the view that any reduction in work hours resulting from such a scheme would be large enough to jeopardize its economic feasibility. This economic aspect of the feasibility assessment would, of course, also depend on many other considerations. One of them concerns the extent to which an initial work reduction of people with less attractive jobs would push wages upward and/or improve working conditions and, in turn, help stimulate individuals with such occupations to work more. Another important aspect is the cost and relative importance of competing redistributive measures that we find desirable (a question to which I return below). But let me now turn to the broader assessment of feasibility called for above. To widen our focus in this direction, I will identify a number of mechanisms through which the basic income, because of its unconditionality, has great potential to help support the *relevant* ethos, as characterized in criteria 1–3 above.[1]

Participation, Time, and the Ethos of Contribution

First, the preference expressed by a person who does not wish to spend much time in employment under a basic income regime need not be a preference to escape a life of contribution, as in the extreme case of Joe, but simply to contribute less in the form of full-time employment. Any plausible account of the virtues of contribution on which the stable realization of (radical-liberal) justice depends is much wider than paid work. As argued at several stages in the preceding chapters, it must, for example, take into account efforts in support of voluntary associations, political activity, local communities, cultural activities, and informal care work.

Basic income adherents can thus respond by arguing that once we take into account concerns to avoid that the communal ties, human capital, and the cultural structure that form the background of people's choices become impoverished, this assessment is likely to turn out differently. Of course, it would be naïve to expect that a basic income would be sufficient to generate a flourishing ethos of contribution along these lines. However, if linked to a social infrastructure of participation (see sections 2.7, 4.8, and 6.7 in chs 2, 4, and 6), and a broader set of supportive policies, a basic income system has a number of clear advantages (relative to work-test schemes) to support the above objectives.

Unconditional payments provide not only cash but also greater potential (for those who wish) to access *time*. For that reason it offers people—regardless of their employment history, current job situation, or health status—means for useful nonmarket participation, such as those mentioned above (Gorz 1999; Standing 2011, 178–182). Under distributive schemes based on a work-test, whether of the social assistance or social insurance kind, any activities such as full-time education or active forms of voluntary work will typically clash with the conditions of being either *available* for a full-time job or being *incapable* of performing paid work. Of course, details vary between welfare states and particular schemes. However, time-consuming and demanding forms of civil society activity or political action are typically incompatible with the conditions under which work-based forms of income security is admitted (Hirst 1994; Jordan 1992, 157).

As Brian Barry puts it, "there is surely something crazy about the stipulation that those drawing unemployment benefit must be 'available for work' at any moment, which rules out their using the time to improve their qualifications, engage in community work, or help a neighbour while earning a bit extra" (Barry 2001, 65–66). By contrast, if people in a basic income regime wish to engage in time-consuming activities outside the formal labor market—say volunteering for a good cause—they are perfectly free to do so without losing their payment.

They can do so even if this makes them unavailable for paid work (violating an "availability for work" condition) or if it indicates that they are in fact capable of performing paid work (violating an "incapability of work" condition). They don't need to ask for anybody's permission or approval. Insofar as a possible reduction in the total volume of paid work under a basic income program is matched by an increase of vital unpaid contributions such as those listed, there would be no need to worry from the point of view of contributive virtues, all things considered.

Unconditional Payments, Critical Deliberation, and the Common Good

Expanding opportunities for socially valuable forms of participation beyond the wage-based economy is important also to the more specific concerns of supporting conditions for political deliberation. With a basic income to rely on, the social conditions needed for being an active and well-informed citizen may become (more) accessible to all. As Carole Pateman observes in her defense of the basic income option, this would no longer require heroic efforts (Pateman 2003, 133).

It is important to see, however, that the argument for a link between basic income, democratic renewal, and public-spirited virtues does not rest solely on the fact that such a program would remove certain practical obstacles and time constraints for engaging in relevantly civic activities. As illustrated by the example of Joe above, the basic income may, in principle, be used to withdraw from public spaces and weaken the prospects for gainful interaction across groups. At the same time, a good workplace can ideally be an excellent school of citizenship in which people get to know and understand people they would not otherwise have met, and be made to develop virtues of responsibility and solidarity.

For this link to be established more firmly, then, this view seems to depend on an argument about the potential of a workplace-independent share of resources to help reshape the general *political culture*, and *workplace conditions*, in order to stimulate a broader and more active concern for the common good. One suggestion to explain this step, offered by Zygmunt Bauman, emphasizes the role of a basic income to remove certain fundamental sources of anxiety and insecurity tied to the satisfaction of one's basic everyday needs (Bauman 1999).

I will here spell out three possible mechanisms of importance for this argument to hold and place them in relation to the aims of this chapter. First, in the everlasting day-to-day quest for basic (nonstigmatizing) economic security, civic reflection and the state of the world may quite understandably be secondary concerns. People may reasonably be more occupied with urgent personal needs (such as putting food on the table) and short-term personal interest than ethical reflection.

The daily quest for self-reliance and successful business—in a world of fear and insecurity about the satisfaction of one's basic needs—could easily paralyze deliberation and action for the common good. With a reliable independence-promoting and brute-luck-equalizing program in place, and with one's basic needs securely satisfied through such a distributive scheme, people can afford to think about other things than urgent personal needs or positional competition to make ends meet. To put the point crudely: they can afford to be moral.

Second, the step toward decoupling basic income security and the social bases of self-respect from the employment contract could also remove fundamental economic, existential, and psychological barriers to criticize the particular productive activities, or production units, that one may otherwise depend on for a living.[2] One can afford to add pressure on holders of economic power to act in accordance with justice.

A vital republic depends on the existence of a vigilant citizenry ready to scrutinize the ends and methods of productive activities and to check tendencies of injustice and corruption amongst political and economic elites. With an unconditional tier of distribution, people gain some independence in relation to the labor market and work-tested schemes. Hence, they are endowed with important resources to put greater emphasis on the moral reasons to undertake (or avoid) particular forms of employment. The power to exploit people's vulnerability and urgent needs by "buying" their loyalty to, and silencing opposition against, morally dubious projects is thereby counteracted (I return to this point in the section on postproductivism below).[3]

This argument relates to a third relevant mechanism, namely, the possible impact of unconditional transfers on the possibility to engage in critical deliberation and protest in order to support the conditions of equality of status. As we have seen, anybody concerned with basic autonomy needs to pay close attention to the interaction between institutional arrangements and social structure, and, in our present context, between social policy and societal ethos. The achievement and maintenance of social arrangements in which one's access to basic autonomy is respected and recognized depend, among other things, on the existence of a robust protection against the denial of voice and demeaning treatment.

There is a sense in which anyone that depends fully on someone else's willingness to employ her, or to provide her with income security (on a conditional basis), lacks a very important foundation for the development and exercise of *independent political judgment.* Under conditions where the requirements of employment-based contribution operate within a social and economic macro-framework within which many are exposed to the whims of an employer they depend on for their livelihood, the employment contract will clearly tend to strengthen rather than challenge norms of subservience (cf. Pateman 2006, 109–111).

This point may be generalized to any relation in which someone is personally depending on another for attaining the basic means for survival and well-being, whether it is an employer, a person who admits the payment of conditional welfare checks, or a husband or wife whose income one depends on. A distributive framework in which people will need to bow and scrape before one another in order to secure their basic needs will seriously hamper the prospects for achieving and maintaining a societal climate in which people can form and maintain a nonsubservient self-conception.

Instead, the latter must be a society in which people can articulate and express their wishes and opinions freely, and in which their status as equals is thus mutually recognized and reinforced in their daily lives. So, while we have important grounds for why a desirable social ethos (according to our radical-liberal standards) needs to be supportive of a firm commitment to social contribution, the above remarks underscore that our way of specifying and supporting those virtues and activities must never be detached from the broader conditions needed for the protection of basic autonomy.

In conclusion, once we operate with a nonproductivist version of the ethos of contribution, and once the characterization of the relevant ethos is informed by a broader concern for solidarity-guided and basic autonomy-protecting dispositions, a number of powerful arguments become available for why a "basic income society" would help generate its own support. Taken together, then, these arguments suggest that a politics of basic income—in the right normative context, and with the relevant supporting policies—can activate important mechanisms to help generate and support the civic virtues on which its stable realization depends.

7.3. REAL FREEDOM, PERCEIVED LEGITIMACY, AND THE ENCOMPASSING MODEL

Let me now place the abstract radical-liberal criteria of justice under consideration in relation to three empirically thicker welfare models in the context of *nonideal theory*, that is, a real-world context in which we assume that such standards of justice are not yet fully realized or complied with. The radical-liberal ideals of stakeholding and unconditional basic income may potentially fit into, and build upon, many contemporary welfare regimes that have either been (to some extent) realized or defended as desirable and realistic options in empirically oriented research on welfare states.

However, ideals of unconditional universalism can be given widely differing political interpretations and transition paths in nonideal theory depending on the broader normative and institutional framework in which they are placed. In the following, I will discuss some of the key challenges that the quest for such a political real-world justification must confront and identify a number of issues in the intersection of philosophy, welfare state theory, and policy assessment that will be important to address in future research.

Given a concern to maximize the opportunities of the least advantaged within a conception committed to principles of individualized and universal forms of resource provision, the so-called encompassing model provides a promising starting point. According to Walter Korpi and Joakim Palme, comparative research gives strong empirical evidence for the hypothesis that reducing inequality and poverty is best achieved by an encompassing welfare model (Korpi and Palme 1998; cf. Rothstein 1998).

The basic characteristics of the encompassing welfare model are described as follows: "eligibility is based on contributions *and* citizenship. Universal programs covering all citizens and giving them basic security are combined with earnings-related benefits for the economically active population. This model reduces the demand for private insurance and has the potential of encompassing all citizens within the same program" (Korpi and Palme 1998, 669).

The so-called paradox of redistribution presented by Korpi and Palme suggests that "the more we target benefits at the poor and the more concerned we are with creating equality via public transfers to all, the less likely we are to reduce poverty and inequality" (1998, 661). To make sense of this puzzling claim we must understand that the core idea of this argument is that the relative success of the encompassing model in relation to these objectives is explained by the power dynamics of coalition-building between the least advantaged and the middle classes. This can help put a robust political and economic structure in place that effectively makes the budget size available for state redistribution much higher compared to arrangements more closely targeted at the poor.

Some of the arguments for such a regime have obvious affinities with the arguments in the literature on basic income and the stakeholder society, with the latter's emphasis on universal coverage and basic security for all. However, if the paradox of redistribution is correct, it also presents an important political feasibility challenge to the expansion of universal and unconditional programs. To spell out this challenge, I will distinguish between two possible interpretations of such an encompassing Swedish-style welfare model with respect to its implications for cash transfers to people who are able to work.

The first interpretation is that the categories of "citizen" and "contributor" must, insofar as possible, be made to coincide by linking universal programs to work-tests in order to secure that this coalition-building and legitimacy-supportive mechanism remains firmly in place. This seems to generate an immediate rejection of basic income. Such a reading underscores the interpretation that the encompassing welfare regime, with its combination of generous social insurance programs and a high volume of paid work, is distinctively "productivist."

On this account of the model, it requires a political agenda with a very clear focus on full employment, and policies of *recommodification* and *social investment*, which serve to make people self-supporting and, arguably, help them realize their maximum productive abilities. Why, then, would the arguments for the paradox of redistribution lead us to reject basic income?

A basic income may potentially weaken the coalition-building power structure stressed by this argument if it implies a move from the encompassing model to (what Korpi and Palme call) a *basic security model*, in which the responsibility of the state with regard to income security is limited to the aim of securing universal access to relatively low, flat-rate benefits. Even if we would accept basic income as desirable in ideal theory, this challenge provides a clear threat in nonideal theory. In the latter context, we must take into account that many people may not be responsive to considerations of distributive justice.

The political scenario with which this objection is concerned is that significant deviation from schemes based on accustomed living standards would remove, or seriously weaken, reasons based on personal needs and self-interest for the middle class to support a universal welfare state for their own social protection. So, this view holds that it is strategically crucial to protect a central role for generous, earnings-related social insurance and to make sure that this group will not depend heavily on private insurance for the protection of their income security and access to high-quality welfare services.

This, the argument goes, is of great importance to make sure that there is a broad and solid acceptance of relatively high levels of taxation and redistributive institutions. All this suggests that it would be politically shortsighted and counterproductive to promote the expansion of universal, flat-rate basic security programs *at the expense* of maintaining (or implementing) a strong earnings-related social insurance based on accustomed living standards.

There is, however, a second possible interpretation of the encompassing model that softens this political skepticism in relation to basic income policies considerably. This latter view holds that the argument for citizenship and (paid) contribution as necessary conditions of eligibility should be taken to mean that the encompassing model combines two different layers of distributive justice. The justification of one layer is based on the arguments for *universal wealth sharing* between all citizens (and, thus, supports a basic income-type arrangement), whereas the other additional set of policies is mainly based on considerations of *reciprocity* (justifying contribution-based, earnings-related benefits).

This account is strongly consistent with the normative principles explored in this book, but it is also, I think, consistent with the motivation behind the arguments offered in defense of the encompassing model. Indeed, how could we effectively provide "universal programs," giving "all" basic security, unless we opt for something like an unconditional basic income? Furthermore, most welfare states categorized as "encompassing" by Korpi and Palme actually combine elements of the basic income approach and the earnings-related social insurance approach. Universal flat-rate benefits to children and students, as well as a guaranteed pension for people above a certain age, are crucial parts of actual welfare regimes that they categorize as encompassing.

In addition, there are many in-kind benefits and services, such as highly subsidized universal health care, educational resources, and, of course, police protection (just to name a few examples), to which all members of society are entitled, irrespective of previous earnings, work record, or willingness to work. As emphasized in Per Janson's exploration of the Swedish basic income debate, few people in such welfare states would seriously consider making people's access to *these* rights conditional on their willingness to work (Janson 2003, 98–101).

On this second interpretation, then, the question is not *if* there should be a basic income component in the encompassing welfare model. Rather, the question is how generous and expansive this component should be. How should it, in the context of nonideal theory, be specified in relation to (and balanced against) reciprocity-based social insurance schemes in order to be perceived as legitimate and remain consistent with strategic coalition-building to serve the long-term objectives of social justice?

Under present conditions, there are several arguments for why certain basic income or basic capital proposals would fit naturally into a so-called transitional labor market and enhance the operation of an encompassing model in its conventional productivist form. In such an ideal it is found normal and desirable that people opt out of paid work during some periods of their lives in order to undertake necessary care work (e.g., parental leave), retrain, take a sabbatical leave, or engage in voluntary work (Schmid 2000; Schmid and Gazier 2002). Opportunities for lifelong learning can make workers more productive and motivated to work for longer parts of their lives. The option to temporarily and voluntarily opt out of employment may also help prevent burnout and keep workers healthy.

As long as such a case for a basic income in support of mobility and smooth transition is guided by a welfare state ideal in which social investment and building capability for labor market participation are primary concerns, this agenda fits smoothly into a productivist account of the encompassing model (cf. Esping-Andersen 2002). Gösta Rehn, one of the most important theorists of the Swedish model, famously argued that we should prefer "the security of the wings" to the "security of the shell."

Institutions that link basic security very tightly to a person's present job and, thus, aim to protect jobs rather than incomes can effectively block individually and socially beneficial mobility (Rehn 1977). Partly dissociating people's incomes from their jobs—and ensuring that there is always a solid workplace-independent income to rely on—clearly seems desirable from this viewpoint. This helps make people willing to embrace economic change and the "creative destruction" of capitalism, even if that will threaten their current jobs. Their concern for income security gives them no need to desperately protect and hold on to an occupation they do not like, or which is no longer in demand and may not survive for long without state subsidies.

In view of these arguments, a distributive mechanism that allows voluntary career breaks can play a very important role to help people find a place in the economy suited to their interests and productive abilities. Universal access to a workplace-independent income can facilitate skill improvement as well as establish a secure foundation to fall back upon when starting up a new business project. In short, it could provide a central element of an economic background structure in support of the kind of risk-taking, entrepreneurship, and flexibility that is necessary for a dynamic, vibrant, and nonprotectionist economy (cf. Van Parijs 1995, 222–223).

Still, within the context of such a two-tiered form of egalitarian productivism, substantial and permanent basic income payments could only be accepted with important qualifications. Adherents of such a productivist, encompassing model may prefer to keep a basic income for adults (who are able to work) mildly conditional in order to ensure that people use their time for purposes that serve long-term productivity and do not reject the importance of paid work.

The relevant type of basic income guarantee (complementing earnings-related, work-based transfers) could, for instance, take the form of a small initial payment for social investment at the age of maturity, a basis from which to start one's productive life or to rely on through periods of transition (Le Grand and Nissan 2003). Another relevant option would be a *time-limited* basic income that could be activated for economic investment, reschooling, temporary recreation, or as a residual security buffer (White 2003b, 90–93). The arguments for such arrangements express an egalitarian concern for the health, bargaining power, and long-term productive abilities of the work force. At the same time, however, they remain consistent with the productivist ideal of full-time employment for all who are able to work, and a general commitment to the world of employment.

7.4. Environmental Sustainability and the Challenge of Postproductivism

However, many of my arguments in the context of ideal theory have been explicitly directed against any fundamental connection between liberal-egalitarian justice and productivist ideals. If we are in search for a solid foundation—and political guidance—for a welfare state ideal motivated by the long-term objective of providing a substantial basic income to all, the considerations generated in dialogue with the encompassing model are helpful but limited.

A different framework for understanding social rights in real-world policy debates—more consistent with such normative starting points—may be provided by welfare theorists who advocate various versions of a "postproductivist" welfare regime (e.g., Fitzpatrick 2003; Goodin 2001; Offe 1992; Van der Veen and Groot 2006; see also Birnbaum 2009). While the encompassing model is open to a limited basic income component along the lines suggested, authors such as Robert Goodin and Claus Offe present us with a theoretical framework in which a substantial basic income is explicitly presented as a possible cornerstone of a feasible and desirable universal welfare model.

For those who place the promotion of work incentives in focus, a fully universal and unconditional basic income has clear advantages relative to social-assistance-based transfers. In contrast to the latter, under which welfare recipients often face confiscatory effective marginal tax rates, the basic income offers a foundation to which income from other sources can be freely added. Nevertheless, if we are hoping to (within an egalitarian framework) maximize the total volume of paid work, the basic income proposal is unlikely to be embraced as an ideal policy instrument.

After all, it will give people who are unmotivated or unsatisfied with their jobs the opportunity to work less, or even drop out of paid work without losing the basis of subsistence. It is often defended as an instrument to increase the overall level of employment and to make it possible to work at higher ages, while *at the same time* making a reduced workweek and voluntary career breaks more feasible options.

But the expanded freedom from employment will seem highly problematic or provoking only if we do not place the quality of paid work, or people's personal independence in relation to employment, in the foreground, or if we think that useful activities outside the sphere of paid work do not require time, recognition, and support on a systematic basis.

A *postproductivist* welfare regime, as characterized by the above thinkers, shares many of the essential characteristics of the encompassing model, such as the commitment to principles of universalism, egalitarianism, and welfare payments as individual rights. Moreover, the strategy for economic feasibility relied upon in this model is also guided by the objective of facilitating labor market flexibility and smooth labor force transition through universalistic distributive means.

The objective for postproductivists, however, is explicitly to provide a path toward a universalistic welfare regime under which the freedom from toil (i.e., the Marxian "realm of necessity") and the servitude of involuntary employment are highlighted as very central objectives. As our societies grow richer, postproductivists hold that it is no longer desirable or necessary to push everyone into the firm structure of full-time work throughout their active ages, that is, irrespective of people's preferences with regard to the forms of employment they can access.

Like egalitarian productivists, then, postproductivists are strongly concerned with opportunities for meaningful forms of paid work. Their ideal, however, is to shift emphasis toward useful and personally rewarding activities rather than paid work as such, and to advance the possibilities of a shorter working week and less rigid patterns of employment through the different stages of life.

Of course, it is undeniable that a substantial volume of paid work is crucial to the long-term feasibility of any reasonably generous welfare state. However, while taking the importance of stimulating a sufficient work effort into account, postproductivism also affirms the desirability of collectively opting for a more relaxed approach to paid work and holds that access to discretionary time (i.e., time that is free to spend as one pleases) is a very important dimension of freedom (see also Goodin et al. 2008).

If guided by radical-liberal ideals and if provisionally attached to the encompassing model (for the reasons stated), what are the fundamental reasons for reinterpreting such a model in the direction of postproductivism? As I see it, the case for such a shift tends to be shaped by three central standpoints: (1) the normative claim that we should ascribe fundamental moral importance to the values of "real freedom" and the conditions to ensure that people are free from exploitable dependency; (2) the empirical claim that "economic productivity can be sustained at moderately high levels on the basis of far less than full employment, full-time for absolutely everyone of working age" (Goodin 2001, 15–16; cf. Engler 2005).

Finally, the desirability and urgency of actually making use of that possibility is supported by (3) the empirical claim that any job growth in the richer parts of the world that is based on accelerating or status quo levels of economic growth tend to be ecologically unsustainable. We live in a world of global climate change and alarming levels of environmental degradation where our economic activities do not respect the nonnegotiable, planetary boundaries within which human societies can operate safely (Rockström et al. 2009).

In this context, fast growth as an instrument for job creation will lead us to incur a heavier global ecological footprint to block the path for the radical reorientation needed for sustainable economic expansion in poorer parts of the world, and to secure ecological requirements for intergenerational justice (Barry 2005; Jackson 2009; Offe 1992, 71; on the complex relationship between economic growth, basic income, and environmental sustainability, see also Van Parijs 1992a, 26–28 and Van Parijs 2009c). Taken together, these claims add up to the conclusion that narrowly productivist interpretations of welfare universalism are morally misguided, economically unnecessary, and ecologically unsustainable.

By placing discretionary time, the conditions for independence, and environmental sustainability in the foreground, a policy anchored in such a framework is less likely than productivist perspectives to have objections to *partial* basic income payments. In such a welfare regime, the security and independence in relation to people's present jobs are not only promising by serving to support an economically rational transition, but may also serve the objective of making people less personally dependent on environmentally harmful policies or global material expansion that may be necessary to create or maintain those jobs. After all, how can we afford to criticize ecologically destructive elements of the production process, or to slow down our economies, if our very existence and prospects for recognition depend on access to those particular jobs?[4]

This provides another reason for why postproductivists are likely to be less troubled by the objection that a general commitment to the world of paid work, production, and material consumption might weaken, that is, if a basic income would tend to stimulate part-time employment and more discontinuous patterns of work. Insofar as that reorientation would result in a strengthened commitment to nonmaterial pursuits and more local, service-intensive activities, this might, overall, provide an important argument *in favor* of such a policy (see, e.g., Barry 2005, 229–230; Boulanger 2009; Van Parijs 2009c).

My above exploration of the principle of wealth sharing has focused on the arguments about "gifts" in the form of inherited resources and job assets. However, the postproductivst viewpoint can help us identify alternative or complementary ways to fund a substantial basic income based on this type of justification. Under present conditions, one might, for example, consider whether access to certain scarce natural assets (that have previously been given away for free) must fall under the principle of wealth sharing.

In works by authors such as Gar Alperovitz, Peter Barnes, David Bollier, and Iain McLean, there are a wide range of proposals for dividends on the sale or lease of publicly owned resources or "common assets" to fund basic income policies. A number of arguments have been advanced for using new forms of land taxation, the revenue from broadcasting licences, oil and mining royalties, or taxes on the pollution of the global atmosphere.

Like our arguments on *wealth sharing* in chapters 4–6, these tend to be based on moral intuitions about reclaiming and distributing a given set of scarce assets to which all are (or so it is argued) equally entitled (Alperovitz 2005; Barnes 2001; Bollier 2002; 2006; Howard and Widerquist 2012).[5] If we are placing ecological boundaries and our unequal ecological footprints at the center of a gift-equalizing approach to justice, it is interesting to notice the recent suggestions that energy taxation, personal carbon trading, and perhaps even transferable birth licenses belong to the set of measures needed to prevent some from monopolizing scarce *environmental* assets to which all may be equally entitled.

Jan-Otto Andersson observes that the distributive implications of ecological taxes in this spirit may often be particularly painful to the poor. As he puts it: "In a very unequal world ecological taxes will absolve the rich from their extravagant life styles... whereas poor people may not be able to afford even the necessities of life" (Andersson 2009, 4). Hence, while green taxes are necessary for sustainability, Andersson concludes that they seem socially justified only if combined with a basic income.

At the same time, it must be observed that this relationship is not without friction. Paul-Marie Boulanger and Gideon Calder have recently pointed out that connecting these two reforms too tightly would introduce a clear tension between sustainability and a high basic income. Under such a scheme the revenue from green taxes would, after all, be "directly proportionate to the amount of polluting activity" (Calder 2009). The success of green taxes to achieve their environmental objectives may, thus, undermine the necessary tax base for the basic income to survive (Boulanger 2009).

In sum, the postproductivist framework helps articulate and guide important qualifications to the encompassing model from the point of view of radical liberalism. The concern for maximizing the budget set (i.e., what is available for redistribution) must never be dissociated from the ultimate purposes—or long-term sustainability—of social justice. If, in nonideal theory, our political opportunities to address conditions for basic autonomy-respecting, maximin distribution of real freedom are potentially violated or restricted by the means necessary to maximize the budget set, the next step must be to explore the interaction between *budget set maximization* and *opportunity to pursue objectives of justice* in order to identify the most optimal, achievable arrangement.

Suppose that the paradox of redistribution is correct and that postproductivist priorities rest on accurate empirical assumptions. A crucial task for the nonideal theorist's project of "transitional justice" (Simmons 2010, 22) will then be to identify an encompassing policy path that provides the basis for a legitimacy-producing basic income while at the same time facilitating a postproductivist reorientation of the universal welfare state.

7.5. GENDER EQUITY AND THE UNIVERSAL CAREGIVER MODEL

Taking the structural exploitation objection into account (section 6.5 in ch. 6), the normative weight attached to decommodification and minimizing conditionality in the postproductivist rationale of basic income, will now draw our attention to a further challenge. Universal *individual* social rights and the recognition of work performed in the household and civil society associations are important objectives in feminist thought. On the other hand, productivist adherents of the encompassing model can now point out that the commodification of such work has often been an important mechanism of "defamilialization" and, thus, for liberating women from dependency and domination in the patriarchal family (Orloff 1993; cf. Sainsbury 1996, 36ff.).

Clearly, addressing the distribution of domestic work and strengthening women's status in the labor market are matters of profound importance to social justice and central to the set of objectives I have sought to articulate in terms of equality of status and basic autonomy (Brighouse and Wright 2008; Gornick and Meyers 2003; 2008). A postproductivist reinterpretation of the encompassing model, with a basic income—or similar policies of strong universalism—at its core, might seem empty-handed when facing this objective. As discussed briefly in chapter 6, there is empirical support for the view that some basic income-type arrangements may even contribute to reinforcing rather than counteracting a traditional division of labor between men and women.[6]

Perhaps this must, after all, lead supporters of radical-liberal commitments to embrace an uncompromisingly employment-based interpretation of the encompassing model? An assessment of whether or not a basic income is currently desirable from a feminist viewpoint requires attention to a wide range of complex issues. Nancy Fraser's work on the ideal of a *universal caregiver model* offers a useful orientation point in this context. Her arguments in defense of this model address feminist objectives in a way that is strongly consistent with a path for social justice and welfare universalism that is both encompassing *and* postproductivist.

It is concerned with providing a workable welfare model in a world of unstable employment and diverse family conditions in which gender equity is one of the prime objectives. Such an ideal challenges masculinist accounts of social contribution, narrowly based on paid work, while also placing women's exposure to exploitable dependency at the center of attention. It emphasizes the need for a much more equal distribution of informal care work, leisure, and opportunities for participation in the public sphere, between men and women (Fraser 1996, 222).

It sides with postproductivists and their concern for pursuing egalitarian objectives in ways that respect not only universalism and individualism but *also* minimizing of conditionality in antipoverty programs. This is embraced as an important condition for protecting the basis of women's personal independence and, thus, the voice and power associated with access to a reliable economic fallback position. In contrast to a "universal breadwinner model" of gender equity—universalizing a traditional male emphasis on career and individual achievement in the labor market—the universal caregiver model is not tied to an ideal in which all would ideally conform to the market activities, values, and motivations associated with traditional male roles.

Instead, it serves to strengthen the opportunity for both men and women to combine caring, working, and social participation in all domains of social life "while also leaving time for some fun" (Fraser 1996, 236). From these remarks it seems clear that Fraser's model offers a helpful link between the abstract ideal of radical liberalism and the project of connecting feminist objectives to the assessment of basic income in the context of real-world politics. This framework is also well equipped to take on board the qualifications I have raised with respect to the metric of "real freedom" and basic income in chapter 6.

So, what role might be allowed for basic income-type policies within a practical interpretation of radical liberalism that is sensitive to such a set of concerns? Important arguments in support of basic income in this context are that such an instrument could (a) support the non-market foundations of the labor market and recognize such activities by incorporating that policy within a normative context that accepts a concept of contribution that reaches far beyond wage-contracts, (b) help equalize incomes between men and women, (c) strengthen the bargaining position and material independence of women in relation to bosses and partners, and more generally, in relation to the institution of marriage, (d) help renegotiate working conditions to achieve a work-life balance more suited to an ideal in which people are normally *both* paid workers and caregivers (Alstott 2001; McKay and VanEvery 2000; McKay 2005; Pateman 2003; 2006).

Given the existing gender division of labor, the distribution of market income, unpaid care work, and occupational status, more women than men tend to be placed in the circumstances of market vulnerability, dependency, and income disadvantage associated with weaker labor market attachment. Hence, there are likely to be more women than men among those who would benefit the most from a basic income reform in terms of income, security, and personal independence (Elgarte 2008). Under conditions where some may channel more efforts than others into other socially valuable activities than paid work, the basic income could thus serve to protect critical material interests of those who do so (Robeyns 2000; 2001).

By challenging traditional productivist interpretations of work that tend to conceal contributions in the household and civil society, such a policy could play an important role in realizing the universal caregiver model's aim of reshaping gender roles and strengthening a positive valuation of activities and values that have traditionally been carried out by women (Zelleke 2008). However, a basic income policy is not the only strategy for advancing such objectives. Moreover, the potential gender conservatism of some basic income proposals alerts us to the need for careful empirical, contextually sensitive analyses of whether (and, if so, in which broader political framework) such a policy would be likely to help achieve the desired long-term objectives.

7.6. Competing Options for Universal Caregiving

Even though the politics of basic income has some clear and important advantages relative to income protection policies based on work-conditionality and/or household status, it is, more precisely, vulnerable to feminist criticism of two different kinds. First, one objection holds that informal work is not *sufficiently* recognized by the basic income proposal since basic income is paid both to those who make a substantial valuable social contribution and those who do not. The second objection suggests that the basic income appears too soft with regard to the gendered division of paid and unpaid labor, and that we must therefore accept alternative reforms to attack that division more resolutely.

The first objection starts from the observation that a universal basic income program makes no distinction between a busy volunteer or full-time caregiver, on the one hand, and someone who is busy playing video games or surfing all day, on the other. The need to recognize and provide material security and independence to those who perform socially necessary care work and social economy activities can be met without endorsing a basic income. For such reasons some prefer a distributive solution linked more directly to the performance of care work, such as a caregiver wage (Krebs 1998).

In response to this objection we must begin by stressing that the radical-liberal justification of basic income does not regard such a scheme as a wage for care work. It is a program for consistently (i.e., without discrimination or exception) securing the basis of people's basic autonomy and for equalizing (in an efficiency-sensitive way) their access to "real freedom." Hence, these options have different and, to some extent, complementary objectives. Nevertheless, social resources are scarce and—as we have seen throughout this book— a basic income is often defended *in part* as an instrument to stimulate (and provide income protection for people who perform) useful non-market contributions.

Focusing on this overlap between the objectives of these two policy options, I think the relevant response from the basic income camp has two elements. The first is to accommodate some of these concerns by accepting the need for combining basic income with targeted transfers to caregivers and universal access to professional care. The second is to provide compelling reasons for why the basic income option seems preferable to very far-reaching models of targeted remuneration.

The market, and society at large, will continue to depend heavily on informal nonmarket contribution in any feasible, liberty-respecting social order (see also sections 3.3 and 6.7 in chs 3 and 6). As observed by Tony Fitzpatrick, then, "most carework will always remain informal, performed for reasons of emotional belonging" (Fitzpatrick 2003, 98). If the activities of informal care work, volunteering, political activity, and so on were marginalized, we would (where possible) need to find costly ways to compensate for that loss. There is clearly a very strong case for distributive schemes that are specifically directed to people who make substantial contributions beyond the realm of paid employment, such as those who care for an elderly partner or relative (this, of course, is also crucial to protect the basic autonomy of people with special needs).

However, beyond a certain point, trying to transform informal contributions into paid work, or recognizing such activities by way of targeted monetary compensation, seems impossible or unattractive. In part, this is because the citizens of a liberal society are likely to disagree in the attempt to identify which particular informal activities should count as a relevant contribution, and also because the contributions in question are often inherently motivating and difficult to distinguish sharply from leisure activities.

They tend to be bound up with friendship, love, and personal enjoyment, and people are drawn to them whether or not they are paid to perform the relevant tasks. The very idea of incorporating the relevant forms of "voluntary" work and activities into the logic of standard wage-contracts (i.e., something that must be done in order to earn a living) is not very promising in cases where the activities under discussion rely for their existence or value on the motivations of personal affection, spontaneity, or ideological conviction.

There are well-known problems with the idea of paying people to produce love or friendship. In many cases, allowing the absorption of such activities into the sphere of normal paid jobs would not only seem intrusive but also alter the meaning of these relations and activities in ways that threaten to destroy, or diminish, their value (Gorz 1999). In sum, targeted programs and comprehensive commodification strategies can never come close to capturing all of the relevant activities and may often change the motivation of such activities in damaging ways. In addition, once such programs grow comprehensive and eat themselves far into the sphere of personal relationships, they would need to involve a costly and intrusive bureaucracy to sort productive from unproductive activities.

We must also observe, however, that such arguments on the limits to the expansion of targeted payments and waged work can be misused. Actual impulses to provide care for free or to find socially useful informal activities "inherently rewarding" are—in our societies—more often expressed by and encouraged for women than men. Hence, they could easily be exploited by individuals who do not share such caring impulses or by governments and institutions that find it convenient to rely on such dispositions *instead* of funding adequately paid jobs or targeted transfers to provide universal and high-quality care. But that qualification, which flows from our more general and fundamental concern with structural exploitation (see section 6.5 in ch. 6), does not affect the arguments on the appropriate balance between different forms of provision. This reservation is concerned with the *gendered structure* of these contributions and their distribution, not their motivational basis, form, or value.

There are further limitations of the alternative under consideration. The particular option of a comprehensive caregiver wage program can easily become a household trap for women. It can, more specifically, be counterproductive to the aim of universalizing caregiving through at least two different mechanisms. First, if the wage is directly linked to the performance of care and the role as caregiver, the person who receives this wage will risk losing it if she wants to engage in (other forms of) employment or education and, thus, mix *different roles* and *forms of care* in a flexible way.

For that reason, a conditional payment directed specifically to those who perform household work may easily deter such individuals from accepting employment and lock them into the role as caregiver. Second, the presence of targeted caregiver-programs in a gender structured division of labor, where the recipients of such wages will much more often be women than men, can easily be used as an excuse for men not to do their fair share of household work and thereby stand in the way of desirable role sharing. After all, another person would now explicitly be paid for doing that work (Elgarte 2008; Van Parijs in Couillard 2002; Zelleke 2008).

In the case of a basic income, any income from (other forms of) work is simply added to the universal payment and no similar disincentive for paid work is thus involved. The unconditionality of basic income brings extended opportunities for people to engage in such activities, but it is not given *for* doing so. In that sense it does not interfere with the nonprofit motivation of many such activities. Nor does it rely on the project of finding a universally accepted normative basis for distinguishing and monitoring the *particular forms* of caring, cultural, educational, and other informal activities that are socially useful (and require recognition) from those that are not.

What about our second objection? Many of those who would accept the arguments against substantial reliance on caregiver-wages, or of allowing labor markets to absorb the bulk of such informal activities, may now claim that we should embrace a different mix of universalistic arrangements instead of the basic income option. In order to facilitate and recognize informal care while simultaneously breaking down the gendered division of paid and unpaid work, one might consider an alternative agenda (e.g., Ferrarini 2006; Gornick and Meyers 2008).

This may include policies such as generous *individualized* schemes for parental leave (i.e., nontransferable between parents), a basic income for children, universal access to well-funded, high-quality day care, regulations for a shorter standard working week, and other policies in support of women's labor market participation. In short, there might be other ways of accommodating the values of universal caregiving (or, in the words of Gornick and Meyers, an "earner-carer" model) while avoiding possible disadvantages of flat-rate cash benefits.

If my general remarks in chapter 6 are well-founded, basic income supporters must take on board parts of the agenda suggested by such an interpretation of the universal caregiver model (I return to this point briefly in the final section of the chapter). However, from the viewpoint of radical-liberal standards, this is unlikely to give compelling reasons for rejecting basic income rather than reshaping the broader policy context in which this proposal should be incorporated.

The alternative (non-basic income) agenda, suggested by this path, would face some of the real-libertarian—and other liberal-egalitarian—objections against a preference-insensitive distribution of jobs and other external assets, as well as some economic efficiency arguments against inflexible forms of allocating labor. But rather than restating the general justice-based case for basic income and discussing its more general attractions, let us, again, focus on the overlap between the concerns of these two policy agendas and, thus, the particular issues of informal work and exploitable dependency emphasized by the universal caregiver model.

Even assuming that the gender patterns under consideration have been substantially altered in order to equalize the relevant set of opportunities between men and women, the need to (somehow) provide opportunity, independence-protecting security, and recognition for those individuals who devote a major part of their time to perform such work in the social economy or household spheres would remain.

In any society that accepts basic liberties, freedom of occupational choice, and substantial ethical pluralism, and in which individuals are thus free to choose what kind of work they wish to engage in, and how much to work, there are likely to be categories of individuals (men or women) who are more oriented toward socially useful non-remunerated activities than others. Hence, there is likely to remain a substantial number of people who would be heavily dependent on the market incomes of other individuals in the absence of basic income or similar policies of strong universalism.

Those who spend much time outside paid work then remain dependent on those who earn market incomes, without monetary recognition of their contribution, and, thus, very likely to lack sufficient protection of their basic autonomy. Hence, these individuals are exposed to the forms of vulnerability to exploitation and, ultimately, abuse associated with that condition of dependency. Accepting that substantial socially necessary contributions are necessarily or preferably provided outside the formal labor market, and taking into account the set of assumptions stated, could lead us to consider two options to prevent this vulnerability wherever there is an asymmetrical division of unpaid and paid labor.

The first option is to give each member of a household a legal entitlement to the earnings of their partners and, thus (following Susan

Okin's proposal), "to have employers make out wage checks equally divided between the earner and the partner who provides all or most of his or her unpaid domestic services" (Okin 1989, 180–181; Rawls 2001a, 167). In order to ensure an exit option and independence for both partners, this may be combined with strict rules to ensure both partners of postdivorce households the same standards of living for at least as long as asymmetrical division of labor within the household was agreed upon (Okin 1989, 183).

The second option is to integrate this concern with the broader aims of protecting the conditions for basic autonomy and the universal redistribution of brute-luck advantages (including, but not reducible to, the privileges accessed through favorable jobs) in the form of a basic income. I will identify a number of considerations to support that the former seems either inadequate or insufficient and hence defend the attractiveness of the latter option.

Okin's strategy is addressed specifically to the case of unpaid domestic workers within a household in which they depend fully on the salary of their husband or wife. This means, first, that it will do nothing to address exploitable dependency in relationships in which partners live separately and/or where both parties prefer not to have their mutual economic expectations based on the model of marriage.[7]

This restriction also means that the person who performs the valuable informal work will not access a steady, significant wage income through such an arrangement when he or she is not a full-time caregiver of this household, for example, when this work is divided within a larger family unit, between relatives, neighbors, close friends, and so on. More fundamentally, this mandatory division of wage checks will not reach individuals whose informal contribution does not consist in domestic labor but, instead, various forms of public civil society work (on the link between basic income and the empowerment of the "social economy," see Wright 2010, ch. 7).

If we are liberals, in the sense that we seek to acknowledge and respect the diversity of possible family arrangements, an ideal welfare state must allow for great flexibility in order to be sensitive to different family structures. At the same time, we must not abandon the concern to universally protect people from the stated kinds of vulnerability and disadvantage.

It is also worth noticing that if the case for dividing wages between partners under asymmetrical division of responsibility is largely based on the need to reward and recognize informal and unpaid work, it looks arbitrary for the following reason: the person who happens to live with a high-income earner receives a much higher income than the person who lives with a low-income earner, while both are doing the same kind and amount of work.

Of course, it is reasonable for most people to *insure* themselves against sudden drops in accustomed living standards. Sometimes it makes sense to make this kind of insurance mandatory (for example, to protect a person's exit option and bargaining power). As a principle of distributive justice for informal work, however, "to each according to the size of his or her partner's wage" looks far from plausible.

A universal and individualized scheme would capture and redistribute some of the relevant privileges to support the least advantaged while also giving them basic protection from exploitable dependency in whatever relations and unpaid activities they engage. Placing this latter concern in relation to the aim of addressing injustice under nonideal conditions while simultaneously providing a transition path toward ideal justice suggests the following. The lack of a robust protection for personal independence should not (as discussed in relation to caregiver wages above) be addressed in ways that may lock people into fixed roles and, thus, block a transition toward the desired patterns of role sharing.

7.7. REPLACING OR REFORMING THE WELFARE STATE?

I shall now bring together some of the general implications of the above analysis for the politics of basic income in the context of nonideal theory. The introduction of a full and permanent basic income (i.e., that would be sufficient to cover basic needs) is a radical and costly reform that would face significant political and economic challenges. It may also have many unforeseeable consequences within a wide range of policy areas. For such reasons, most basic income supporters think that the first short-term step to aim for would be to introduce some form of partial, time-limited, or mildly conditional, forms of basic income (while at the same time working to improve the macro-conditions for the realization of more far-reaching goals).

However, in attending to short-term restrictions of political feasibility and how they induce a search for alternatives to a pure or full basic income, the following question about long-term objectives arises. Should we essentially think of an unconditional tier of distribution as a radical alternative to the welfare state or as part of a development of existing welfare state structures?

Charles Murray's *In Our Hands* (2006) recently defended the idea of a grand libertarian restructuring of the welfare state with the aim of replacing a wide range of existing arrangements with a universal basic income. A very different brand of antistatist, replacement-oriented ideas are present in "associationalist" versions of such proposals. For example, Paul Hirst has linked the basic income proposal to a strategy for moving a significant share of services from the state to voluntary associations. On this view, many people could rely on a "well-funded" basic income to work as volunteers or "providing for their welfare at home" (Hirst 1994, 183–184).

Bruce Ackerman and Anne Alstott explicitly connect their account of liberalism and the stakeholder society to the rejection of the welfare state project of social democracy. They argue that an unconditional stake in cash (Ackerman and Alstott 1999; 2006, 45–46) and/or a basic income (Alstott 1999) would be much more consistent with liberal commitments than many of the narrowly work-based programs and services associated with the welfare state.[8]

By contrast, other more modest versions of the basic income proposal and similar ideas have been advanced as a powerful basis for *complementing and reforming* arrangements associated with the social democratic tradition. It would build on but move beyond the existing welfare state, thus "renewing the Left's ambition to build a society in which both economic and political power are more widely dispersed" (Dowding, De Wispelaere, and White 2003, 5; cf. Pearce, Paxton, and White 2006, 190).

In this final section I want to conclude by stating a general case for this latter approach. In social models where there is little space for increasing the level of taxation, a politically feasible basic income *must* clearly replace some other arrangements that are presently in place. Of course, for a wide range of transfers it is very natural and attractive to do so. For example, the lion's share of social assistance schemes, the nonearnings-related part of unemployment insurance and student grants, as well as parts of retirement pensions and disability benefits, and other transfer programs would become redundant when there is a basic income for all to rely on.

The same could be said for some of the wage subsidies and other traditional measures to address unemployment as well as some support presently targeted at corporations, agriculture, regional development, or the cultural sectors. This holds insofar as a basic income would play an important role for securing labor market opportunities for all (also making it easier to make a living in poorer regions of a political community), to starting up one's own business, or protect income security in times of economic transition, studies, or low demand for one's services.

Any substantial and socially meaningful basic income would clearly involve replacement of some existing programs and, thus, imply a nontrivial degree of simplification of any welfare-state arrangements. However, it should be clear by now that—when confronting current political and economic constraints—the idea of a generous basic income as an alternative to the welfare state is not the option I take to be the more promising one, all things considered. One point of basic income is certainly the prospects of simplification, but Tony Walter is right to stress that it is not *the* point (Walter 1989, 61).

The various reasons articulated in this chapter suggest that the most fruitful and sensible way to think of basic income, and similar policies, in the context of real-world politics is to include it as part of a broader and more complex policy package. But if we should not opt for a generous basic income scheme *instead of* such welfare-state arrangements, but rather (at least initially) stick to more moderate, partial, time-limited or even mildly conditional forms of basic income, one will need to face an obvious objection about the value of such a reform.

Why introduce yet another distributive scheme in addition to a highly complex and differentiated set of arrangements for income security? After all, the level of income that such a program could offer would (for political feasibility reasons) realistically be so low that it is unlikely to allow all to *fully* escape the need for means-tested social assistance and the various poverty traps, activity-restrictions, and other independence-constraining conditions associated with welfare dependency. Would not accommodating the advantages of maintaining many other welfare programs, and opting for more modest versions of basic income, come at the unacceptable cost of losing some of the most crucial gains of basic income?

In response, let me now briefly draw out some conclusions of the preceding analysis for the attractions, and policy advantages, of such an approach. To be more precise, we may distinguish between two claims about the advantages of a complementary approach relative to a replacement approach. The first claim is that such a mixed, gradualist strategy is that the combination of basic income and *earnings-related social insurance* is preferable to a basic income arrangement without a strong social insurance component. The second claim is that a basic income that builds on a wide range of *"in kind" benefits and services* that have been implemented in many existing welfare states is preferable to one that replaces or (if less developed) offers a basic income instead of such welfare services.

Basic income and social insurance. If adherents of the encompassing model are right, a universal welfare state in which a basic income would replace (or implemented instead of) earnings-related social insurance is less likely to be resistant to objections from political feasibility and perceived legitimacy. Also, a basic income strategy without or instead of social insurance arrangements has fewer resources to improve the material prospects of the least advantaged in ways that could simultaneously weaken the gendered distribution of informal care work. The reason is that the specific way of constructing the latter programs can provide incentives (e.g., by earmarking payments and/or incorporating bonuses) to help shape group patterns in the desired direction.

It is true that the implementation of a modest basic income would not realistically do away *completely* with the poverty traps or stigmatization associated with traditional forms of social assistance or any activity restrictions in social insurance schemes. However, it could take us very far in the right direction according to the standards of radical liberalism. By definition, a partial basic income (see section 1.3 in ch. 1) is insufficient on its own to cover all of one's basic material needs. As we have observed above, however, it could replace a wide range of means-tested benefits, as well as tax exemptions, and integrate them into one individualized and universal scheme.

It would aim to promote individual independence and labor market opportunities while also holding inequalities in check in a watertight and nonstigmatizing scheme. This program would serve to prevent the need for intrusive forms of means testing and help simplify welfare arrangements as a whole. Such a distributive solution could thereby help in crucial ways to secure background justice and address forms of market vulnerability unaddressed by any existing battery of work-based social rights (Atkinson 1996).

However, the case for such a mixed strategy not only suggests that social insurance may be needed in order to legitimize basic income but also that a strengthened basic income component may help legitimize any existing social insurance-based schemes and make them run more smoothly (cf. Van Parijs 1996/2006, 475). The general idea is that if such a universalistic scheme were in place, efforts to make people respect the rules of work-based schemes would become fairer and more successful.

In order to remain legitimate and true to their underlying insurance-based justification, social insurance schemes should not be expanded to cover cases of need for which they are not intended.[9] To explain, it is understandable if people who tend to be net contributors to social insurance schemes are less enthusiastic about being part of such a system *if* they have grounds to believe that others will fail to comply with the conditions on which it is based and may often (try to) activate social insurance payments for illegitimate purposes (i.e., claim benefits even if they do not actively apply for work, or if they claim to be incapable of working but could work if they really wanted to).

At the same time, it is also understandable *if* people in need are less willing to consistently play by existing rules, for example, by actively applying for jobs they have no chance to get, when such arrangements operate in a nonideal context, in which a distributive scheme that provide all with an opportunity-equalizing foundation is lacking. People who feel that society has no place for them, or who remain stuck in (or could only access) jobs they hate, or who have not been able to find a job and therefore failed to (legitimately) qualify for social insurance-based security, or—for any other reasons—find themselves in a situation of desperate need and/or degrading dependency, could no doubt be tempted to try activate any existing scheme to make their situation bearable.

Straightforward eligibility criteria for social insurance and strict enforcement of such criteria are more justified if everybody can access basic income security and, partly because of that, more easily find a job (thereby ensuring that job search activity is meaningful). A basic income—which is not justified as an insurance-based measure, but (at least in part) as an instrument to provide all with a share of given wealth to which nobody has a justified prior claim—is a promising instrument for addressing such threats to a legitimate and stable social insurance arrangement.

The relevant mechanisms have been mentioned many times by now. Such a radicalized form of universalism could play the role of an implicit wage-subsidy and offer expanded options for part-time work, thereby making it easier for people to qualify for (and abide by the conditions for) work-based security. In contrast to most work-conditional schemes, it would also give opportunities for *legitimately* taking a sabbatical leave or to quit a bad job while still having some basic income security to rely on.

Basic income in cash or kind? The second claim of the mixed strategy is that a basic income with a wide range of universal and unconditional in-kind benefits and services is preferable to a more radical replacement strategy. One of the most obvious reasons for such a view is linked to our feminist objections against libertarian forms of basic income. As discussed above, basic income-type programs for income security (e.g., in experiments with negative income tax) and

state-funded schemes for sabbatical leave have often, where implemented, tended to be used more often by women than men to reduce
working time for the purpose of doing more unpaid care work.

This illustrates how a basic income strategy without, or instead of,
many other central components of traditional welfare state services
(such as universal access to high-quality child care, schooling, and
health care) may well contribute to the reinforcement of traditional
gender roles. For the reasons I have stated, such an outcome will
probably fail to deliver a stable, basic autonomy-respecting account
of liberal equality, and would be vulnerable to the structural exploitation objection. Hence, if there is a very weak role for social rights
to subsidized services in existing welfare states, it is far from obvious that an unconditional basic income in cash is the option that we
should give priority, all things considered.

However, the outcome of a basic income policy within this dimension would clearly depend crucially on the broader norms and expectations in place of the society under study, the technical details of the
scheme, and the institutional and normative context to which it is tied
(Pateman 2003; 2006; Zelleke 2008). This underscores the need for
caution about an all-or-nothing approach to basic income (Birnbaum
2005; 2007). On the other hand, the strategic gender interests under
consideration must not be advanced in ways in which the *least* advantaged (such as relatively poor women exposed to market vulnerability,
precarious work, and, thus, with low bargaining power) are asked to
bear the costs of transition. Hence, denying them resource rights on
equal terms, or in ways that sacrifice other central requirements of
social justice, is clearly not a promising option.

In the context of a liberal-egalitarian conception of justice, the
features of the existing gender order that are unfair—or have a negative structural impact on background conditions of justice—would
need to be addressed in ways that also attend to the practical needs of
women under present conditions, whatever ethical commitments or
values they identify with (Okin 1989). A basic income strategy allied
to the endorsement of a strong in-kind component in the agenda for
welfare universalism has the potential to do so through the various
mechanisms I have already discussed at length.

It does so while also linking smoothly with the objective of promoting a broader societal ethos in support of a position of personal
independence and foundations of critical deliberation from which
people can expose, resist, and challenge exploitative relations. Hence,
rather than concluding that the case for an opportunity-equalizing
and basic autonomy-protecting basic income should be rejected, it

would be more natural to explore how such gender patterns can be addressed by combining it with reforms in family policy (and other policy areas) under which those who are privileged (and economically way above any basic needs threshold) under existing conditions would bear the heaviest transition costs.

In policy terms, such an interpretation of radical liberalism would need to consider a basic income proposal combined with measures to facilitate solidarity-fostering interaction across groups, and knowledge-enabling forms of participation. This may include gender-equalized arrangements for parental leave schemes (such as a fully individualized programs in which months are nontransferable between parents), various forms of affirmative action, subsidized high-quality day care, universal access to the economic means for higher education, and ways of linking the basic income to new arenas for political participation (on the latter, see, e.g., Standing 2011, 180–181).

The identification of sensible options for concrete policy clearly depends very strongly on empirical assumptions and contextual circumstances. But the guiding aim would be to identify liberty-respecting policies that provide firm incentives to promote or maintain gender (or other group) patterns that help secure and stabilize the structural conditions of equality of status without stigmatizing individual choices.

A crucial political task for adherents of radical liberalism and the politics of basic income will be to design proposals that are supportive to the objectives of political legitimacy, sustainability, and gender equity. I have argued in this chapter that basic income proposals that seek to build on and develop the social insurance and in-kind benefits of existing welfare state institutions are far better suited to serve these objectives than radical replacement strategies.

Notes

1 Basic Income, Liberal Egalitarianism, and the Study of Social Justice

1. To illustrate, it is interesting to notice that the idea of an unconditional basic income guarantee was the central component of Robert van der Veen's and Philippe Van Parijs's "A Capitalist Road to Communism" (1986) while also playing an important role in Milton Friedman's neoliberal vision in *Capitalism and Freedom* (1962), in the form of a negative income tax.

2. One basis for specifying such descriptions of social reality is the argument that there is a new and distinctive class divide in many contemporary welfare states not reducible to inequalities in access to means of production between "capitalists" and "workers." This is a divide between those that hold good and attractive jobs (thus having access to stable, meaningful, well-paid positions and adequate social protection through earnings-related insurance arrangements and other employment-based forms of security), and those that do not. The latter groups tend to rely for their income on precarious forms of employment, residual safety nets, or the help they might be able to access from families and friends (Van Parijs 1987/1993).

3. Such changes in the structure of labor markets, family conditions, and community life imply that social risks are less standardized than they used to be and come to differ more greatly across situations and individual circumstances. All this adds relevance to the search for forms of income distribution that are as flexible as possible, and—in the words of Robert Goodin—"minimally presumptuous" about the sources of help people might be able to access, thereby allowing them to activate universal income support in a way that effectively allows them to cater for particular needs in particular situations (Goodin 1992; 2001).

4. The most notable European exception in the past few years is Germany, where there has been considerable interest in the basic income proposal in different parts of the political spectrum. In a nation such as Sweden, which is one of the welfare states of the world most strongly associated with the ideal of welfare universalism, basic income proposals have played a marginal role in public political debates and often been ridiculed by its opponents (Birnbaum 2005; Janson 2003). Basic

income proposals have been debated more broadly and intensely at various stages in Finland, Denmark, and the Netherlands (Andersson and Kangas 2005; Christensen 2000; Van der Veen and Groot 2000). Beyond the European context, the Alaska Permanent Fund, consisting primarily of resources from oil, has paid substantial annual dividends to each permanent resident of Alaska, USA, since the early 1980s (Goldsmith 2010; Howard and Widerquist 2012). Even though the basic income of Alaska does not come anywhere close to covering basic needs, it distributes substantial amounts to every individual on an unconditional basis. The value of those payments reached a peak in 2000 when distributing nearly $2000 to each individual (see www.apfc.org). One of the most interesting examples of political basic income initiatives in recent years is that of Brazil. The long-term objective of providing all permanent residents with an unconditional basic income, by gradually expanding existing programs against hunger and poverty, was signed into law in January 2004. Initiatives of basic income movements in South Africa (Standing and Samson 2003) and Namibia, in which basic income experiments were recently conducted, have been other focal points of discussions in recent years (for the latter, see www.bignam.org). The newsletters and websites of Basic Income Earth Network (BIEN) and The U.S. Basic Income Guarantee Network (USBIG) provide regular updates on political developments related to basic income (see www.basicincome.org, www.binews.org, and www.usbig.net, respectively).

5. Hence, a straightforward way of attacking unemployment is to lower barriers to the labor market by allowing lower wages and more flexible forms of employment, thus making it easier both to hire and fire employees. Such a political alliance between principles of workfare and labor market liberalization generally accepts a higher level of material inequality and job insecurity, either as consistent with justice or as a legitimate cost for the greater or more urgent good of promoting employment, participation, and social cohesion.

6. Accounts of egalitarian liberalism in this radical vein have been conceptualized and specified in different directions under labels such as real-libertarianism (Van Parijs 1995), the stakeholder society (Ackerman and Alstott 1999), and social republicanism (Dowding, De Wispelaere, and White 2003). See also Krouse and McPherson (1988), Paxton and White (2006), and Ackerman et al. (2006).

7. Many of the relevant contemporary debates and perspectives on justice and the social minimum evolve from, or draw heavily on, the Rawlsian framework. Examples of central ideas in contemporary thinking on social justice largely deriving from the Rawlsian framework (to which I will return throughout this book) are luck-egalitarianism, nonperfectionism, justice as reciprocity and society as a fair system of social cooperation, equality of resources (as opposed to equality of welfare), democratic equality, and the idea of maximin-guided distribution.

8. This means I will have little to say with respect to approaches that do not share these starting points, such as various utilitarian, right-libertarian, and/or strongly perfectionist approaches to distributive justice. Introducing such (and other) perspectives could no doubt generate many arguments with considerable force. Even leaving such non-Rawlsian approaches to one side, however, will give us enough tasks to deal with.

9. While a basic income guarantee that takes the form of large, infrequent payments may be squandered at the local casino on the day of payment and, thus, be insufficient to cover one's basic needs at a particular moment, the level of such a payment can still be related to such a standard and be defined as "full," "partial," or, if very low, "transitional" (Fitzpatrick 1999, 36).

10. This idea runs as follows: if a level of economic abundance could be reached that made it possible to satisfy all needs and wishes that are set against each other under moderate scarcity, the problem of justice would not arise, or, at least, the concern for specifying the demands of justice would largely seem to have lost its relevance. Similarly, if a perfect harmony of interests (regardless of the level of economic abundance) could be achieved due to a universal willingness of the participants in a scheme of social cooperation to let their personal interests coincide with some higher common end, we may similarly seem to have reached a stage beyond justice. As John Rawls puts it: "The justice of practices does not come up until there are several different parties…who do press their claims on one another, and who do regard themselves as representatives of interests which deserve to be considered" (Rawls 1971/1999, 205).

11. There is considerable theoretical disagreement and debate on the relation between facts and justice (Cohen 2008; Mason 2004; Miller 2001; Räikkä 1998). John Rawls and many of his followers have argued that the objective of a theory of justice should be to provide some form of realistic utopia, taking fundamental facts about human nature, human societies, and feasibility into account (Rawls 2001b). Against this view, G. A. Cohen has worked out a powerful criticism, according to which ultimate principles of justice are always fact-independent and must be carefully distinguished from the broader (and more empirically demanding) project of identifying optimal rules of social regulation (Cohen 2003; Cohen 2008; cf. Swift 2003). It is debatable whether, and if so, to what extent facts help constitute (correct principles of) justice (see Miller 2008). However, it is uncontroversial to say that facts matter in crucial ways to the analysis of how best to specify *the implications of fundamental principles of justice for existing societies,* and *the exploration of what set of public institutions, policies and social ideals that broadly liberal-egalitarian principles— fact-sensitive or not—would recommend.* For present purposes I leave open whether the latter, fact-sensitive and broadly Rawlsian project

(on which this book focuses), is best described as a study of ideal principles of justice and their implications or, more broadly, as a study of competing candidates for offering just and applicable "rules of social regulation."

12. While the connection between principles of justice and particular policies may sometimes be very tight, my notion of broad compliance with certain general ideals and arrangements need not imply full compliance with one specific list of detailed principles. As mentioned above, in connection with Sen's theory, we may often share a strong commitment to the same policies and values while at the same time having rather different ways of linking such commitments to abstract principles. Conversely, we may also subscribe to the very same set of principles while at the same time having radically diverging views (due to differences of interpretation and empirical assumptions) about the right set of institutions or policies to adopt.

13. It is important to distinguish between neutrality in the moral justification of principles of justice and neutrality in the consequences that justice may have for various conceptions of the good. No theory of justice can be neutral in the effects it has on the opportunities for different conceptions of the good to gain support. A theory of justice is always a substantive moral theory and, as such, it is clearly not compatible with ethical conceptions that are unable to coexist with the imperatives of justice. Neutrality on the good is not moral neutrality. Conceptions of the good that require or encourage violations of other people's rights (for example, by sexual abuse or other forms of assault cannot hope to live and prosper under just institutions. No society can contain all kinds of life within it, or give equal opportunities for all ways of life to flourish. What a theory of justice can do, however, is to avoid referring to thick conceptions of the good in the justification of moral principles on matters of basic justice. Neutrality-based morality contrasts with perfectionist doctrines that build their political ideals on a particular conception of human perfection and explicitly rank competing social arrangements from the point of view of that specific, ethical view.

14. For example, most of us have strong intuitions against constraining the set of options of those who are more healthy or productive than others for the purpose of improving the prospects of those who are less favorably endowed, say by demanding compulsory transfers of bodily organs to less advantaged or—more mildly—imposing a duty to work at some highly productive occupation they may not like, in order to maximize tax revenue (Cohen 1995; Nozick 1974; Fried 2004; Otsuka et al. 2005). Rawls's own interpretation of social justice seeks to avoid such a trade-off between fundamental liberties and material equality by ascribing certain equal basic liberties lexicographical ("lexical") priority in relation to objectives of economic equality. It is not settled, however, how best to specify the

normative status of basic liberties in relation to egalitarian objectives within the Rawlsian framework.

15. In many of these debates on social justice, the exploration of basic income will also help clarify theoretical views and concepts and help expose attractions and limitations to competing accounts of justice. As we have seen, the idea of basic income for all pushes the limits of liberal neutrality (should we be neutral in relation to different conceptions of the value of work and leisure or are preferences for work implicated by the demands of justice?), luck-egalitarian (choice-based) accounts of individual responsibility (to what extent should people be held economically responsible for disadvantages resulting from a voluntary decision not to work?), and the normative basis of liberal community and the nature and purposes of a fair scheme of social cooperation (are liberal views on community and cooperation inexorably tied to paid work as an obligation or can even those who do not contribute productively have justice-based resource claims?). Hence, I agree strongly with Philippe Van Parijs when he points out that exploring the justification of basic income "is not a matter of simply applying to this particular issue some pre-conceived libertarian or egalitarian ideal. In the very process of relating basic income to such ideals, one is forced to question, clarify and reformulate some of the most central principles of modern political philosophy" (Van Parijs 1992a, 8).

16. For helpful discussion on basic income, migration, and the scope of justice, see Howard (2006), Van Parijs (1995, ch. 6), Van Parijs (2003b) and Van der Veen and Van Parijs (2006, 11–14).

17. In many cases it may be difficult to realize the full implications of the principles we (provisionally) accept and to relate critically to one's own initial moral judgments. The construction of various thought experiments and hypothetical examples are valuable in this context as they can help us become aware of the full implications of certain principles or assumptions in particular cases and, hence, to help assess whether we are (on reflection) justified in holding them.

2 EQUALITY OF STATUS AND ITS PRIORITY: A RAWLSIAN CASE FOR BASIC INCOME

1. The first principle covers a wide range of familiar and (mostly) uncontroversial political and civil liberties such as freedom of thought, freedom of speech, liberty of conscience, the right to vote and participate in politics, freedom of assembly, freedom of association, rights protecting the liberty and integrity of the person, and free choice of occupation.

2. Rawls argues that "when we feel that our plans are of little value, we cannot pursue them with pleasure or take delight in their execution. Nor plagued by failure and self-doubt can we continue in our endeavours" (Rawls 1971, 440).

3. On the close link between the basic liberties and self-respect, see Shue (1975).

4. For Laborde, "minimal" is meant to emphasize that this requirement does not suggest the endorsement of "maximal" autonomy in the form of a liberal-perfectionist, autonomy-oriented conception of the good life.

5. The Rawlsian account of self-respect is complex and harbors several ambiguities (see, e.g., J. Cohen 1989; Darwall 1977; Eyal 2005; Massey 1983). As illustrated by recent debates over the value of non-domination (e.g., Pettit 1997; Raventós 2007; Laborde 2008; Lovett 2010; White and Leighton 2008) and, more broadly, attempts to develop "relational" accounts of the egalitarian ideal, in which the value of respect takes center stage (e.g., Anderson 1999; Satz 2010; Scheffler 2003, 2005; cf. Wolff 1998), there are also different paths for specifying the exact nature of the links between equality of status, independence, and self-respect. My argument in this chapter sides with all the latter contributions in the sense that it ascribes great importance to equality of status and self-respect. It should also be general enough to remain consistent with different ways of spelling out the core values at stake and their philosophical justification. It clearly differs, however, from those versions of republicanism and relational egalitarianism that deny that brute-luck inequality of economic life prospects is a very important aspect of justice in its own right, that is, *irrespective* of how this inequality affects relations of power, status, and domination. For further discussion, see also sections 5.6–5.7.

6. In specifying the meaning of the first part of the second principle, Rawls also emphasizes the freedom to choose occupation with access to a "diverse set of opportunities" (Rawls 1982/1999, 363, 366; 2001a, 58). In the context of justice as fairness, then, substantive (and not merely formal) freedom of occupational choice (access to "powers and prerogatives") is an important objective in its own right. In the Rawlsian view constructed here, however, I accommodate this concern by including it as one important element of a policy aimed to secure the recognitional bases of self-respect.

7. Considering that Catriona McKinnon has also developed a self-respect-based Rawlsian justification of basic income, it is worth pointing out that the foundations of my argument are different in at least two important respects. McKinnon (2003) treats income and wealth as valuable only as a social basis of self-respect, and, unlike my view, her argument does not seem to be based on the assessment of *life prospects*. My Rawlsian argument deals with income, wealth, leisure time, and self-respect as distinct and independently valuable primary goods. Competing arrangements are assessed by examining the prospects of the least advantaged over a life course under every scheme and the relevant primary goods are balanced in a way that gives special weight to the social bases of self-respect.

8. For some of Meade's arguments in defense of a social dividend, see Meade (1993).
9. Considering that powerful responsibility-based objections to basic income have been formulated, it is interesting to notice that Wolff's argument points to a potential trade-off between *the enforcement* of responsibility and the protection of self-respect. Now, if conditions that undermine self-respect should be avoided "at almost any cost" (Rawls 1971, 440), the demeaning aspects of welfare-dependency should make defenders of such objections question whether possible violations of individual responsibility under a basic income scheme would really provide a *decisive* reason to reject it.
10. With the words of Gar Alperovitz: "liberty to speak out depends on a guarantee that one's means of livelihood will not be undermined" (Alperovitz 2001, 108).
11. In fairness to competing options, it must be admitted that the feasible implementation of a full basic income, that is, at a level which is high enough to cover one's basic needs, without a poverty trap, is likely to require higher average marginal tax rates than most existing packages of conditional schemes. However, anyone who attaches priority to the interests of the least well-off in a way that is sensitive to the set of concerns identified in sections 2.3–2.4 needs to give us a powerful argument for why we should not move in that direction, and why that cost is not worth paying.
12. It is also questionable whether massive, individually targeted wage-subsidies, making explicit that certain subsidized jobs are earmarked for a distinct category of unskilled "low-productivity" people who would not otherwise get a job, can play a role equivalent to other jobs from the point of view of self-respect (Van Parijs 2003a, 220).

3   ARE ONLY CONTRIBUTORS ENTITLED TO SOCIAL RIGHTS? COOPERATION, RECIPROCITY, AND THE BOUNDARIES OF SOCIAL JUSTICE

1. Whether people who do not cooperate in the relevant way may have justified distributive claims on other grounds than social justice is, of course, left open by this view.
2. To be more precise, it does not follow that the only individuals who would be entitled to justice-based transfers are those who offer their services in the market (self-employed or wage-workers), or who are preparing/qualifying to do so (e.g., students, unemployed people who are actively seeking a job), or who have provided a relevant work contribution in the past (retired).
3. "All these things which in the complex division of labor in a market society are undertaken by others form an infrastructure on which I depend as a producer in the market" (Plant 1993, 47). Referring to the research of Nancy Fraser and Linda Gordon, Plant holds that

"the idea of dependency is itself an ideological construction which puts more socially-based or structural ideas such as inequality off the agenda." To overcome arbitrary divisions of labor, and the "independence/dependence dichotomy," Fraser and Gordon asks us to "redefine work so that it is understood to include non-wage-earning labor...reconsidering a variety of labor such as housework and child care, children's activity in attending school, the labor of artists, and the effort that goes into nurturance of friends and maintenance of social networks" (Fraser and Gordon 1994, 25).

4. The same intuition seems to be at work in Philippe Van Parijs's rejection of Rawls's way of addressing the claims of Malibu surfers as perfectionistic. It does not allow people who don't work to claim a real share in an "exogenously generated benefit" (Van Parijs 1995, 98).

5. A purely luck-egalitarian view may hold that talented individuals have ability-based duties of redistribution in relation to less talented individuals simply because they are more favorably endowed by nature (or other circumstances beyond their control) than the latter. But if this is the claim, reciprocity looks redundant since this talent-sensitive duty exists because of the mere presence of (natural) brute-luck inequality and *not* as a result of a reciprocity-based relationship.

6. In light of this difficulty, one possibility would be to suggest that we should accommodate this requirement as a part of an ethos of justice, internalized by citizens (i.e., affecting their choice of occupation), instead of interpreting them as duties to be enforced by *state institutions*. This, however, will seem like a costly concession to anyone (like myself) who thinks that it is one of the central tasks for a theory of justice to offer a foundation for workable, interpersonal comparisons, and action-guiding considerations for the institutional design of public tax-and-benefit schemes. For *this purpose* we need an identifiable target that allows the relevant parties to know and understand their rights and duties, and, thus, enable them to verify to one another—according to objectively available information—that they are fulfilling their duties. This is not to say that all the principles or requirements of justice must satisfy such a desideratum of publicity, because not every aspect of justice requires precision of this kind (Cohen 2008). I still believe, for instance, that an ethos of justice has an important, supportive role to play in our efforts to facilitate and maintain the institutional and structural preconditions of social justice.

7. Also, we cannot take for granted that those who can access some high-income job (thus having a high potential income at some particular moment in time) can access a wide range of jobs in lower-income segments of the labor market.

8. The most obvious examples where this seems highly unjust are probably situations in which there is a massive market demand for jobs that some people could easily access but may have very good reasons to reject, say tasks involving prostitution, pornography, or other sexual

services. Surely, it would be absurd to suggest that a person A, having (but rejecting) such a lucrative option, should pay a higher income tax at a given job than person B, whose endowment and actual occupation are identical to that of A, apart from the fact that she/he could not get such a well-paid job in the sex industry. Perhaps one could avoid this outcome by making an argument for why a plausible conception of productive contribution, or a plausible way of specifying the requirements of a society of equals (protecting people's bodily integrity and self-respect), must lead us to conclude that no such jobs would count as productive or remain available in a just liberal-egalitarian society. Whether or not that is true, there is no similar reply to my pianist example.

9. It should be emphasized that the problem with talent-based taxation for most egalitarian liberals who reject liberty constraining egalitarianism is not the idea of targeted transfers to compensate for (assessable components of) unfavorable personal endowments as such, that is, that people who are favorably endowed in terms of health, and so on, are obliged to give (as a matter of justice) to those who are not. The point is that the fund offering resources for such targeted egalitarian policies should not be generated or justified in ways that violate integrity rights or the principle of unconstrained occupational freedom protected by the basic liberties under consideration.

10. In many situations it is plausible to hold that we have duties of contribution based on the principle that we are obligated not to free ride on the burdens of others for producing and maintaining some morally weighty public good from which we stand to benefit (Arneson 1982; Rawls 1971, 112; Segall 2005, 339; Van Parijs 1996; 1997). People may also have obligations grounded on reciprocity-based requirements of fair play in a variety of situations in which they enjoy the social benefits of a particular household, voluntary association, or insurance-based scheme.

4 WHY UNCONDITIONAL TRANSFERS ARE NOT EXPLOITATIVE

1. To elaborate, welfare conditionality may, in this view, help express respect and public recognition of the contributions upon which the safety net of a particular community depends. At the same time, it may also help destigmatize recipients. The work-test procedure enables them to show that they are doing their best to make an appropriate contribution in return for benefits and, thus, that their intentions need not be looked upon with suspicion (cf. Anderson 2004).

2. For the arguments to be examined in this chapter, we need not discuss whether these equal starts should amount to a basic capital in the beginning of a person's (adult) life or whether fresh starts, in

the form of a regular basic income, should be agreed to. Van Parijs defends a version of the latter position. For further discussion, see section 5.6 in chapter 5.

3. The proposal for this "baby bond" was initially part of the election manifesto of the Labour Party in 2001, and the fund was launched in January 2005. After the election in 2010, however, the new (Conservative-Lib Dem) coalition government, led by David Cameron, decided to scrap the fund.

4. It should be noticed, however, that while this argument is contingent in certain respects, Van Parijs holds that the unequal conditions under which the real-libertarian case for basic income is justified (he emphasizes inequality of access to valuable jobs in particular) would also be present under socialist forms of ownership (Van Parijs 1995, 193–194).

5. If we are guided by a liberal concern for the opportunity to live by one's particular conception of the good, I think this should also give a presumption in favor of *individual* resource shares in cases where it makes sense to divide resources. The possibility for me to use resources for doing whatever I might want to do will clearly be limited in fundamental ways if my actual opportunity to use them, and my decisions on *how* to use them, will constantly depend on the consent of many others (who may have radically different conceptions of the good).

6. This criterion for selective compensation, called undominated diversity, demands that our distributive fund of given assets be used for selective transfers to ensure that "what is given to one person over her lifetime, whether as internal or external resources, should not be unanimously preferred to what is given to another." In *Real Freedom*, self-ownership is ascribed a soft priority in relation to undominated diversity, and undominated diversity is ascribed a soft priority in relation to value equalization of external assets. This means that "a major improvement of the satisfaction of an inferior principle may justify a minor deterioration of the satisfaction of a superior principle" (Van Parijs 2003b, 202; 1995, 25–26). More recently, Van Parijs has remarked that undominated diversity now seems "inessential" to him, and in this context, he suggests that we should decide how much of the universal grant we must use to deal with handicaps and health disadvantages (and how this should be done) by applying a veil-of-ignorance exercise in a decentralized way that is sensitive to "local circumstances and preferences" (Van Parijs 2009b, 159–160).

7. Hence, the real-libertarian notion of gifts incorporates the typical "left-libertarian" demands of equality with respect to *natural* assets, but it is much more inclusive. It also reaches well beyond the category of inherited wealth, which is typically the focal point in the discourse on "the stakeholder society" (e.g., Ackerman and Alstott 1999).

8. Van Parijs holds that scarcity rents should be identified in ways that disregard whether or not those bidding on the resources are actually

qualified to perform these jobs. To make qualification irrelevant to rightful claims on job assets invites the objection that people should be held economically responsible for making or not making efforts to acquire marketable skills. I address this complication in chapter 5.

9. According to *insider-outsider theory* of unemployment, people in employment can receive wages above the market-clearing equilibrium because of the costs associated with hiring, training, and firing employees. According to *efficiency wage theory*, it is rational for firms to pay more than what is necessary to attract employees, since doing so will improve labor productivity. For example, this wage may lead people in employment to shirk less since it will increase the cost of losing one's job. Alternatively, there might be positive effects on motivation and loyalty from knowing that the wage one receives exceeds the level necessary to attract a worker to the position (Van Parijs 1995, 107–108).

10. This interaction between technological inheritance arguments and brute-luck arguments in Van Parijs's theory is present in the following way of expressing the notion of value equalization. The idea that most of what the "tappers" receive "must be viewed as a gift...should be clear when comparing the yield of paying the same number of visits to a rich aunt and to a poor one, or the payoff of a given physical and mental effort in Manhattan and in Peshawar" (Van Parijs 2003b, 206).

11. Of course, if there are no such gifts in the relevant economy to (re)distribute, a basic income may still be justified, all things considered. With such a weaker argument for basic income, we would have to stick to some version of the "balance of fairness" reply discussed above. This view concedes that the basic income may involve objectionable forms of exploitation but holds that it provides us with *other* advantages that would (on balance) outweigh such moral costs (White 2006a; cf. Wolff 2004).

12. I examine the account of responsibility in *Real Freedom* and its paternalist element more closely in chapter 5, in particular in section 5.6.

13. Hence, in this view, genuine endorsement of a particular way of life is not simply "additive" but "constitutive" to a good life. No component (event or achievement) may add value to a person's life against her own opinion that it does not (Dworkin 2000, 248–249, 268ff.).

14. As explained by Dworkin, his resourcist—nonperfectionist and responsibility-sensitive—account of disadvantage takes the actual mix of ethical preferences (suitably filtered to prevent the impact of unjust attitudes and adaptive preferences) or the general state of the world's resources as "parameters of justice," that is, as facts of the world "that fix what it is fair or unfair for me to do or to have," rather than something that may itself be fair or unfair (Dworkin 2000, 298). For an argument in defense of welfare as the currency of justice, see Arneson (2000).

15. It must be noticed that this emphasis on the social costs of individual nonwork would not only be an argument against a basic income or basic capital scheme but also against the acceptability of access to any kind of inheritance, gifts, capital income, or indeed wage rates that may provide substantial freedom to reduce the total amount of time spent in paid work. As members of society become wealthier, some will inevitably be given the opportunity to select more freely how much to work. Unless restrictions are imposed on holders of such wealth on how to use those resources, or unless they were prevented from receiving it in the first place, more citizens will control assets that give them the option not to engage in employment for longer periods of their lives (whether for productive or nonproductive, commercial or noncommercial purposes).

16. To take another example from the basic income literature, Samuel Brittan (from a different normative point of view) relies on the technological inheritance argument as follows: "Hayek went so far as to say that if there were no other way it would be better to grant an independent income to one householder in a hundred chosen by lots than not to have it at all. In the 40 years and more since his Constitution of Liberty was published, productivity in the developed world has made great strides. Are we not now approaching a position where some nonwage income could be available not to one in a hundred but to all citizens?" (Brittan 2001).

17. Indeed, given that there is likely to be a clash between increasing or status quo levels of consumption of scarce material resources in the wealthier countries of the world and global ecological sustainability, some version of the opposite claim is far more likely to be true. The requirements of sustainability and global justice demand affluent, high-consuming economies to restrict rather than expand total output per capita in order for global development to operate safely within the biophysical constraints for economic growth (e.g., Barry 2005; Cohen 2000, 113).

18. On Van Parijs's view, full-time jobs have been turned "from unavoidable toil to valuable assets" (Van Parijs et al., 2000, 53; see also Van Parijs 1987/1993).

19. To illustrate, Van Parijs notes that "everything we know suggests that nearly all people seek to make some contribution" (Van Parijs 2001b, 25; cf. Pateman 2003, 142). And Samuel Brittan reminds us that "most of the old upper bourgeoisie also worked and regarded their own independent means as either a nest egg to fall back upon or as a supplement to their professional or business incomes" (Brittan 2001).

20. For an analysis of Rawlsian stability and basic income in relation to the real-libertarian criterion of sustainability (also discussing a previous version of my argument in this book), see Midtgaard (2008).

5 Jobs as Gifts: A Reconstruction and a Qualified Defense

1. As Williams shows, it is not clear whether or how *Real Freedom* offers a justification of value equalization that does not ultimately appeal to envy-elimination. For Van Parijs's response, see Van Parijs (2003b).

2. I assume that there is a mechanism in place to assess and tax some of the privilege enjoyed by the castle holder in order to equalize access to the value of external assets, and to make sure that castle holders belong to those who *willingly* (taking taxation of hypothetical market value into account) hold on to the asset in question. In other words: they are free to leave it if they decide that the price is not worth paying. On the role of the market, scarcity, and informal exclusion in Real Freedom, see also Sturn and Dujmovits (2000) and Van Parijs's reply in Van Parijs (2001a).

3. For critical examination of the independent interest criterion, see also Widerquist (2006b).

4. For a critique of *Real Freedom* based on such a talent-sensitive account of responsibility, see Arneson (2003).

5. For a powerful attempt to address inequality of marketable talent along these lines, see Dworkin (2000; 2002; 2004; 2011).

6. This theme is central in Van Parijs (2009a; 2009b). I examine these arguments, and rival views, more fully in Birnbaum (2010a).

7. For a different way of specifying this intuition in the real-libertarian framework, see Midtgaard (2000; 2007) and Van Parijs's reply in Van Parijs (2001a).

8. We should observe that choices that some philosophers attach to the category of option luck (the economic outcome for which we must be held responsible) are not only unavoidable but also present in every sphere of life. Decisions about effort and involvement within seemingly noneconomic realms of life have similar economic consequences as deliberate economic choices, and are also economically risky in this sense. Choosing to spend time and effort with some particular friends, relatives, social networks, potential partners, and so on, rather than with others, has different economic consequences depending on whether the persons and employers who come to like us are rich or poor, successful, well-educated or not, and so on. In the absence of redistribution, a given level of effort in any social sphere may have radically different economic results depending on such circumstances.

9. Again, if partly justified on the basis of various practical considerations, the predictable maximin distribution of job assets and other scarcity rents is still, in a sense, a case of pragmatic imperfection rather than ideal justice. But if that observation is to form the basis of a relevant objection in the context of an institutional ideal, it must be shown that this imperfection is avoidable and—in other words—that

such limitations are shortcomings of the ideal *relative to some better, applicable ideal for the kinds of societies we address.*

10. For helpful remarks on age-differentiation of basic income payments, and to what extent room should be left to convert part of the basic income into capital grants, see Fitzpatrick (2007).

11. For valuable discussion on paternalism in this context, and the possible hybrid models between basic income and basic capital (and various forms of conditionality) to which it may lead, see also White (2006b).

12. It will also, however, provide grounds for a few qualifications against it, to be identified in chapter 6.

13. For the argument that luck-egalitarianism and relational egalitarianism (the latter is often referred to as "democratic equality") are complementary, see also Brown (2005; 2009) and Wolff and de-Shalit (2007).

6 Why Do People Work If They Don't Have To? Basic Income, Liberal Neutrality, and the Work Ethos

1. I introduce Van Parijs's views on the work ethos in section 6.3.

2. However, at least one passage notes the relevance of a strong work ethic for the objective of promoting the highest sustainable basic income. In this context, *Real Freedom* mentions that it is "conceivable" that "a real-libertarian case could be made for some type of regime because of the ethos it tends to generate" (See Van Parijs 1995, 251, n.49).

3. This remark was made in response to my presentation at the Hoover Chair of Economic and Social Ethics, UCLouvain, April 24, 2007.

4. Interestingly, in their 1986 piece "A Capitalist Road to Communism," Van der Veen and Van Parijs remarked in a footnote that "if the motivation to work is provided by fear of nonmaterial penalties (social disapproval, contempt, resentment, etc.), it is questionable whether alienation has really been abolished" (Van der Veen and Van Parijs 1986/2006, 5, n.5).

5. For useful remarks on liberal neutrality and the enforcement of norms and virtues, see Rawls (2001a, 116–119).

6. For remarks on this theme, see Fraser and Gordon (1994), Plant (1993), and Pateman (2006).

7. The idea in this argument is that involuntarily unemployed and involuntarily employed can swap places and the basic income can be activated as a wage subsidy in seeking employment or in running one's own business. It could also be relied upon or used to expand the market for part-time jobs.

8. See Ackerman and Alstott (2006), Van Parijs (2001a), and (in a right-wing version of basic income) Murray (2006). The general feminist concern is that the spontaneous distribution of work and leisure under a basic income scheme does little to change, and could

well reinforce, traditional gender roles and statistical discrimination based on gender-based expectations with respect to work commitment and unpaid caring responsibilities (Robeyns 2000; 2001). For relevant discussions, see also McKay (2005), Pateman (2006), and the special issue of *Basic Income Studies* 3 (2008), guest-edited by Ingrid Robeyns, "Should Feminists Endorse Basic Income?" http://www.bepress.com/bis/vol3/iss3/.

9. In contrast to the latter, a distributive scheme of this kind helps place everyone in a position of basic material independence from which they can confidently speak, act, and criticize without fear that the basis of their livelihood will be withdrawn. It can, thus, help to offer people a secure material basis from which they can articulate and express their own wishes (to partners, parents, or employers) without jeopardizing access to the basic necessities of life. I discuss and defend this argument in chapter 2 of this book.

10. This is a significant deviation from Van Parijs's views. Van Parijs explicitly argues that "it is not the job of the institutions of a just society to lay down what each participant in a cooperative venture should do and not do. People may choose to durably enter a relationship in which they know there will be plenty of free riding, or in which they know they will be in a submissive position" (Van Parijs 2001a, section 10). In such passages he argues that institutions should not try to influence women's choices or to restrict the choices open to them. In accepting that more women than men may choose to lighten their double shift under a basic income scheme by spending less time in paid work, he responds that: "who could seriously think that working subject to the dictates of a boss for forty hours a week is a path to liberation" (Van Parijs 2001b, 20). More broadly, Van Parijs emphasizes that deviations from equal cash grants to address nonpecuniary disadvantages must be responsive to "local circumstances and preferences" (Van Parijs 2009a, 159). Again, all this raises the question of whether real-libertarianism holds the resources necessary to *challenge* (and not passively reflect) injustices when they are based on preferences, norms, and social structure rather than economic inequality. The case for a basic autonomy-constrained interpretation of real freedom sides with Van Parijs's neutralist rejection of paternalistic arguments that tell women (or men!) that they need recognition through paid work rather than through nonmarket options they may be more interested in pursuing. It does not reject or stigmatize anybody that identifies with gender-conservative options or ascribe to those that make them a false consciousness. It holds, however, that we must be concerned with the structural impact and the social patterns that result from isolated choices insofar as that outcome will tend to systematically affect people's access to a position of basic autonomy. If, through such a social outcome, people are prevented from making valuable and well-informed use of their

options as confident, materially, and socially empowered choosers, such patterns and structures are objectionable from the point of view of justice.

11. In this context, it should be observed that Ronald Dworkin provides a number of considerations for why at least some elements of this broader agenda must be integrated into a plausible version of resource-egalitarianism. His discussion in *Sovereign Virtue* of the principles of authenticity (2000, 160) and independence (2000, 161) is general, and it is not clear what kind of practical conclusions they might yield with respect to social equality, self-respect, and adaptive preferences. However, it clearly aims to identify *resource-egalitarian* reasons for why the participants of his ideal auction procedure must be effectively free to form and reflect on their preferences, as well as influencing the views of others ("the principle of authenticity"), and for why racist and sexist preferences, expressing contempt or dislike for the individuals of some particular group, must not be allowed to influence the outcome of the auction ("the principle of independence"). In effect, this will redefine opportunity costs in order to protect people from "systematic prejudice" (Dworkin 2000, 161–162).

12. This option is interesting as a transitional means to help articulate, legitimize, and enforce the demands of a broader ethos of contribution. On the other hand, extending contribution tests to the context of informal educational and cultural activities, care, and various forms of volunteer work is associated with some rather obvious and well-known problems, such as introducing a great degree of administrative complexity, a number of arbitrary distinctions between contributors and noncontributors, and bureaucratic surveillance of familial relationships. For a useful discussion, see De Wispelaere and Stirton (2007).

13. One of the central arguments of many basic income supporters for why their strategy would help reinforce work commitment is that greater independence in relation to the labor market could help to gradually improve the quality of work. The exit option provided by a substantial basic income could be expected to add pressure on employers to improve the intrinsic attractiveness of less well-paid jobs in order to attract workers and make it necessary for them to offer higher wages and, thus, provide added incentives for labor-saving technology to replace less attractive jobs that would become more difficult to fill.

14. I thank Robert van der Veen for his remarks in this direction.

7 SOCIAL JUSTICE IN PRACTICE: ON THE POLITICAL IMPLICATIONS OF RADICAL LIBERALISM

1. In the present context, these arguments are meant to respond to the stability objection against basic income. However, these arguments may also give independent reasons in favor of universal and

unconditional distributive schemes for anyone concerned with the republican objectives of political equality, nondomination, and civic virtue. For a sketch, see, e.g., Birnbaum and Casassas (2008).

2. An early version of this argument, examining the relationship between work obligations and the military industry, was developed by Danish author Johannes Hohlenberg in the 1930s, see Hohlenberg, Birnbaum, and Christensen (2007) and Christensen (2010).

3. If the moral standards by which a person is required to earn her basic economic security, and meet public moral standards, depend on her being silent with respect to the moral and ethical ends of activities in demand, that will be an effective mechanism to block ethical deliberation on the ends of productive activities, whether in civil society, the market, or the political forum. Do not ask for what purpose you do things, or whether the means utilized for the specified ends are morally acceptable. Ask whether the income you get from that activity is sufficient to earn a living on your own.

4. As argued by Claus Offe: "The productivist link that ties social security to economic growth and budgetary growth dividends operates as an effective brake upon more stringent varieties of policies aiming at environmental protection, as the clients of this type of welfare state will naturally be inclined to prefer economic growth over the preservation of natural resources" (Offe 1992, 71).

5. Some of the sentences in this section are reproduced from Birnbaum (2009).

6. For example, this prediction is supported by empirical evidence in several European nations from programs that provide a state-supported scheme for career break or sabbatical leave (offering the possibility to voluntarily opt out from the labor market with a guaranteed income for a limited period of time) (Fröberg et al. 2003; Robeyns 2000, 123) and by evidence from the negative income tax experiments conducted in the USA and Canada during the 1970s (Burtless 1986; Keeley 1981; Robins 1985). On the limitations of low, flat-rate transfers in the context of family policy, specifically with regard to parental leave take-up and the prospects of challenging gender inequality, see Ferrarini (2006, 157–160).

7. Okin argues in a footnote that her proposal should not be restricted to couples who are legally married (Okin 1989, 180), but should apply to any relationship that produce children and where the relevant division of labor is present.

8. Ackerman and Alstott argue that such a policy would not—in contrast to social-democratic programs—exclude any citizen from the distributive scheme, and it would better respect people's interests and choices by providing an account of justice that widens our political horizon beyond a work- and workplace-based agenda (e.g., beyond earnings-related social insurance, work-subsidies, day care services, subsidies for higher education, etc.). It would thereby bring attention to justice

for mothers and caretakers, and to people without a capacity or taste for higher studies (Ackerman and Alstott 2006). In the Swedish context, a particularly radical version of basic income as an alternative to the welfare state was articulated in an internal report on basic income of the Green Party 2000, suggesting that all or most other forms of cash transfers—including earnings-related social insurance—should be replaced by a monthly basic income to all (see Reinikainen 2005). Similar views are defended in Ekstrand (1995; 1997).

9. The contingent consent on which the legitimacy of such schemes is based may be interpreted as something like this: "I am a willing contributor to the scheme because I know that some other day I am the one in need of support (due to sickness, involuntary unemployment, accident, etc.). If I am in trouble I can count on others' support, in the way they can count on mine. However, it only makes sense for me to remain loyal to this reciprocity-based scheme of risk-sharing as long as I can be confident that others will contribute and play by the rules."

REFERENCES

Ackerman, Bruce. 1980. *Social Justice in the Liberal State*. New Haven: Yale University Press.

Ackerman, Bruce. 2003. "Radical Liberalism." In Dowding, De Wispelaere, and White. 2003.

Ackerman, Bruce and Anne Alstott. 1999. *The Stakeholder Society*. New Haven: Yale University Press.

Ackerman, Bruce and Anne Alstott. 2006. "Why Stakeholding?" In Ackerman, Alstott, Van Parijs, and Wright. 2006.

Ackerman, Bruce, Anne Alstott, and Philippe Van Parijs. 2006. *Redesigning Distribution: Basic Income and Stakeholder Grants as Cornerstones for an Egalitarian Capitalism*, edited by Erik Olin Wright. London & New York: Verso.

Alperovitz, Gar. 1994. "Distributing our Technological Inheritance." *Technology Review* 97 (7): 30–36.

Alperovitz, Gar. 2001. "On Liberty." In Cohen and Rogers. 2001.

Alperovitz, Gar. 2005. *America beyond Capitalism: Reclaiming Our Wealth, Our Liberty, and Our Democracy*. Hoboken: John Wiley & Sons.

Alstott, Anne. 1999. "Work vs. Freedom: A Liberal Challenge to Employment Subsidies." *Yale Law Journal* 108 (5): 967–1058.

Alstott, Anne. 2001. "Good for Women." In Cohen and Rogers. 2001.

Anderson, Elizabeth. 1999. "What is the Point of Equality?" *Ethics* 109 (2): 287–337.

Anderson, Elizabeth. 2001. "Optional Freedoms." In Cohen and Rogers. 2001.

Anderson, Elizabeth. 2004. "Welfare, Work Requirements, and Dependant-Care." *Journal of Applied Philosophy* 21 (3): 243–256.

Andersson, Jan-Otto. 2009. "Basic Income from an Ecological Perspective." *Basic Income Studies* 4 (2): Article 4.

Andersson, Jan-Otto and Olli Kangas. 2005. "Universalism i arbetslinjens tid: inställningen till grundinkomst i Sverige och Finland." *Tidskrift för Politisk Filosofi* 9 (3): 6–33.

Arneson, Richard. 1982. "The Principle of Fairness and Free-Rider Problems." *Ethics* 92 (4): 616–633.

Arneson, Richard. 1990. "Is Work Special? Justice and the Distribution of Employment." *American Political Science Review* 84 (4): 1127–1147.

Arneson, Richard. 2000. "Welfare Should Be the Currency of Egalitarian Justice." *Canadian Journal of Philosophy* 30 (4): 497–524.

Arneson, Richard. 2003. "Should Surfers Be Fed?" In Reeve and Williams. 2003.

Atkinson, Anthony B. 1996. "The Case for a Participation Income." *Political Quarterly* 67 (1): 67–70.

Attas, Daniel and Avner de-Shalit. 2004. "Workfare: The Subjection of Labour." *Journal of Applied Philosophy* 21 (3): 309–320.

Baker, John. 1992. "An Egalitarian Case for Basic Income." In Van Parijs 1992.

Barnes, Peter. 2001. *Who Owns the Sky? Our Common Assets and the Future of Capitalism.* Washington D.C.: Island Press.

Barry, Brian. 1982/1997. "Humanity and Justice in Global Perspective." In *Contemporary Political Philosophy: An Anthology*, edited by Robert Goodin and Philip Pettit. Oxford: Blackwell.

Barry, Brian. 1989. *A Treatise on Social Justice, Volume 1: Theories of Justice.* London: Harvester-Wheatsheaf.

Barry, Brian. 1995. *A Treatise on Social Justice. Volume 2: Justice as Impartiality.* Oxford: Clarendon Press.

Barry, Brian. 1997. "The Attractions of Basic Income." In *Equality*, edited by Jane Franklin. London: Institute for Public Policy Research.

Barry, Brian. 2001. "UBI and the Work Ethic." In Cohen and Rogers. 2001.

Barry, Brian. 2005. *Why Social Justice Matters.* Cambridge: Polity Press.

Barry, Norman. 2006. "Defending Luck Egalitarianism." *Journal of Applied Philosophy* 23 (1): 89–107.

Bauman, Zygmunt. 1999. *In Search of Politics.* Cambridge: Polity Press.

Becker, Lawrence. 1986. *Reciprocity.* London: Routledge.

Beitz, Charles. 1999. *Political Theory and International Relations.* Princeton: Princeton University Press.

Birnbaum, Simon. 2001. "Inkomst utan arbete?" Thesis for Degree of Master. Department of Political Science, Stockholm University.

Birnbaum, Simon. 2005. "Universell grundinkomst och den svenska välfärdsstaten: Mot en ny generation av inkomsträttigheter?" *Statsvetenskaplig tidskrift* 107 (4): 323–350.

Birnbaum, Simon. 2007. "Social republikanism och andelssamhället." In *Retten til basisindkomst*, edited by Karsten Lieberkind, Christian Ydesen and Erik Christensen, Göteborg: NSU Press.

Birnbaum, Simon. 2009. "Introduction: Basic Income, Sustainability and Post-Productivism." *Basic Income Studies*, 4 (2): Article 3.

Birnbaum, Simon. 2010a. "Rättvis fördelning och den generella välfärdens gränser: Om differensprincipen, aktivering och rätten till en inkomst." *Tidskrift för politisk filosofi* 14 (1): 7–32.

Birnbaum, Simon. 2010b. "Två föreställningar om jämlikhet: Om rättvisa, självrespekt och välfärdspolitik." *Tidskrift for velferdsforskning* 13 (2): 70–82.

Birnbaum, Simon and David Casassas. 2008. "Social Republicanism and Basic Income." In White and Leighton. 2008.

Block, Fred. 2001. "Why Pay Bill Gates?" In Cohen and Rogers. 2001.

Bollier, David. 2002. *Silent Theft: The Private Plunder of Our Common Wealth.* London: Routledge.

Bollier, David. 2006. "Using Stakeholder Trusts to Reclaim Common Assets." In Paxton, White and Maxwell. 2006.

Boulanger, Paul-Marie. 2009. "Basic Income and Sustainable Consumption Strategies." *Basic Income Studies* 4 (2): Article 5.

Bowles, Samuel and Herbert Gintis. 1998/1999. "Is Egalitarianism Passé? Homo Reciprocans and the Future of Egalitarian Politics." *Boston Review* 23 (6): 4–10.

Brighouse, Harry and Erik O. Wright. 2008. "Strong Gender Egalitarianism." *Politics and Society* 36 (3): 360–372.

Brittan, Samuel. 2001. "In Praise of Free Lunches." *Times Literary Supplement*, August 24, 2001.

Brock, Gillian. 2009. *Global Justice: A Cosmopolitan Account.* Oxford: Oxford University Press.

Brown, Alexander. 2005. "Luck Egalitarianism *and* Democratic Equality." *Ethical Perspectives* 12 (3): 293–339.

Brown, Alexander. 2009. *Personal Responsibility. Why It Matters.* London: Continuum.

Browne, Jude and Marc Stears. 2005. "Capabilities, Resources and Systematic Injustice: A Case of Gender Inequality." *Philosophy, Politics and Economics* 4 (3): 355–373.

Burtless, Gary. 1986. "The Work Response to a Guaranteed Income. A Survey of Experimental Evidence." In *Lessons from the Income Maintenance Experiments,* edited by Alicia Munnell. Boston: Federal Reserve Bank of Boston.

Calder, Gideon. 2009. "Mobility, Inclusion and the Green Case for Basic Income." *Basic Income Studies* 4 (2): Article 8.

Caney, Simon. 2005. *Justice Beyond Borders: A Global Political Theory.* Oxford: Oxford University Press.

Carens, Joseph. 1981. *Equality, Moral Incentives and the Market: An Essay in Utopian Politico-Economic Theory.* Chicago: University of Chicago Press.

Carens, Joseph. 1986. "Rights and Duties in an Egalitarian Society." *Political Theory* 14 (1): 31–49.

Casal, Paula. 2007. "Why Sufficiency Is Not Enough." *Ethics* 117 (2): 296–326.

Casassas, David. 2007. "Basic Income and the Republican Ideal: Rethinking Material Independence in Contemporary Societies." *Basic Income Studies* 2 (2): Article 9.

Christensen, Erik. 2000. *Borgerløn: Fortællinger om en politisk idé.* Højbjerg: Hovedland.

Christensen, Erik. 2010. *Borger i tre verdener: Johannes Hohlenbergs økono-misk-politiske filosofi.* Odense: Syddansk universitetsforlag.

Cohen, G. A. 1989. "On the Currency of Egalitarian Justice." *Ethics* 99 (4): 906–944.

Cohen, G. A. 1995. *Self-Ownership, Freedom, and Equality.* New York: Cambridge University Press.

Cohen, G. A. 2000. *If You're an Egalitarian, How Come You're so Rich?* Cambridge, MA: Harvard University Press.

Cohen, G. A. 2003. "Facts and Principles." *Philosophy and Public Affairs* 31 (3): 211–245.

Cohen, G. A. 2004. "Expensive Taste Rides Again." In *Dworkin and His Critics*, edited by Justine Burley. Oxford: Blackwell.

Cohen, G. A. 2008. *Rescuing Justice and Equality*. Cambridge, MA: Harvard University Press.

Cohen, Joshua. 1989. "Democratic Equality." *Ethics* 99 (1989): 727–751.

Cohen, Joshua and Joel Rogers, eds. 2001. *What's Wrong with a Free Lunch?* Boston: Beacon Press.

Couillard, Pascal. 2002. "Basic Income: Origins and Prospects. An Interview with Philippe Van Parijs." *The Newsletter of the United States Basic Income Guarantee Network* (USBIG), July 2002. http://www.usbig.net/.

Cunliffe, John and Guido Erreygers, eds. 2004. *The Origins of Universal Grants: An Anthology of Historical Writings on Basic Income and Basic Capital*. Basingstoke: Palgrave Macmillan.

Dagger, Richard. 1997. *Civic Virtues: Rights, Citizenship, and Republican Liberalism*. Oxford: Oxford University Press.

Dagger, Richard. 2006. "Neo-Republicanism and the Civic Economy." *Politics, Philosophy & Economics* 5 (2): 151–173.

Daniels, Norman. 1996. *Justice and Justification: Reflective Equilibrium in Theory and Practice*. Cambridge: Cambridge University Press.

Darwall, Stephen. 1977. "Two Kinds of Respect." *Ethics* 88 (1): 36–49.

De Wispelaere, Jurgen and Lindsay Stirton. 2004. "The Many Faces of Universal Basic Income." *Political Quarterly* 75 (3): 266–274.

De Wispelaere, Jurgen and Lindsay Stirton. 2007. "The Public Administration Case against Participation Income." *Social Service Review* 81 (3): 523–549.

Dowding Keith, Jurgen De Wispelaere, and Stuart White, eds. 2003. *The Ethics of Stakeholding*. Basingstoke: Palgrave Macmillan.

Dworkin, Ronald. 2000. *Sovereign Virtue: The Theory and Practice of Equality*. Cambridge, MA: Harvard University Press.

Dworkin, Ronald. 2002. "Sovereign Virtue Revisited." *Ethics* 113 (1): 106–143.

Dworkin, Ronald. 2004. "Ronald Dworkin Replies." In *Dworkin and His Critics*, edited by Justine Burley. Oxford: Blackwell.

Dworkin, Ronald. 2011. *Justice for Hedgehogs*. Cambridge, MA: Harvard University Press.

Ekstrand, Lasse. 1995. *Den befriade tiden*. Göteborg: Korpen.

Ekstrand, Lasse. 1996. *Arbetets död och medborgarlön*. Göteborg: Korpen.

Elgarte, Julieta. 2008. "Basic Income and the Gendered Division of Labour." *Basic Income Studies* 3 (3): Article 4.

Elster, Jon. 1986. "Comment on Van der Veen and Van Parijs." *Theory and Society* 15 (5): 709–721.

Elster, Jon. 1988. "Is There (Or Should There Be) a Right to Work?" In *Democracy and the Welfare State*, edited by Amy Gutmann. Princeton: Princeton University Press.

Engler, Wolfgang, B. 2005. *Bürger, ohne Arbeit: für eine radikale Neugestaltung der Gesellschaft*. Berlin: Aufbau-Verlag.

Esping-Andersen, Gøsta. 2002. "Why We Need a New Welfare State." In *Why We Need a New Welfare State*, edited by Gøsta Esping-Andersen. Oxford: Oxford University Press.

Eyal, Nir. 2005. "'Perhaps the Most Important Primary Good': Self-Respect and Rawls's Principles of Justice." *Politics, Philosophy and Economics* 4: 195–219.

Farrelly, Colin. 1999. "Justice and Citizen's Basic Income." *Journal of Applied Philosophy* 16 (3): 283–296.

Farrelly, Colin. 2007. "Justice in Ideal Theory: A Refutation." *Political Studies* 55 (4): 844–864.

Ferrarini, Tommy. 2006. *Families, States and Labour Markets: Institutions, Causes and Consequences of Family Policy in Post-War Welfare States*. Cheltenham: Edward Elgar.

Fitzpatrick, Tony. 1999. *Freedom and Security: An Introduction to the Basic Income Debate*. Basingstoke: Macmillan.

Fitzpatrick, Tony. 2003. *After the New Social Democracy. Social Welfare for the Twenty-first Century*. Manchester-New York: Manchester University Press.

Fitzpatrick, Tony. 2007. "Streams, Grants and Pools: Stakeholding, Asset-Based Welfare and Convertibility." *Basic Income Studies* 2 (1): Article 6.

Forget, Evelyn. 2011. "The Town with No Poverty. Using Health Administration Data to Revisit Outcomes of a Canadian Guaranteed Annual Income Field Experiment." Winnipeg: University of Manitoba. http://econ.duke.edu/uploads/assets/Workshop%20Papers/HOPE/forget-cea.pdf (accessed March 28, 2011).

Fraser, Nancy. 1996. "Gender Equity and the Welfare State: A Postindustrial Thought Experiment." In *Democracy and Difference*, edited by Seyla Benhabib. Princeton: Princeton University Press.

Fraser, Nancy and Linda Gordon. 1994. "'Dependency' Demystified: Inscriptions of Power in a Keyword of the Welfare State." *Social Politics* 1 (1): 4–31.

Fried, Barbara. 2004. "Left-Libertarianism: A Review Essay." *Philosophy & Public Affairs* 32 (1): 66–92.

Friedman, Milton. 1962. *Capitalism and Freedom*. Chicago: University of Chicago Press.

Fröberg, Daniela, Linus Lindqvist, Laura Larsson, Oskar Nordström Skans, and Susanne Ackum Agell. 2003. "Friåret ur ett arbetsmarknadsperspektiv." *Rapport 2003:7*. Uppsala: Institutet för arbetsmarknadspolitisk utvärdering (IFAU).

Galston, William. 2001. "What About Reciprocity?" In Cohen and Rogers. 2001.

Galston, William. 2005. "Conditional Citizenship." In *Welfare Reform and Political Theory*, edited by Lawrence Mead and Christopher Beem. New York: Russell Sage Foundation.

Giddens, Anthony. 1998. *The Third Way: The Renewal of Social Democracy*. Cambridge: Polity Press.

Goldsmith, Scott. 2010. "The Alaska Permanent Fund Dividend: A Case-Study in Implementation of a Basic Income Guarantee." Paper presented at the 13th Basic Income Earth Network Conference. São Paolo, Brazil.

Goodin, Robert. 1992. "Towards a Minimally Presumptuous Social Welfare Policy." In Van Parijs. 1992.

Goodin, Robert. 2000. "Crumbling Pillars: Social Security Futures." *Political Quarterly* 71 (2): 144–150.

Goodin, Robert. 2001. "Work and Welfare: Towards a Post-Productivist Welfare Regime." *British Journal of Political Science* 31 (1): 13–39.

Goodin, Robert, James Mahmud Rice, Antti Parpo, and Lina Eriksson. 2008. *Discretionary Time: A New Measure of Freedom*. Cambridge: Cambridge University Press.

Gornick, Janet and Marcia Meyers. 2003. *Families that Work: Policies for Reconciling Parenthood and Employment*. New York: Russell Sage Foundation.

Gornick, Janet and Marcia Meyers. 2008. "Creating Gender Egalitarian Societies: An Agenda for Reform." *Politics & Society* 36 (3): 313–349.

Gorz, André. 1999. *Reclaiming Work: Beyond the Wage-based Society*. Cambridge: Polity Press.

Groot, Loek. 2004. *Basic Income, Unemployment and Compensatory Justice*. Dordrecht: Kluwer Academic.

Hirst, Paul. 1994. *Associative Democracy: New Forms of Economic and Social Governance*. Oxford: Polity Press.

Hohlenberg, Johannes. 2007. "Anthroposophical Reflections on Basic Income." Edited and introduced by Simon Birnbaum and Erik Christensen. *Basic Income Studies* 2 (2): Article 6.

Howard, Michael. 2006. "Basic Income and Migration Policy: A Moral Dilemma?" *Basic Income Studies* 1 (1): Article 4.

Howard, Michael and Karl Widerquist, eds. 2012. *Alaska's Permanent Fund Dividend: Examining its Suitability as a Model*. New York: Palgrave Macmillan.

Hum, Derek and Wayne Simpson. 1993. "Economic Response to a Guaranteed Annual Income: Experience from Canada and the United States." *Journal of Labor Economics* 11 (1): S263–S296.

Jackson, Tim. 2009. *Prosperity without Growth: Economics for a Finite Planet*. London & Washington: Earthscan.

Janson, Per. 2003. *Den huvudlösa idén: medborgarlön, välfärdspolitik och en blockerad debatt*. Lund: Arkiv.

Jordan, Bill. 1992. "Basic Income and the Common Good." In Van. 1992.

Kangas, Olli. 1998. "Rättvis fördelning och socialpolitiska modeller. Rawls i internationell jämförelse." *Tidskrift för politisk filosofi* 2 (1): 5–24.

Keeley, Michael. 1981. *Labour Supply and Public Policy: A Critical Review.* New York: Academic Press.

Keynes, John Maynard. 1963. "Economic Possibilities for Our Grandchildren." *Essays in Persuasion.* New York: Norton.

Kildal, Nanna, ed. 2001. *Den nya sociala frågan.* Göteborg: Daidalos.

Kildal, Nanna and Stein Kuhnle, eds. 2005. "The Nordic Welfare Model and the Idea of Universalism." In *Normative Foundations of the Welfare State: The Nordic Experience*, edited by Nanna Kildal and Stein Kuhnle. London: Routledge.

Knight, Carl and Zofia Stemplowska, eds. 2011. *Responsibility and Distributive Justice.* Oxford: Oxford University Press.

Korpi, Walter and Joakim Palme. 1998. "The Paradox of Redistribution and Strategies of Equality: Welfare State Institutions, Inequality, and Poverty in the Western Countries." *American Sociological Review* 63 (5): 661–687.

Krebs, Angelica. 1998. "Love at Work." *Acta Analytica* 13 (20): 185–194.

Krouse, Richard and Michael Macpherson. 1988. "Capitalism, Property-Owning Democracy, and the Welfare State." In *Democracy and the Welfare State*, edited by Amy Gutmann. Princeton: Princeton University Press.

Kymlicka, Will. 1992. "Introduction." In *Justice in Political Philosophy*, edited by Will Kymlicka. Aldershot: Elgar.

Kymlicka, Will. 2002. *Contemporary Political Philosophy*, 2nd Edition. Oxford: Oxford University Press.

Laborde, Cécile. 2006. "Female Autonomy, Education and the Hijab." *Critical Review of International Social and Political Philosophy* 9 (3): 351–377.

Laborde, Cécile. 2008. *Critical Republicanism.* Oxford: Oxford University Press.

Larmore, Charles. 1996. *The Morals of Modernity.* Cambridge: Cambridge University Press.

Layard, Richard. 2005. *Happiness: Lessons from a New Science.* London: Penguin Books.

Le Grand, Julian and David Nissan. 2003. "A Capital Idea: Helping the Young to Help Themselves." In Dowding, De Wispelaere, and White. 2003.

Lindensjö, Bo. 2004. *Perspektiv på rättvisa.* Göteborg: Daidalos.

Lovett, Frank. 2010. *A General Theory of Domination and Justice.* Oxford: Oxford University Press.

Lundquist, Lennart. 1993. *Det vetenskapliga studiet av politik.* Lund: Studentlitteratur.

Marx, Karl. 1998. *The German Ideology* [1845]. Amherst, NY: Prometheus Books.

Mason, Andrew. 2004. "Just Constraints." *British Journal of Political Science* 34 (2): 251–268.

Massey, Stephen J. 1983. "Is Self-Respect a Moral or a Psychological Concept?" *Ethics* 93 (2): 246–261.

McKay, Ailsa. 2005. *The Future of Social Security Policy: Women, Work and a Citizens' Basic Income*. New York: Routledge.

McKay, Ailsa and VanEvery Jo. 2000. "Gender, Family, and Income Maintenance: A Feminist Case for Citizens Basic Income." *Social Politics* 7 (2): 266–284.

McKinnon, Catriona. 2003. "Basic Income, Self-Respect and Reciprocity." *Journal of Applied Philosophy* 20 (2): 143–158.

Mead, Lawrence. 1987. *Beyond Entitlement: The Social Obligations of Citizenship*. New York: Free Press.

Mead, Lawrence. 1992. *The New Politics of Poverty: The Nonworking Poor in America*. New York: Basic Books.

Mead, Lawrence. 2005. "Welfare Reform and Citizenship." In *Welfare Reform and Political Theory*, edited by Lawrence Mead and Christopher Beem. New York: Russell Sage Foundation.

Meade, James. 1964. *Efficiency, Equality and the Ownership of Property*. London: Allen & Unwin.

Meade, James. 1993. *Liberty, Equality and Efficiency*. London: Macmillan.

Meade, James. 1995. *Full Employment Regained? An Agathotopian Dream*. Cambridge: Cambridge University Press.

Midtgaard, Søren F. 2000. "Ambition-Sensitivity and an Unconditional Basic Income." *Analyse & Kritik* 22 (2): 223–236.

Midtgaard, Søren F. 2007. "John Rawls' teori om retfærdighed og idéen om en ubetinget borgerløn." In *Retten til basisindkomst*, edited by Karsten Lieberkind, Christian Ydesen, and Erik Christensen. Göteborg: NSU Press.

Midtgaard, Søren F. 2008. "Rawlsian Stability and Basic Income." *Basic Income Studies* 3 (2): Article 5.

Mill, John Stuart. 1965. *Collected Works. Vol. 3, Principles of Political Economy* [1848], edited by John M. Robson. Toronto: University of Toronto Press.

Mill, John Stuart. 1989. *On Liberty* [1859]. Cambridge: Cambridge University Press.

Miller, David. 1995. *On Nationality*. Oxford: Oxford University Press.

Miller, David. 2001. *Principles of Justice*. London: Harvard University Press.

Miller, David. 2007. *National Responsibility and Global Justice*. Oxford: Oxford University Press.

Miller, David. 2008. "Political Philosophy for Earthlings." In *Political Theory: Methods and Approaches*, edited by David Leopold and Marc Stears. Oxford: Oxford University Press.

Mills, Charles. 2005. "'Ideal Theory' as Ideology." *Hypatia* 20 (3): 165–184.

Moon, Donald. 1988. "The Moral Basis of the Democratic Welfare State." In *Democracy and the Welfare State*, edited by Amy Gutmann. Princeton: Princeton University Press.

Moellendorf, Darrel. 2002. *Cosmopolitan Justice*. Boulder, CO: Westview Press.

Moellendorf, Darrel. 2009. *Global Inequality Matters*. Basingstoke: Palgrave Macmillan.

Munnell, Alicia. ed. 1986. *Lessons from the Income Maintenance Experiments*. Boston: Federal Reserve Bank of Boston.

Murray, Charles. 2006. *In Our Hands: A Plan to Replace the Welfare State*. Washington: American Enterprise Institute Press.

Musgrave, Richard. 1974. "Maximin, Uncertainty, and the Leisure Trade-off." *Quarterly Journal of Economics* 88 (4): 625–632.

Nozick, Robert. 1974. *Anarchy, State and Utopia*. New York: Basic Books.

Nussbaum, Martha. 2003. "Rawls and Feminism." In *The Cambridge Companion to Rawls*, edited by Samuel Freeman. Cambridge and New York: Cambridge University Press.

Offe, Claus. 1992. "A Non-Productivist Design for Social Policies." In Van Parijs. 1992.

Okin, Susan Moller. 1989. *Justice, Gender, and the Family*. New York: Basic Books.

O'Neill, Martin. 2009. "Liberty, Equality and Property-Owning Democracy." *Journal of Social Philosophy* 40 (3): 379–396.

Orloff, Ann Shola. 1993. "Gender and the Social Rights of Citizenship: The Comparative Analysis of Gender Relations and Welfare States." *American Sociological Review* 58 (3): 303–328.

Otsuka, Michael, Vallentyne, Peter, and Steiner, Hillel. 2005. "Why Left-Libertarianism Is Not Incoherent, Indeterminate, or Irrelevant." *Philosophy & Public Affairs* 33 (2): 201–215.

Page, Edward A. 2007. "Fairness on the Day after Tomorrow: Justice, Reciprocity and Global Climate Change." *Political Studies* 55 (1): 225–242.

Pateman, Carole. 2003. "Freedom and Democratization: Why Basic Income is to be Preferred to Basic Capital." In Dowding, De Wispelaere and White. 2003.

Pateman, Carole. 2005. "Another Way Forward: Welfare, Social Reproduction, and a Basic Income." In *Welfare Reform and Political Theory*, edited by Lawrence Mead and Christopher Beem. New York: Russell Sage Foundation.

Pateman, Carole. 2006. "Democratizing Citizenship: Some Advantages of a Basic Income." In Ackerman, Alstott, Van Parijs and Wright. 2006.

Paxton, Will and Stuart White, eds, with Dominic Maxwell. 2006. *The Citizen's Stake: Exploring the Future of Universal Asset Policies*. Bristol: The Policy Press.

Pearce, Nick, Will Paxton, and Stuart White. 2006. "Conclusion: What is The Best Way Forward for The Citizen's Stake?" In Paxton, White, and Maxwell. 2006.

Pettit, Philip. 1997. *Republicanism: A Theory of Freedom and Government*. Oxford: Oxford University Press.

Pettit, Philip. 2007. "A Republican Right to Basic Income." *Basic Income Studies* 2 (2): Article 10.

232 ◈ REFERENCES

Phelps, Edmund. 1997. *Rewarding Work: How to Restore Participation and Self-Support to Free Enterprise.* Cambridge, MA: Harvard University Press.

Phelps, Edmund. 2001. "Subsidize Wages." In Cohen and Rogers. 2001.

Plant, Raymond. 1993. "Free Lunches Don't Nourish: Reflections on Entitlements and Citizenship." In *New Approaches to Welfare Theory*, edited by Glenn Drover and Patrick Kerans. Aldershot: Edward Elgar.

Pogge, Thomas. 1989. *Realizing Rawls.* Ithaca and London: Cornell University Press.

Premfors, Rune. 2000. *Den starka demokratin.* Stockholm: Atlas.

Rakowski, Eric. 1991. *Equal Justice.* Oxford: Oxford University Press.

Raventós, Daniel. 2007. *Basic Income: The Material Conditions of Freedom.* London: Pluto Press.

Rawls, John. 1971/1999. "Justice as Reciprocity." In Rawls. 1999.

Rawls, John. 1971. *A Theory of Justice.* Cambridge, MA: Harvard University Press.

Rawls, John. 1974/1999. "Reply to Alexander and Musgrave." In Rawls. 1999.

Rawls, John. 1975a/1999. "The Independence of Moral Theory." In Rawls. 1999.

Rawls, John. 1975b/1999. "Fairness to Goodness." In Rawls. 1999.

Rawls, John. 1982/1999. "Social Unity and Primary Goods." In Rawls. 1999.

Rawls, John. 1988/1999. "The Priority of Right and Ideas of the Good." In Rawls. 1999.

Rawls, John. 1993. *Political Liberalism.* New York: Columbia University Press.

Rawls, John. 1996. *Political Liberalism* (Paperback edition). New York: Columbia University Press.

Rawls, John. 1997/1999. "The Idea of Public Reason Revisited." In Rawls. 1999.

Rawls, John. 1999. *Collected Papers.* Edited by Samuel Freeman. Cambridge, MA; and London: Harvard University Press.

Rawls, John. 2001a. *Justice as Fairness: A Restatement.* Cambridge, MA: Belknap.

Rawls, John. 2001b. *Law of Peoples* (Paperback edition). Cambridge, MA; and London: Harvard University Press.

Reeve, Andrew and Andrew Williams, eds. 2003. *Real Libertarianism Assessed: Political Theory after Van Parijs.* Basingstoke: Palgrave Macmillan.

Rehn, Gösta. 1977. "Towards a Society of Free Choice." In *Comparing Public Policies*, edited by J. J. Wiatr & R. Rose. Wroclaw: Ossolineum.

Reinikainen, Jouni. 2005. "Social rättvisa per medborgarlön? Den egalitära liberalismen i miljöpartiets distributiva ideal." *Statsvetenskaplig tidskrift* 107 (4): 351–375.

Robeyns, Ingrid. 2000. "Hush Money or Emancipation Fee? A Gender Analysis of Basic Income." In Van der Veen and Groot. 2000.

Robeyns, Ingrid. 2001. "Will a Basic Income do Justice to Women?" *Analyse & Kritik* 23 (1): 88–105.

Robeyns, Ingrid, ed. 2008. "Should Feminists Endorse Basic Income?" *Basic Income Studies*. Special Issue 3 (3).

Robeyns, Ingrid and Adam Swift, eds. 2008. "Social Justice: Ideal Theory, Nonideal Circumstances." *Social Theory and Practice*. Special Issue, 34 (3).

Robins, Philip. 1985. "A Comparison of the Labor Supply Findings from the Four Negative Income Tax Experiments." *Journal of Human Resources* 20 (4): 567–582.

Robins, Philip, Robert G. Spiegelman, Samuel Winer, and Joseph G. Bell, eds. 1980. *A Guaranteed Annual Income. Evidence from a Social Experiment*. New York: Academic Press.

Rockström, Johan, Will Steffen, Kevin Noone, Åsa Persson, F. Stuart Chapin, Eric F. Lambin, Timothy M. Lenton et al. 2009. "A safe operating space for humanity." *Nature* 461 (September 24, 2009): 472–475.

Roemer, John. 1994. *Egalitarian Perspectives*. New York: Cambridge University Press.

Rothstein, Bo. 1998. *Just Institutions Matter: The Moral and Political Logic of the Universal Welfare State*. Cambridge: Cambridge University Press.

Rothstein, Bo. 2000. "Universell välfärdsstat och medborgarinkomst—en kritisk analys." In *Den nya sociala frågan*, edited by Nanna Kildal. Göteborg: Daidalos.

Russell, Bertrand. 1932/1996. *In Praise of Idleness*. London: Routledge.

Räikkä, Juha. 1998. "The Feasibility Condition in Political Theory." *Journal of Political Philosophy* 6 (1): 27–40.

Sainsbury, Diane. 1996. *Gender Equality and Welfare States*. Cambridge: Cambridge University Press.

Sangiovanni, Andrea. 2007. "Global Justice, Reciprocity, and the State." *Philosophy & Public Affairs* 35 (1): 3–39.

Satz, Debra. 2010. *Why Some Things Should Not Be for Sale. The Moral Limits of Markets*. Oxford: Oxford University Press.

Schaller, Walter E. 1998. "Rawls, the Difference Principle, and Economic Inequality." *Pacific Philosophical Quarterly* 79 (4): 368–391.

Scheffler, Samuel. 2003. "What is Egalitarianism?" *Philosophy & Public Affairs* 31 (1): 5–39.

Scheffler, Samuel. 2005. "Choice, Circumstance, and the Value of Equality." *Politics, Philosophy & Economics* 4 (1): 5–28.

Schmid, Günter. 2000. "Transitional Labour Markets: A New European Employment Strategy?" In *Innovative Employment Initiatives*, edited by Bernd Marin, Danièle Meulders and Dennis Snower. Aldershot: Ashgate.

Schmid, Günter and Bernard Gazier, eds. 2002. *The Dynamics of Full Employment: Social Integration through Transitional Labour Markets*. London: Edward Elgar.

Schweickart, David. 2002. *After Capitalism*. Lanham: Rowman & Littlefield Publishers.

Segall, Shlomi. 2005. "Unconditional Welfare Benefits and the Principle of Reciprocity." *Politics, Philosophy and Economics* 4 (3): 331–354.

Sen, Amartya. 1980/1987. "Equality of What?" In *Liberty, Equality and Law*, edited by Sterling M. McMurrin. Salt Lake City: University of Utah Press.

Sen, Amartya. 1991. *Development as Freedom.* Oxford: Oxford University Press.

Sen, Amartya. 1992. *Inequality Reexamined.* New York: Russell Sage Foundation.

Sen, Amartya. 2009. *The Idea of Justice.* London: Penguin.

Shue, Henry. 1975. "Liberty and Self-Respect." *Ethics* 85 (3): 195–203.

Simmons, John. 2010. "Ideal and Nonideal Theory." *Philosophy and Public Affairs* 38 (1): 5–36.

Simon, Herbert A. 2001. "UBI and the Flat Tax." In Cohen and Rogers. 2001.

Standing, Guy. 1999. *Global Labour Flexibility: Seeking Distributive Justice.* Basingstoke: Macmillan.

Standing, Guy. 2001. *Beyond the New Paternalism, Basic Security as Equality.* London: Verso.

Standing, Guy, ed. 2004. *Promoting Income Security as a Right: Europe and North America.* London: Anthem Press.

Standing, Guy. 2011. *The Precariat: The New Dangerous Class.* London and New York: Bloomsbury.

Standing, Guy and Michael Samson, eds. 2003. *A Basic Income Grant for South Africa.* Lansdowne: University of Cape Town Press.

Steiner, Hillel. 1994. *An Essay on Rights.* Oxford: Blackwell.

Sturn, Richard and Rudi Dujmovits. 2000. "Basic Income in Complex Worlds: Individual Freedom and Social Interdependencies." *Analyse & Kritik* 22 (2): 198–222.

Swift, Adam. 2003. "Social Justice: Why Does it Matter What the People Think?" In *Forms of Justice, Critical Perspectives on David Miller's Political Philosophy*, edited by Daniel A. Bell and Avner de-Shalit. Oxford: Rowman & Littlefield.

Tan, Kok-Chor. 2004. *Justice without Borders. Cosmpolitanism, Nationalism and Patriotism.* New York: Cambridge University Press.

Tersman, Folke. 1993. *Reflective Equilibrium: An Essay in Moral Epistemology.* Stockholm: Almqvist & Wiksell International.

Vallentyne, Peter. 1997/2003. "Self-Ownership and Equality: Brute Luck, Gifts, Universal Dominance and Leximin." In Reeve and Williams. 2003.

Vallentyne, Peter and Hillel Steiner, eds. 2000a. *The Origins of Left-Libertarianism: An Anthology of Historical Writings.* New York: Palgrave.

Vallentyne, Peter and Hillel Steiner, eds. 2000b. *Left-Libertarianism and Its Critics: The Contemporary Debate.* New York: Palgrave.

Vanderborght, Yannick and Philippe Van Parijs. 2005. *L'allocation universelle.* Paris: La Découverte.

Van der Veen, Robert. 1998. "Real Freedom versus Reciprocity: Competing Views on the Justice of Unconditional Basic Income." *Political Studies* 46 (1): 140–163.

Van der Veen, Robert. 2004. "Basic Income versus Wage Subsidies: Competing Instruments in an Optimal Tax Model with a Maximin Objective." *Economics and Philosophy* 20 (1): 147–183.

Van der Veen, Robert and Loek Groot, eds. 2000. *Basic Income on the Agenda.* Amsterdam: Amsterdam University Press.

Van der Veen, Robert and Loek Groot. 2006. "Post-Productivism and Welfare States: A Comparative Analysis." *British Journal of Political Science* 36 (4): 593–618.

Van der Veen, Robert and Philippe Van Parijs. 1986/2006. "A Capitalist Road to Communism." *Theory and Society* 15 (5): 635–655. Reprinted in *Basic Income Studies* 1 (1): Article 6.

Van der Veen, Robert and Philippe Van Parijs. 2006. "A Capitalist Road to Global Justice: Reply to Another Six Critics." *Basic Income Studies* 1 (1): Article 13.

Van Donselaar, Gijs. 1997. *The Benefit of Another's Pains. Parasitism, Scarcity, Basic Income.* Doctoral dissertation. Amsterdam: University of Amsterdam.

Van Donselaar, Gijs. 2003. "The Stake and Exploitation." In Dowding, De Wispelaere, and White. 2003.

Van Donselaar, Gijs. 2009. *The Right to Exploit. Parasitism, Scarcity, Basic Income.* Oxford: Oxford University Press.

Van Parijs, Philippe. 1987/1993. "A Revolution in Class Theory." In *Marxism Recycled*, edited by Philippe Van Parijs. New York: Cambridge University Press.

Van Parijs, Philippe. 1991. "Why Surfers Should be Fed: The Liberal Case for an Unconditional Basic Income." *Philosophy and Public Affairs* 20 (1991): 101–130.

Van Parijs, Philippe. 1992a. "Competing Justifications of Basic Income." In Van Parijs. 1992.

Van Parijs, Philippe, ed. 1992b. *Arguing for Basic Income: Ethical Foundations for a Radical Reform.* London: Verso.

Van Parijs, Philippe. 1995. *Real Freedom for All. What (if Anything?) Can Justify Capitalism.* Oxford: Oxford University Press.

Van Parijs, Philippe. 1996. "Free Riding Versus Rent Sharing: Should Even David Gauthier Support an Unconditional Basic Income?" In *Ethics, Rationality and Economic Behaviour*, edited by Francesco Farina, Frank Hahn, and Stefano Vanucci. Oxford: Oxford University Press.

Van Parijs, Philippe. 1996/2006. "Basic Income and the Two Dilemmas of the Welfare State." In *The Welfare State Reader*, 2nd edition, edited by Christopher Pierson and Francis G. Castles. Cambridge: Polity.

Van Parijs, Philippe. 1997. "Reciprocity and the Justification of an Unconditional Basic Income. Reply to Stuart White." *Political Studies* 45 (2): 327–330.

Van Parijs, Philippe. 1998/1999. "Fairness." *Boston Review* 23 (6): 15–16.

Van Parijs, Philippe. 2001a. "Real Freedom, the Market and the Family: A Reply." *Analyse & Kritik* 23 (1): 106–131.

Van Parijs, Philippe. 2001b. "A Basic Income for All." In Cohen and Rogers. 2001.

Van Parijs, Philippe. 2001c. "Reply." In Cohen and Rogers. 2001.

Van Parijs, Philippe. 2003a. "Difference Principles." In *The Cambridge Companion to Rawls*, edited by Samuel Freeman. Cambridge and New York: Cambridge University Press.

Van Parijs, Philippe. 2003b. "Hybrid Justice, Patriotism and Democracy: A Selective Reply." In Reeve and Williams. 2003.

Van Parijs, Philippe. 2009a. "Egalitarian Justice, Left Libertarianism and the Market." In *Hillel Steiner and The Anatomy of Justice: Themes and Challenges*, edited by S. de Wijze, M. Kramer, and I. Carter. London: Routledge.

Van Parijs, Philippe. 2009b. "Basic Income and Social Justice: Why Philosophers Disagree." The Joseph Rowntree Foundation/University of York Annual Lecture. http://www.jfr.org.uk/sites/files/jfr/van-parijs-lecture.pdf.

Van Parijs, Philippe. 2009c. "Political Ecology: From Autonomous Sphere to Basic Income." *Basic Income Studies* 4 (2): Article 6.

Van Parijs, Philippe, Laurence Jacquet, and Claudio Caesar Salinas. 2000. "Basic Income and its Cognates: Partial Basic Income versus Earned Income Tax Credit and Reductions of Social Security Contributions as Alternative Ways of Addressing the 'New Social Question.'" In Van der Veen and Groot. 2000.

Walter, Tony. 1989. *Basic Income: Freedom from Poverty, Freedom to Work.* London: Boyars.

White, Stuart. 1997. "Liberal Equality, Exploitation, and the Case for an Unconditional Basic Income." *Political Studies* 45 (2): 312–326.

White, Stuart. 2000. "Social Rights and the Social Contract–Political Theory and the New Welfare Politics." *British Journal of Political Science* 30 (2): 507–532.

White, Stuart. 2003a. *The Civic Minimum.* Oxford: Oxford University Press.

White, Stuart. 2003b. "Freedom, Reciprocity and the Citizen's Stake." In Dowding, De Wispelaere, and White. 2003.

White, Stuart. 2003c. "Fair Reciprocity and Basic Income." In Reeve and Williams. 2003.

White, Stuart. 2004. "What's Wrong with Workfare?" *Journal of Applied Philosophy* 21 (3): 271–284.

White, Stuart. 2006a. "Reconsidering the Exploitation Objection to Basic Income." *Basic Income Studies* 1 (2): Article 4.

White, Stuart. 2006b. "The Citizen's Stake and Paternalism." In Ackerman, Alstott, Van Parijs, and Wright. 2006.

White, Stuart. 2007. *Equality*. Cambridge: Polity Press.

White, Stuart and Daniel Leighton, eds. 2008. *Building a Citizen Society. The Emerging Politics of Republican Democracy*. London: Lawrence and Wishart.

Wicksell, Knut. 1905. *Socialiststaten och nutidssamhället: Några socialekonomiska betraktelser*. Stockholm: Albert Bonniers Förlag.

Widerquist, Karl. 1999. "Reciprocity and the Guaranteed Income." *Politics & Society* 27 (3): 387–402.

Widerquist, Karl. 2005. "A Failure to Communicate: What (If Anything) Can We Learn from the Negative Income Tax Experiments?" *The Journal of Socio-Economics* 34 (1): 49–81.

Widerquist, Karl. 2006a. *Property and the Power to Say No: A Freedom-based Argument for Basic Income*. D.Phil. Thesis, University of Oxford.

Widerquist, Karl. 2006b. "Who Exploits Who?" *Political Studies* 54 (3): 444–464.

Widerquist, Karl, Michael A. Lewis, and Steven Pressman, eds. 2005. *The Ethics and Economics of the Basic Income Guarantee*. Aldershot: Ashgate.

Williams, Andrew. 1999/2003. "Resource Egalitarianism and the Limits to Basic Income." In Reeve and Williams. 2003.

Williams, Andrew. 2006. "Basic Income and the Value of Occupational Choice." *Basic Income Studies* 1 (1): Article 8.

Wolff, Jonathan. 1998. "Fairness, Respect and the Egalitarian Ethos." *Philosophy and Public Affairs* 27 (2): 97–122.

Wolff, Jonathan. 2004. "Training, Perfectionism and Fairness." *Journal of Applied Philosophy* 21 (3): 285–295.

Wolff, Jonathan. 2010. "Fairness, Respect and the Egalitarian Ethos Revisited." *Journal of Ethics* 14 (3-4): 335–350.

Wolff, Jonathan and Avner de-Shalit. 2007. *Disadvantage*. Oxford: Oxford University Press.

Woodcock, George. 2004. *Anarchism: A History of Libertarian Ideas and Movements*. Peterborough: Broadview Press.

Wright, Erik Olin. 2005. "Basic Income as a Socialist Project." *Rutgers Journal of Law & Urban Policy*, 2 (1): 196–203.

Wright, Erik Olin. 2006. "Basic Income, Stakeholder Grants, and Class Analysis." In Ackerman, Alstott, Van Parijs, and Wright. 2006.

Wright, Erik Olin. 2010. *Envisioning Real Utopias*. London: Verso.

Zelleke, Almaz. 2008. "Institutionalizing the Universal Caretaker through a Basic Income?" *Basic Income Studies* 3 (3): Article 7.

Index

Ackerman, Bruce, 94, 199, 221
adaptive preferences, 160, 215, 220
Alaska Permanent Fund, 94, 126, 206
alienation, 147, 218
all purpose means, 23, 103
   see also primary goods
Alperovitz, Gar, 188, 211
Alstott, Anne, 94, 199, 221
ambition-sensitivity, 132–5
   see also option luck
Anderson, Elizabeth, 25
autonomous sphere, 6

Barry, Brian, 31, 106–8, 177
basic autonomy, 9, 32, 35, 36,
   49, 50, 56, 63, 89, 138, 141,
   161–5, 166, 167, 169, 171,
   175, 179, 180, 189, 190,
   193, 196, 197, 203, 219
basic capital, 13, 123, 135–9, 159,
   171, 184, 213, 216, 218
basic income (BI)
   and bargaining power, 52, 54, 132,
     139, 165, 185, 191, 198, 203
   defined, 11–12
   and environmental sustainability,
     6, 76–7, 155, 185–9, 221
   and gender injustice, 71–2,
     159–60, 164–5, 190–8, 201,
     202–4, 219–20, 221
   and global justice, 27–9, 187–8,
     209, 216
   as instrument against
     unemployment, 4–6, 12, 52–6,
     57–63, 70, 156, 177, 184–5,
     186–8, 199–200, 202, 218

   in kind, 101, 136, 163,
     183, 202–4
   and labor market flexibility, 4–6,
     28, 52–3, 132, 156, 184,
     186, 194, 196–7
   and negative income tax, 11,
     13–14, 70, 175, 205
   political feasibility of, 172–3,
     180–3, 189, 198, 200,
     201, 204
   political initiatives for, 205–6
   and political participation, 6,
     106–7, 178–80, 204
   reforming vs. replacing the
     welfare state, 36–7, 164–5,
     173, 198–204, 221–2
   and social assistance, 11–12, 13,
     52, 177, 186, 199, 200–1
   and social insurance, 5, 11–12,
     13, 37, 52, 177, 182–3,
     200–2, 222
   vs. basic capital, 135–9
   see also basic income guarantee,
     and throughout
basic income guarantee (BIG)
   defined, 11
   ex ante vs. ex post models of,
     13–14
   experiments with, 70, 175,
     202, 221
   full vs. partial, 13, 100, 188,
     198, 201, 207
   interval between payments, 13,
     136, 207
   permanent vs. time-limited, 13,
     185, 198, 200